BAMBOOZLED

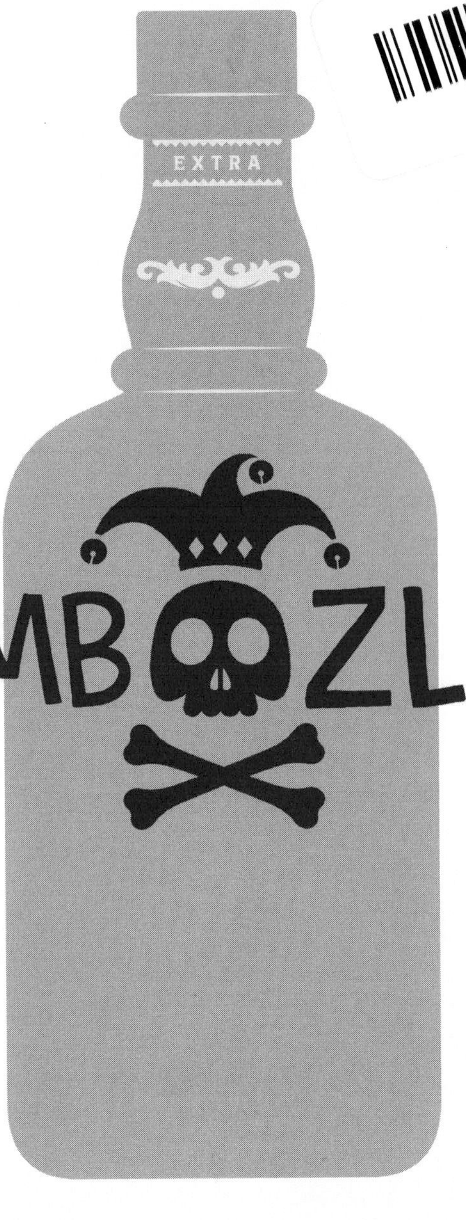

Clovercroft Publishing

BAMBOOZLED

HOW ALCOHOL
MAKES FOOLS OF US ALL

The guide to getting
EVERYTHING you want in life
by giving up alcohol!

Ken Makimsy Middleton

Clovercroft Publishing

Bamboozled: How Alcohol Makes Fools of Us All

©2023 by Ken Middleton
All rights reserved. No part of this book may be reproduced or transmitted in any form or by any means, electronic or mechanical, including photocopying, recording or by any information storage and retrieval system, without permission in writing from the copyright owner.

Clovercroft Publishing

Published by Clovercroft Publishing, Franklin, Tennessee
Published in association with Shane Crabtree of Clovercroft Publishing
www.clovercroftpublishing.com

Cover and Interior Design by Melinda Martin
Printed in the United States of America

ISBN: 978-1-954437-86-9 (paperback)

Disclaimer: The author of this book does not dispense medical advice or prescribe the use of any technique as a form of treatment for physical, emotional, or medical problems without the advice of a physician, either directly or indirectly. The intent of the author is only to offer information of a general nature to help you in your quest for emotional and spiritual well-being. In the event you use any of the information in this book for yourself, the author and the publisher assume no responsibility for your actions.

To my wife, Lena.

I tell everyone that quitting drinking was
the second best decision I ever made only to marrying you.

You are my absolute best friend,
and being able to be on this journey of life with you
is a gift that I will always cherish.

Thanks for your undying support
and always being my biggest cheerleader.

143 . . .

AMAZON REVIEW REQUEST

Please STOP to read

Amazon reviews are the lifeblood of any author to get their work out to the world and make a difference.

Many people wait until the end of the book to ask for a book review, but I fancy myself a bit of a contrarian by nature, so I'm asking NOW instead.

I'm not asking for you to give me a book review without reading any aspect of the book, but I don't think you need to read the entire book before doing so. Often, many people just forget by the time they get to that part or, unfortunately, don't make it to the end of the book for whatever reason.

Considering that, I'm asking that if you are learning or getting anything helpful from this book at any part that is making an impactful difference, go and leave a book review at that time.

It's so easy to do, takes less than two minutes, and goes a long way in helping more people discover this book and, hopefully, gain something from it too.

Thanks so much for doing this in advance. You're a rockstar!

CONTENTS

INTRODUCTION

Yeah, I'm Talking to You

"Everything you want in life
is probably on the other side of giving up alcohol."

- KEN MAKIMSY MIDDLETON

Let me clear up one thing right off the bat: this book is NOT meant for alcoholics.

I wanted to start with this statement because this is a common first thought (and misconception) when people read the title of this book and its tagline, "The guide to getting EVERYTHING you want in life by giving up alcohol."

What I mean by this is if you are someone who has a serious problem with alcohol and you need professional medical or psychological help, then I cannot say that this book would be the *best* resource for you. There are a lot of strategies in here that can help, but I must be honest: This book is for individuals who would not yet describe themselves as "serious drinkers," but who still feel that alcohol may be holding them back from realizing their full potential.

Now, let me confirm what was probably your second thought about this book's contents: This book IS about alcohol.

More explicitly, this book is about exploring the history of alcohol and the lies we have been told for years.

It's about how it has been the magic elixir for generations, making some people's dreams come true, while simultaneously destroying the dreams of others.

The reason I chose the title *Bamboozled* is because it represents the numerous ways we've been tricked by alcohol for so long. "Bamboozle" has numerous synonyms—beguile, misinform, deceive—that directly relate to the different ways we think alcohol makes our lives better when, instead, it is only preventing us from making it as good as it could be.

Most people want to live a life in which they have overall solid health without any ailments or diseases, an abundance of wealth that allows them to do what they want when they want, and great, loving relationships with all of their family and friends.

The problem is that, secretly and subtly, alcohol hinders one's ability to obtain and keep all three of these over time, while also creating a host of other problems that can sabotage one's life in a number of ways.

We need to recognize the truth of this warning and understand that living a life of alcohol-consciousness can prevent or stop this from happening and give us the ability to create any future we desire.

What is alcohol-consciousness?

Throughout this book, you will hear me use the term *alcohol-consciousness* instead of the more commonly known term *sobriety*. That is because the purpose of this book is not to inspire you to give up alcohol because you have some type of addiction. As shared earlier, this book is not generally for alcoholics. Instead, its purpose is to help you (the casual, "normal" drinker) recognize the tremendous negative effects that come with the decision to drink alcohol consistently.

It's about truly understanding these effects and how they will impact your long-term future. Then you can make the decision to drink or not drink with that information squarely in mind each and every time.

Comparable to how someone who doesn't eat fried foods or drink sugary drinks would be considered health-conscious, this book's purpose is about you truly grasping the tradeoffs that you make each time you decide to drink and going into that decision eyes wide open.

It is my hope that by doing so, you (the reader) will eventually see the way you have been tricked by alcohol to believe something that is not true and will then make the decision that you will no longer be bamboozled by its lies.

This Is For You

There are many people who can probably benefit from a life of not drinking alcohol, as the numerous negative effects of it are expansive.

However, for those who find alcohol to be an amazing friend and "easer" of life, this is for you.

For those who find alcohol to be one of the great inventions of mankind and who could not see any way of living life without it, this is for you.

For the person who uses drinking in almost every aspect of life and with almost every social interaction, this is for you.

Basically, the individual who reads this title and thinks either one of two things:

1. There is no way you can give up alcohol because it is too ingrained in your life and you would suffer from this decision, OR
2. You have always felt that alcohol did not allow you to become your full best self and perhaps you should give it a break…

This is for you.

The reality is that alcohol is as dangerous as any other drug in the world, but it is promoted by one of the greatest PR marketing machines of all time, so many people just don't recognize this as being the case.

The fact that the phrase "alcohol AND drugs" actually is very well known and accepted is evidence of this, but we'll dive more into this later.

The stats are staggering enough, but they don't even come close to the true harm that alcohol does to the lives of individuals on a daily basis.

About 95,000 people[1] (approximately 68,000 men and 27,000 women) die from alcohol-related causes annually, making it the third leading cause of preventable death in the US.

The first is smoking and the second is poor diet and physical activity, and we'll share later how drinking probably affects both of these as well.

Globally, this number balloons to 3 million people,[2] according to the World Health Organization. This equates to 5.3% of all deaths, a number that is sad when thinking how preventable these deaths are.

While these numbers are sad and tragic, they don't focus on the majority of people who are harmed by alcohol in a more insidious and long-term manner. This group consists of the 2.3 billion people[3] who drank alcohol casually throughout the world who never end up in these statistics but are held back every day by not being able to grow to the level of which they are capable.

There is a very good chance that you are in this group of people if you're reading this book now. Its content will explain to you why this is the case and how you can break free of alcohol's ensnarement to give yourself the chance to become the very best version of yourself.

How This Book Will Help

This book will help you either give up alcohol completely or start your alcohol-consciousness journey so that you can live the life of your dreams.

We'll walk through the corridors of history to understand how this happened over time.

We'll walk through the origin of alcohol and how it was viewed as a spiritual aid to get one closer to God. We'll then uncover how this changed to it being seen as poison that could ruin lives and destroy a person entirely and then eventually evolve to the "harmless as long as you're careful" view that society has of it today.

We'll dive into how society has made alcohol almost a part of our everyday lives in order to be viewed as a "normal" individual. We'll explore the culture of heavy drinking in college, how this graduates to work "happy" hours, and then permeates all aspects of our social lives as we mature.

We'll look into how Hollywood and the media has aided this, and how we are primed every day to believe that drinking is not only normal but what the super successful ALWAYS do.

Next, we'll explore the science behind why it is almost inevitable that some people will develop either an addiction to alcohol or a subconscious dependence that will consistently hold that person back from being the best version of themselves.

After that, we'll then explore what life can be like on the other side of this equation.

We'll go on a quick journey to explore what are all the positive benefits of one's life if one decides to give up alcohol.

We'll focus on doing this in five primary aspects of life.

1. Career - We'll look at how drinking alcohol can affect one both positively and negatively early in one's career and how this can typically play out over time.

2. Fitness - We'll discuss how your ability to get in shape and diet appropriately is compromised dramatically by alcohol and review the long-term damage it can do to your body in a number of different ways.

3. Life - We'll discuss how not drinking will give you the opportunity to do a number of things that drinking will not by providing more of something that so many people are looking for as they get older - Time.

4. Aging - Speaking of time, we will focus on how drinking gets worse as one ages and how making the decision to quit at a certain age will pay dividends on one's quality of life as they get older.

5. Finance - We'll do an overview of the financial cost of alcohol to each of us individually and how the decision to drink can have a huge effect on our financial status and future in a number of ways.

6. Relationship - We'll dive into how our love lives are seemingly aided by alcohol by making it easier to "find" love but how it could ultimately be holding us back from finding the true person that we should be with, as well as allowing us to become the person that someone else would want to be with - a double whammy.

Lastly, we'll dive into the concept of The MEDS. For clarity's sake to the reader, this is not related to any type of medication or medical treatment. Instead, this acronym is a holistic strategy that will aid individuals who want to give up drinking for good by providing the concept of two things that will make it a million times easier than trying to do it through willpower alone - Routines and Substitutes.

This step-by-step guide will make it as easy as possible for you to start and stay on track to create the life you desire.

Parable Examples

Throughout this, we will share stories of fictional characters who represent various scenarios in life. While these characters and stories are fictional, they are adaptations of true lives and mistakes I'm sure we've all seen happen with our own eyes because of alcohol.

In these stories, we will share how the characters didn't feel they had a problem with alcohol and how they only recognized how much better life could be when they finally made the decision to give alcohol-consciousness (sobriety) a try.

We will integrate these stories throughout the book, as we go through various parts to drive a point home and give you a real-life example of how theory turned into practice.

The hope is that you will see yourself in these stories and recognize the lies that we tend to tell ourselves with time. These lies keep us in a state of denial and ignorance that prevents us from becoming the true best version of ourselves.

How to Read and Use This Book

Reading this book from beginning to end is the best and recommended way, as much of the material builds upon itself and will make the most sense if you read it from front to back accordingly.

However, after you have read it one time, you can also use it as a reference to address various situations you may go through or specific aspects for which you feel you can use some guidance and advice.

In Part Two, "What Do You Have to Gain By Becoming Alcohol-Conscious?," each chapter is aligned to various aspects of your life, and we'll discuss how a life without alcohol can change those areas dramatically in a positive manner.

At the end, we included an advice appendix. This section contains questions and answers to various situations and experiences you may encounter as you go through the process of becoming alcohol-conscious. We weren't able to cover every situation in the book, so we wanted to include this as a quick reference to provide helpful, practical advice that one could use as well. For the answers that are also included in the book, we provide the reference to the specific chapter for further reading if desired.

Use it as your reference guide to understand what will happen and be prepared to respond to certain situations as they arise.

This is not needed, but I do always recommend reading books a second time if you have the capacity and time, as you'll be surprised at how much you can gain from this practice. However, I would not suggest reading and then immediately rereading the book. Instead, read and digest the lessons given in the book and hopefully begin leading your alcohol-conscious journey. After about three months of implementing various techniques and working toward alcohol-consciousness, come back and pick the book up again to begin comparing what you're going through with many of the lessons and stories from the book.

This second time, you should read it with the thought of capturing specific notes that resonate with you that you want to make sure you remember. You'll be surprised to find during your second reading that you are much more in tune with the material and are really understanding and resonating with what the words are saying.

The first time, it often goes in one ear and out the other, as you are just trying to make sense of all the information that is being thrown at you. However, the second time when you are on your alcohol-conscious journey, you have more of an anchor and frame of reference to approach the material, so you're naturally going to understand and absorb things much better and deeper than the first time around.

You'll be surprised at how you'll look at things differently the second time you pick it up, as you experience the reality of the text real time, firsthand for yourself.

It'll make all the difference in the world.

Now, let's start at the beginning and understand how we got to where we are today by looking at the history of alcohol in detail.

PART I

Why Do You
Do It?

CHAPTER ONE

A Brief History of Alcohol

"A small body of determined spirits
fired by an unquenchable faith in their mission
can alter the course of history."

— MAHATMA GANDHI

Roman Time   Modern Time

Have you ever been drunk out of your mind and suddenly thought, "I wonder how alcohol was ever discovered?"

Haha . . . me neither . . . not something I usually thought about when I was six fireball shots deep and eyeing the cute girl across the bar to muster up the courage to talk to her.

The history of alcohol is not something that I ever thought about until I sat down to write this book.

As I was sitting down to do research on the various stats related to alcohol and how it has affected our lives and society in general for so long, it just hit me that I really didn't know much about how it all started.

After doing a bit of research, I was absolutely blown away. As you'll see, it explains a lot.

As I began to read and better understand how alcohol has very much shaped our society, it helped explain our current view of alcohol as a species and why it has had such a stronghold on so many of us for so long.

As the famous saying goes, you can't understand where you're going until you understand where you come from (I always remember this from a commercial selling the movie *Roots*[4] in a box set on television . . . seems weird now), so here we go.

The Beginning

No one is 100% sure of the actual beginning of alcohol and how it was discovered or created, but there is evidence of traces of beer found in a prehistoric burial site[5] from about 13,000 years ago. It is believed that it was used in a ritual feast to honor the dead, so they were pouring one out for the "homies" a long time ago.

This beer came from a group of people known as the Natufian, who were hunter-gatherers in the eastern Mediterranean.

It has been hypothesized that beer was created primarily during this time for spiritual and ritual purposes. It is even believed by some that this beer dates back to before the cultivation of cereals[6] in that region and could have been the catalyst for this ancient group to actually begin cultivating agriculture.

From there, the next oldest record of alcohol brewing was found in ancient China about 7000 BC. This was produced by fermenting rice, honey, and fruit.

The Chinese recognized the significance of alcohol in their daily lives but understood that overconsumption of it could lead to disastrous effects. (People randomly breaking out in song and doing the macarena or the wobble at weddings comes to mind.) They ascribed the loss of the mandate of heaven from the Xia and Shang dynasty as a punishment for the abuse of the substance.

Next, we go to ancient Persia (modern-day Iran), in which wine became extremely popular and the drink of choice for many. Scientists have discovered wine jars dating back to 5400-5000 BC. We are not entirely sure if they were created for pleasurable consumption, nourishment, or to get mommy through another soccer practice for Sarah in the afternoon, but this process was the best way for them to preserve grapes at the time.

Fast forward to around 3400 BC to ancient Egypt, and we begin to see some of the first documented inclusion of wine in everyday lives. Representative of this was the fact that many Egyptian gods were local, while Osiris, the god of wine, was recognized and worshiped throughout the entire country.

The Egyptians were slowly developing the modern-day interpretation of alcohol by producing different varieties throughout the region.

They were believed to have 17 variations of beer, along with 24 versions of wine. Could you imagine the marketing confusion of trying to pick from this many beers back then? They would probably lose their minds if they saw all the various "special" brews today.

Alcohol was a part of everyone's life, as even day laborers were allowed a ration a day (this would easily still work in a lot of companies today), and alcohol was used in a slew of different ways, including pleasure, medicine, pay, and even funeral services.

Moderation was suggested for both religious and secular reasons and, overall, individuals were warned to stay away from taverns, which were also known as houses of prostitution. Haha . . . bars and prostitution? Who woulda thunk?

It is believed alcohol distillation originated in India around 3000 BC. From 3000 BC to 2000 BC, Sura, a brew brewed from rice meal, sugar cane, wheat, grapes, and other fruits was the drink of choice for many in the region. As alluded to earlier, there was recognition during this time that alcohol was considered a double-edged sword, as there were benefits listed if consumed in moderation, while also warning of various medical ailments that could result from excessive drinking.

By 2000 BC, winemaking had reached the peninsula of Greece, and by 1700 BC, it had worked its way into the accepted everyday lives of society. Over the next 1000 years or so, it became used much in the same fashion as we see it used today, e.g., medicine, celebrations, and everyday meals were all normal functions of wine use.

Wine was seen as such an important part of Greek culture during this time that societies that did not indulge were seen as somewhat lesser-than by the Hellenic group (fuddie duddies).

As you can imagine, the Greek philosophers had a word or two to say about this. Xenophon and Plato both praised the moderate use of alcohol[7] and were critical of over-indulgence, with Plato believing no one under the age of 18 should be allowed to consume it. Hippocrates talked of its medicinal uses[8] and Aristotle was known as someone who was very critical of drunkenness.[9]

On to Rome where, by the 5th century BC, beer and wine were seen as not only normal, but a necessary part of everyday society. It was available to slaves, peasants, women, and aristocrats all the same, and viticulture and wine production spread to all parts of the region.

Medieval Period

As time progressed, alcohol became more ingrained in everyday society, and different cultures figured out how to improve the distillery process to create products with higher alcohol content for greater effectiveness to get us to our happy places much quicker. Yay! . . . Liquor!

It is believed that various Muslim chemists experimented extensively in the 800-900 AD era to improve the process. In Ancient China, it is possible that they also were experimenting with more refined ways of producing alcohol in the 1st and 2nd centuries, but the only true evidence shows this took place during the Hin and Southern Song dynasties between the 10th and 13th centuries.

In Medieval Europe, however, we don't see evidence of more refined methods of distillation until about the 12th century. It was believed that this was adopted from the Middle East, and then fractional distillation[10] was developed by Tadeo Alderatti in the 13th century. This new process of re-evaporation and condensation greatly improved the ability of distilleries to create much higher concentrated alcohol.

As times became more modernized, in 1500, German alchemist Hieronymus Braunschweig published *Liber de arte distillandi* (*The Book of the Art of Distillation*). This was the first book ever published on distillation and was followed up in 1512 by a much more expanded edition.

Due to the boiling of water and growth of yeast for its creation, many people saw alcohol as a way to stave off diseases caused by living in areas of poor sanitation. Water-borne diseases like cholera were avoided by drinking alcohol instead of regular water due to the killing of microorganisms during the creation process.

Can you imagine? It actually *was* safer to drink alcohol than water back then? It must've been wild being a kid back then.

Couple this with the fact that alcohol could be stored for months in only wood containers without spoiling, and it explains why for many trips, alcohol was the main (and for some the only) source of hydration on long sailing voyages across the sea.

Early Modern Period

During this time in history, many religious leaders appeared to be on the same page as it relates to views on the consumption of alcohol. It was seen as a gift from God that should be enjoyed in moderation, but not overly indulged in drunkenness.

Various areas kept track of their consumption, and the numbers are somewhat staggering. During the 16th century, in Valladolid, Spain, alcohol consumption was as high as 100 liters per person per year[11] with Polish peasants said to consume as much as three liters of beer per day. To give you a sense of how over the top these numbers are, the average global consumption of alcohol in 2018 was 6.18 liters per person PER YEAR.[12]

During this same time period, in Coventry, England, the average amount of beer consumed was about 17 pints per week, compared to about three pints today. In Sweden, it is believed that consumption could have been as high as 40 times higher than today, while in Denmark, the usual consumption for sailors seems to be about a gallon per day.

One caveat to all of this is that the strength of the alcohol was much less than what we have today. Whereas today the average beer is anywhere from 3-5% alcohol, during this time, it was in more of the 1% range.

As distillation improved and individuals got more creative and picky about the type of alcohol they wanted to consume, new products such as champagne and different types of liquor began to emerge.

Due to an ongoing conflict (known as the War of the Great Alliance[13]) between England and France around 1690, William of Orange (William III) banned all brandy and wine from France in an attempt to cripple them economically. Many people enjoyed the spirits and wines from France, however, so such a ban was viewed as perhaps more hurtful to the English than their French counterparts.

Therefore, in 1690, the "Act for the Encouraging of the Distillation of Brandy and Spirits from Corn" was passed. This act removed the regulations that the government had placed on the production of alcohol during that time and allowed anyone to be able to do so if they had the means. This, in turn, led to the annual production of spirits reaching nearly one million gallons (a 100% increase) in only four short years and the price of gin even falling below[14] beer.

Fast forward to about 1727, and the annual production was five times that amount, with it more than doubling to over 11 million gallons by 1733.[15] It reached a height of 18 million gallons ten years later, and then slowly began to decrease over time as the Industrial Revolution took place and, more and more, drunkenness was seen as counterproductive to the success of a modernized growing society and economy. Unfortunately, it's just more challenging to get sh*t done when you're drunk all the time.

During that time, alcohol was seen as an important part of society in England and many people who made the trip to America brought large amounts to continue this tradition in the new world.

Also, as the voyage to America was becoming more and more popular and seen as relatively safe, the Transportation Act of 1718[16] was passed. This act allowed the judicial system to send convicted criminals to America as punishment for their crimes and therefore increased the population of individuals who were more inclined to drinking than abstaining.

Couple this with the fact that water contamination was common in trips across the Atlantic, and you can see why drinking alcohol was seen as the safer thing to do for most people at the creation of the thirteen colonies.

Beer was designated X, XX, or XXX according to its alcoholic content, and colonists adhered to the traditional belief that distilled spirits were *aqua vitae*, or the water of life.

The overall consensus was very similar to that of England at the time, in that many people considered alcohol to be a positive thing, although drunkenness was an abuse of it. This was preached by many religious figures as well.

This view continued for some time, with alcohol becoming more and more accepted in society and as a necessary part of everyday life. At its height in 1830, consumption was up to 7.1 US gallons of pure alcohol per person per year. Today, that number is about 2.38 gallons.[17]

As time progressed, the temperance movement began to take hold and the US embarked on the Prohibition movement from 1920-1933.

While for those of us in the US this is a well-known part of American history, most would be surprised to know that we weren't the only country that went down this path during the first quarter of the 20th century.

Canada enacted a brief Prohibition movement from 1918-1920. Based on a wave of patriotism taking place from the First World War, the province of Prince Edward Island enacted a prohibition law to stand with Canadian troops engaged in warfare. I guess they were thinking if the troops can't have any fun, then the people shouldn't either? Or maybe more for the troops? Not sure, but other areas similarly adopted the practice as it spread across the nation. However, they were all repealed by 1948.

Russia (known as the Russian Empire then) went through a Prohibition movement from 1914-1923. Similarly inspired by the First World War to prevent soldiers from being drunk during war engagement, they banned the sale of liquor with high alcohol content. This law had notable results in the nation, as Russia saw a significant decrease in crime in several cities well known for criminal activity until its repeal in 1925. (Seems to make sense. It would be interesting to see how such a decision would play out in today's age.)

Iceland (1915-1935) and Norway (1916-1927) both put bans in place based on a referendum of the people. Pressure from other countries, however, eventually ended both movements, as France was a heavy exporter of alcohol to Norway, and Iceland saw a rebellious movement from those who traveled away from the small country and brought back the views of other countries that disagreed with the movement.

Modern Day

Now, let's fast forward a bit to more modern times and see how we landed where we are today.

Today, how alcohol is viewed is somewhat comparable to how it was viewed in the past. Many people have a love/hate relationship with it, and that may be part of the reason you're reading this book right now.

Over the past 90 or so years since the Prohibition movement, alcohol has become a very common daily part of our lives. Many people thought the sale and taxation of it would be good for the growth of the economy, so it was welcomed back into our lives.

Individuals everywhere partook of it, and with that increase came an increase in the number of individuals who were abusing it. Soon after, a number of different treatment and education courses were created to combat this trend and treat those who needed help.

In 1935, Alcoholics Anonymous was founded by Dr. Bill Wilson and Dr. Bob Smith, and four years later, the book *Alcoholics Anonymous* was published. In 1940, *The Quarterly Journal of Studies on Alcohol* began publication, as it started to become more widely accepted that alcohol addiction was not a moral failing, but there was more science about why this was happening to individuals.

In an effort to find a scientific way to combat addiction, in 1948, chemists created disulfiram[18] (Antabuse), a drug that specifically caused a number of unpleasant reactions to anyone who mixed it with ethanol. This was seen as a supplement to other educational/counseling programs to help individuals stop drinking. Also around this time, doctors began prescribing barbiturates and amphetamines for treatment as well.

You want to stop being addicted to one drug? Here's another drug to help with that.

Alcoholism was first officially recognized by the American Medical Association in 1952, and they recognized there was a way to treat these individuals for their ailment. They stopped short of calling it a disease until about 1967, when it was recognized as a complex disease that could be treated through a combination of counseling and education.

Today, the battle to help individuals stop or control their drinking continues, as it is still very much an important part of everyday society, and excessive drinking is almost seen as a rite of passage during one's college/early adult years. Often drinking habits carry over beyond this period, and many people find they have drinking problems into their mid to late twenties or early thirties.

Some of the numbers from a 2016 study were staggering:

- 136.7 million Americans over age 12 reported using alcohol within the past month.
- 488,000 adolescents aged 12-17 had an alcohol use disorder (2% of the population at the time).
- 3.7 million adults 18-25 had an alcohol use disorder (10.7% of the population).
- 10.9 million adults over age 26 had an alcohol use disorder (5.2% of the population).

Many people think the only individuals who have problems with alcohol are those whom one would consider alcoholics, but the reality is that many people suffer from it.

The reality of today's age is that many individuals have gotten so used to alcohol being a part of their everyday lives that it's hard to imagine living without it. And few things have been more conducive to the proliferation and acceptance of alcohol as a necessary everyday need than the Covid epidemic of 2019.

When the world was becoming increasingly afraid of leaving their homes and parents were forced to be parent, nanny, and teacher all at the same time, the apparent no-brainer response to this was to increase alcohol consumption to deal with the stress.

Shortly after the US officially shut down in March of 2020, alcohol sales were up 54%[19] from the year before, while online sales were up by 262%.

The use of alcohol became an everyday reality for me and it seemed that alcohol was pushed on me to the point that I almost didn't have a choice during that great four-year period of my life in which I went from a scared adolescent child to a not-as-scared, still learning and growing man: college.

CHAPTER TWO

College Days and Haze

"Choices are the hinges of destiny."

— EDWIN MARKHAM

C ollege is pretty amazing.

That's the reality of it. There are very few times in one's life when you can have as much fun and learn as much at the same time as you will in college.

Our college years are the most formative years of our lives for a number of reasons. It's the first time many of us are away from our parents and have the ability to do what we want for the majority of the time.

There are many things that one can try for the first time during college and the decisions we make in regard to those choices can shape the rest of our lives. What fraternity should you pledge? Should you intern at Amazon or Google for the summer? Should you get that tribal tattoo on your right calf like you're thinking? No way, you'll regret that later, right?

For many, choices such as what to major in and what master's program to apply to will be at the forefront of their decisions needed for the future, but the concept of drinking alcohol seems like a foregone conclusion to many.

Alcohol and college are synonymous in a lot of ways, and it's this connection that has put many people at a disadvantage as it relates to giving themselves the best chance at significant success long term in their life. What's ironic about this connection is that many people don't realize that alcohol actually greatly inhibits their ability to maximize their education and learn/grow the most during their college years.

There are many examples of this throughout the annals of college history.

SCOTT AND MITCHELL

Scott and Mitchell were very similar in a lot of ways during high school. They were good friends in high school and both very committed to being successful in the future.

Neither drank in high school, as they were more focused on academics than being the most popular kid in school. They both planned to go to college to become doctors and needed to make sure they got into great pre-med programs, so they could then get into equally great med degree programs.

They had heard horror stories about how some kids had gotten into major trouble with drinking and it had hurt their college chances, so they thought it was best to abstain while in high school.

However, college was an entirely different endeavor. They had done all the hard work to get there, right? So wasn't it time to experience what college truly had to offer by partaking in TRUE college life?

They both grew up on all the different movies and shows that depicted how much drinking was an important part of college, and now they were ready to experience it for themselves.

Freshman year, both Mitchell and Scott started to experiment a bit with alcohol. They lived in a dorm that was alcohol free, but a bunch of sororities and fraternities had freshman welcome parties with tons of alcohol available at the houses.

At Scott's first party, he was excited about the chance to get to see what all the hype was about but wanted to take his time so he didn't get in trouble by making terrible decisions, like some of his high school friends.

During his first party at a frat house, he started to drink slowly by only consuming one beer and seeing how it made him feel before moving on to more than that. After one, he didn't feel much of anything and a few of the fraternity brothers were pressuring him to "step up his game" and not be a "baby."

He knew this type of peer pressure was coming, so he didn't feel overly pressured to drink more at the time, but he had to admit that he started to feel pretty good as the alcohol started to kick in and he felt a tingle throughout his body.

The feeling of a slow buzz started to cover him and he thought that maybe it wouldn't hurt to try a second beer. After the second beer, he started to feel REAL good and began to drink at a tad bit of a quicker pace and started to let his guard down and enjoy the night.

Four hours later, he woke up in his bed, not quite sure how he got there, but he remembered that he had made out with the girl from his physics class and had gotten her number as well.

He remembered that he only had the courage to go up and talk to her because he had been so drunk and just had this feeling of not really caring if she turned him down. She seemed to like him and they enjoyed a fun night together.

To him, that was all he needed to know that this drinking thing was pretty much what others had said it would be, and he was well on the way to a college career of drinking and partying. He joined the fraternity group that he partied with that first night there and eventually became a social committee member.

As a social committee member, he was involved in all of the planning for parties each week or month. As he got more involved in fraternity life, his grades began to slip as he just didn't have as much time to study.

He also realized that many of the concepts that he felt he could grasp well in high school with a bit of hard thinking and focus seemed almost impossible to understand in college. Chemistry wasn't easy for him in high school, but it was something he could understand with a bit of deep thought. Now, he found the spatial concept and theoretical reasoning of organic chemistry very challenging to wrap his head around, and he began to think a medical career may not be for him.

When he got his first-ever D in organic chemistry at the end of the semester, he started to wonder if perhaps he needed to rethink his major. He wasn't overly concerned, however, as he heard that many students didn't initially do well in organic chemistry, and it's something you have to buckle down on to make sure you have the chance to be successful.

He said he would give it another go his sophomore year and make sure that he put in more time studying and focusing on it to ensure he didn't fail. He had taken 15 credit hours this past semester, so he decided he would cut it back to 12 hours to make sure that he could put more time into the subject to be successful.

What he didn't do was consider how much he was drinking as part of the reason he was struggling in the course and never thought about cutting back as a way to increase his chances of success.

Drinking alcohol was part of the college experience, wasn't it? So he couldn't just stop doing it because he got one lousy bad grade. He thought cutting down to 12 hours would be what he needed to go through this time around, and he felt strongly that he was making the right decision.

Mitchell had a very similar experience to Scott. They were pretty much best friends, so guess who was right beside Scott when he had his first drink? Mitchell remembered that feeling of getting his first buzz like Scott and enjoying it immensely.

He had a pretty good night, and even though he didn't come home with a phone number or make out experience like Scott did, he did have a pretty amazing night that he associated with the freedom and confidence that alcohol gave him.

Over the next semester, he and Scott pretty much ran the gamut together, going to all of the campus parties and enjoying college life.

He did okay academically his first semester there, but it was the first time he ever got a B in a class before. He knew that he hadn't been studying as much as he usually would, but he also attributed the B to the hard coursework in college. That's what college was all

about, right? Challenging you more. Pushing you to challenge your-
self and learn more than you had before.

As the second semester rolled around, however, and Mitchell
started the all-consuming class known as organic chemistry, he
started to have some serious questions about his ability to be suc-
cessful with his current approach.

He started noticing many of the same things that Scott did in that
he was having issues with retaining the material and could not quite
comprehend all the information that he needed to understand. He
did fine in high school, so he just wasn't sure why things were so hard
this time around.

As someone who had always been interested in the human mind
and what things can affect how well it functions, Mitchell instantly
started to question whether alcohol was making it more difficult
for him to capture and retain things. He remembered being able to
understand spatial concepts and mathematical theorems in calculus
that were very difficult for some of his classmates to understand
during high school.

At that time, he had attributed much of that to the fact that he
just studied more and spent more time with the material, but now
he started to wonder if this could've also been related to the fact
that many of them drank and consumed other drugs while in high
school as well. Could what they did to themselves at a young age be
happening to him now that he was out of high school?

For that reason, he decided that he needed to put down the alco-
hol for a bit longer or regulate himself much more to ensure it didn't
have an effect on his mind and ability to learn and grow. He decided
that he would not drink and party with the others in college, but
would instead focus on his academics to ensure he was able to learn
the material and achieve his dream of becoming a doctor one day.

Because he made this decision, he was able to squeak out a B in
organic chemistry that next semester, while Scott got his D.

Mitchell tried to convince Scott that partying and consuming alcohol all the time was not helping his brain's ability to process such difficult concepts, but Scott was having way too much fun to listen to him.

Over the next year, Mitchell and Scott started to spend less time together. They weren't in all the same classes anymore because Scott failed OC and had to retake it. This didn't allow him to take a host of more upper-level classes that one needed to take for pre-med. Also, Scott was still partying with the fraternity boys and even thought about pledging, something for which Mitchell just didn't have the time.

The second semester of their sophomore year, Scott decided to join the fraternity officially and that pre-med just wasn't for him. Most of his friends were business majors anyway and had plans to makes lots of money in the future, so going to school for another eight years sounded dumb to him now.

With him now majoring in business and Mitchell still being in pre-med, they started to take fewer and fewer classes together. Mitchell found himself needing to spend more time studying to make sure he was grasping the concepts, while Scott was partying most of his time away.

Mitchell and Scott would still hang out from time to time and Mitchell would even drink with Scott if he felt the event merited it, but he was very careful to monitor how much he drank, as he wouldn't allow it to interfere with his ability to learn and grasp the more difficult concepts in his classes.

As the years went by and the four years were almost up, Mitchell had applied to several med schools where he felt he had a good chance. He asked Scott what his plans were, and Scott said he was going to need an extra semester to finish since he had to drop a few classes along the way that he hadn't passed.

Mitchell didn't think that was a big deal, but when he asked Scott what his plans were once he graduated, Scott still didn't seem to have any clear direction. He said he was thinking about grad school but was so tired of college that he felt he needed a break.

He said he heard of a few companies where his fraternity brothers were working that seemed to pay well and were fun places to work, so he figured he would do the same.

Mitchell went on to med school and became a doctor, having to go to school for six more years total to complete his degree and residency. At 28, he graduated from his residency program and got his first full-time offer making $325,000 per year.

He and Scott continued to stay in touch over the years, but as time progressed, it was less and less.

By the time Mitchell graduated from his program, he last heard that Scott had switched jobs for the third time and was now working as a business analyst for a marketing firm, making around $80,000 per year, not a bad salary for being six years out of college, but not what he thought he would be making when he entered college as a pre-med student.

After Mitchell graduated college, he stopped drinking altogether because he felt like it inhibited his ability to process information as quickly and efficiently, and he just felt with so many people's lives in his hands, he couldn't risk it.

Scott, on the other hand, began to drink more when he graduated, and this was part of the reason that he had not been able to keep a steady job for more than two years. Either he was let go because of performance or did something at a work function that others deemed inappropriate.

As he began searching the internet for his fourth job in six years, he started to wonder how different his life may have been had he decided not to drink so much in college and to do instead what Mitchell did and focus on his studies.

He started to regret a few of the decisions he had made in life at a young age and wondered if he could've done anything differently...

The Role of College in Drinking

For many, college is where their first introduction to the world of alcohol takes place.

Sure, there are some who mature a little faster and are exposed to drinking while in high school, but for the majority, college is where it really ratchets up a notch.

I went to a very small college. When I enrolled at the University of North Carolina at Pembroke in the fall of 1998, there were only about 3,000 students total, about 2,000 of which were commuter students, meaning they didn't live on campus.

This left about only 1,000 students who actually lived there and partook in many of the activities in school. One would think with such a small population that drinking and partying would not be that big of a part of the culture, and one would be VERY wrong.

From the time I got there as a freshman, I felt the pressure to drink. As could be expected, many students had been waiting for some time now to get away from their parents and experience all the partying that they had read about or watched in movies.

If you were not willing to drink, you were seen as a bit of an odd-ball or lame. The concept of drinking is so ingrained in the day-to-day lives of college students that most don't have a chance to make it out of college without having developed a taste or tolerance for the potentially addictive beverage.

The sadness about this is that it's during this stage of our lives that we have so much opportunity to set the foundation for what the rest of our lives will become.

Our minds are still developing and, believe it or not, we have more free time to pursue all the different things that our heart may desire. This is the time of life in which some of the greatest minds in history, e.g. Bill Gates, Steve Jobs, Mark Zuckerberg, were focused on concepts and ideas to create a better world.

Not that there's anything wrong with drinking a beer every now and then, or partaking in various fun activities, but the environment created by college is typically one in which partying can be seen as more important than actual school itself. At some campuses, the badge of top party school[20] is worn with more pride than the academic banners of Harvard and Yale.

Not only do college students drink consistently, but when they do, they often binge drink. Binge drinking[21] is known as any drinking that brings the blood alcohol content level to .08 percent or higher. This typically means consuming up to 4 drinks for a female and 5 drinks for a male in about a 2-hour period.

This behavior happens consistently in college and is one of the reasons that there often appears to be a rash of poor decisions made by college students. Our brains are still developing during our college years,[22] and alcohol can greatly hinder that development.

The Culture of Drinking in College

Many of us can remember watching various movies in which students drinking in college seemed as normal as someone studying. In fact, many believe that part of the allure of college itself is not only the intellectual challenge of learning new material, but also experiencing the party life and doing things that one may never have the chance to do again.

The social scene of college is almost ubiquitously related to alcohol drinking, and many students find themselves part of a culture in which binge drinking is considered the norm as opposed to something that could be potentially dangerous if done in excess.

In a national survey,[23] 2 in 3 students aged 18-22 engaged in binge drinking in the last 30 days.

For many, the concept of binge drinking is just what you do in college because everyone else is doing it.

Whether it's to get ready to go watch a college sporting event, in which tailgating is as much a part of the experience as the game itself, or going to a Greek party in which everyone is expected to drink to pretty much even attend, college events and drinking are somewhat synonymous.

Couple this with the fact that many people are experiencing being away from their parents and normal group of friends for the first time and are riddled with anxiety from meeting new people and the enhanced difficulty of their courses, and you have a world in which alcohol is seen as a source of freedom as well as a social lubricant to allow students to get out of their shells and experience a life that their parents wouldn't allow when they were living at home.

College drinking is about growing up and doing "grown people" things, and drinking as much as desired to show that they are, in fact, full adults.

I was one of those individuals.

For me, the party didn't really get started until I was about four drinks in and potentially had a few shots on top of that. The goal of partying was to get drunk and enjoy the night, so if you wanted to max-imize the amount of fun you had, one invariably wanted to get to that place of euphoria, i.e., drunk, as quickly as possible to make this so.

For some, this has turned into a major issue, as about 20% of col-lege students are believed to have alcohol abuse disorder. On top of that, the statistics[24] involving alcohol related to various criminal activities, injuries, or even death are concerning when considering how much this could have a long-term effect on one's life at such a young age.

While the aforementioned events and circumstances are not ideal, they may not even be the most damaging aspect of how excessive drink-ing in college can hurt an individual's future.

As shared previously, during this time in one's life, the synaptic development of one's brain is at its peak and one has the chance to develop her/his ability to think in a manner that will stay with them for the rest of their lives.

When one decides to excessively consume alcohol during this important development phase, there is a chance that many of the synaptic connections that will help with long-term decision-making are warped in such a way by alcohol that it will delay this person's maturity for some time, if not forever.

Mental development

During the late teens to early twenties (typically 18-25, but it can go well into one's late twenties) period of our lives, our brains are going through what many scientists would call the golden period[25] as it relates to our ability to learn and retain information that can shape our future.

Think Bradley Cooper in *Limitless*.

This has to do with the fact that at this time in your life, your brain has more "synaptic plasticity" (or ability to learn) than at any other time for the rest of your life.

To explain this, when we learn, synapses shoot off in our brain and harden with proteins as we learn different things to stick them in our brain as our memory. During this time in our lives, we have more of it than we will ever have and it sticks with a fervor and strength that allows us to remember things much better and faster. It has even been hypothesized that individuals can noticeably change their IQ during this period in their lives.

This is why it is very possible to see someone go into college and not be the most studious person ever only to emerge as a completely different person because they were willing to put in the hard work and develop during the years of their life that are some of the most important.

Some of the most fantastic works of art, science, and mathematical discoveries all took place during these very young times in people's lives. Einstein came up with his theory of relativity when he was only 26. Charles Darwin made his world-changing discovery of evolution when he was only 28. Mozart, of course, wrote many of his most famous concertos in his twenties (he died at the young age of 35[26]), and Michelangelo did some of his most well-known work, e.g., his sculpture of David,[27] when he was in his twenties as well.

On the flip side, this is also one of the times in which the consumption of alcohol can have the greatest effect on hurting your brain's ability to think and develop over the long term. Studies[28] have shown that the younger you are when you start drinking, the more likely you are to develop serious alcohol dependence as you age.

Because your brain is still developing and is very vulnerable during this time, you can do much more damage to it by introducing foreign chemicals that manipulate its ability to develop in the future.

Think of a piece of clay that has not been baked yet. What happens to it from outside influence during this time of pliability will affect how it looks and how useful it will be in the future. Once this is solidified, it will be much more difficult, if not impossible, to change this in the future.

Also, the more you drink during this highly important development stage of your brain, the more damage you can do to your brain[29] that could hurt your ability to acquire and maintain short- and long-term memories in the future. In fact, alcohol has a profound effect on three primary regions of the brain.

Alcohol and the brain

The first part of our brain affected by alcohol is the hippocampus, or the seahorse-shaped mass in your brain that is responsible for much of our learning and memory. When we drink and experience fuzzy memories or blackouts, it is because alcohol is shorting out this part of our brain during that time of our intense drinking.

Since your brain is still very much developing during this time in your life, there could possibly be permanent damage done that will make it more difficult for you to acquire and retain information in the future. It has been theorized that drinking at a young age affects the size of our amygdala, which is located close to the hippocampus and controls our fear responses (lessens it[30]), hormone secretion, and formation of emotional memories.

In studies,[31] those who drank heavily in their preteen stage (13–21) had significantly smaller hippocampuses than those who did not. Sometimes this could lead to temporary damage that can be repaired, but there is a chance, if drinking is severe enough, that various nerve cells can be permanently destroyed. The clay pot has already been baked into a permanent form.

The second part of our brain affected by alcohol is our frontal lobes in the prefrontal cortex. This is the part of the brain that is responsible for our decision-making and emotions. When we are young and our brains are still developing (15-24 years old), the hardening of the white and gray regions of our brain due to the effects of alcohol can greatly affect our ability to make long-term decisions in the future.

This example shows the insidious nature of how dangerous excessive alcohol consumption is at an early age.

The first decision to drink alcohol is just one bad decision made at that time. However, as the alcohol begins to take hold and warps our decision-making from a long-term perspective, the decision to drink becomes less of a one-time bad decision, as much as something that we do because we've damaged our brain's ability to understand the long-term consequences of making this decision repeatedly.

The third part affected is the reward center of the brain, known as the nucleus accumbens. It experiences a major drop in dopamine during this time in our lives (late teens to early twenties) versus when we were kids.

Remember as a kid when you were able to get excited at seemingly the smallest things? However, as you got older and "grew up," things that used to make you excited didn't seem like anything special anymore. This is part of the reason that teens tend to think everything is "meh" at this time in their lives. Many teens are searching for things to acquire those same types of highs that we used to experience as kids, with alcohol being an easy fix.

This is why the setup in college is so dangerous to so many students and even seems to be somewhat engineered to create a drinker for life.

You have kids who have just experienced a loss of joy that naturally comes from our nucleus accumbens no longer producing dopamine in the same fashion it did in the past, placed in a new environment with something that can help them regain that.

Couple that with putting them with people they don't know, which can naturally cause anxiety, a number of classes with more difficult work than they're used to, and then give them a "this will solve all your problems" elixir that everyone else is drinking to have fun.

How could you NOT drink in this type of set up?

Of course, teenagers are going to drink and since their prefrontal cortex is still forming, the ability to control how much they drink in consideration of the long-term consequences is just not very likely.

One only has to look at the following picture[32] to see how much drinking decreases brain activity in a young teenage brain. The problem with this happening at such an early age is that it is more difficult to reverse as opposed to when one is older (molded clay).

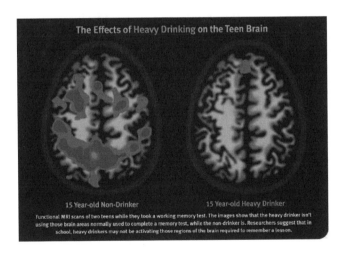

The Effects of Heavy Drinking on the Teen Brain

15 Year-old Non-Drinker   15 Year-old Heavy Drinker

Functional MRI scans of two teens while they took a working memory test. The images show that the heavy drinker isn't using those brain areas normally used to complete a memory test, while the non-drinker is. Researchers suggest that in school, heavy drinkers may not be activating those regions of the brain required to remember a lesson.

Let's review the picture in detail to ensure we really understand what is taking place here. On the left, you have a functional MRI scan of a normal 15-year-old who doesn't drink. As you look at the highlighted regions, it shows the normal activity that takes place in different sections of our brain during a typical incidence of trying to remember or recall something.

There are four main areas that should be highlighted.

As discussed earlier, one of the major sections of the brain that relates to our memory is our hippocampus, as it is extremely important to the transition of our short-term memory to our long-term memory. It is located deep in the brain,[33] hidden within the medial part of the temporal lobe, the section of the brain associated with the encoding of auditory information, and, of course, encoding of your memories.[34] When this isn't functioning properly, we may have learned something recently (perhaps as short as a day to a week ago) that our mind cannot recall now because it never made it to our long-term memory function.

The second area highlighted on the left diagram is our amygdala,[35] which are the two almond shaped clusters located toward the top middle of our brain in the temporal lobe region. While the amygdala is primarily known as an emotional processor responsible for regulating our fear functions,[36] due to the connection between important memories and the emotional response that they evoke, this also becomes a very important piece[37] of the solidification and recall of memories processed.

The third highlighted part is known as the thalamus.[38] It is a large piece of gray matter located in our forebrain on the diagram. This is the part of the brain that captures and interprets everything that comes into our body through our senses (all except smell) before being sent to our cerebral cortex for further processing and interpretation.[39] It helps us know what we're experiencing to decide in what way we should interpret it related to previous data that we already have.

The fourth and final part of the brain that should be lit is the thalamus's "sister" component, known as the hypothalamus.[40] It is coupled with the prefix "hypo" because it is located right below the thalamus on the diagram. While they share part of their names, their functions are totally different. This section of the brain is primarily responsible for the updating of memories and information[41] as you gain new perspectives and supplemental information that could either change or somewhat reshape your initial interpretation of a previous memory. It's the part of the brain that helps us learn and grow, as well as reconsider if something we remembered really happened that way or if our interpretation of it was skewed by external or internal influences.

All four of these areas combine to form what is known as our limbic system,[42] the group of neural pathways that would fill in all the remaining highlighted portions of connectivity between the different parts. As information is moved through each part to facilitate the complex processing of our thoughts for learning and assessment, these pathways should be lit up like the highways of New York City on New Year's Eve. This demonstrates the neurotransmission of mounds of data that should be taking place during this time to show the transition of short-term memory to long-term memory to demonstrate learning.[43]

As you can see, on the right diagram, there is little to no activity taking place. What this represents is that no matter how many times someone reads something or implements different strategies to learn, if they have impaired their brain with heavy drinking at a young age, the areas of the brain that they need to be able to do so just don't work.

When one thinks about this, what's ultimately scarier is the type of drinking college students are encouraged to do is specifically the type of drinking that can create this impairment: binge drinking.

Binge Drinking and the Brain

For college students, the concept of drinking one or two glasses of wine with dinner is about as foreign as not wanting to bury a bone is to a dog. Most kids are not supposed to be drinking anyway, so they have to "pregame" ahead of time, which encourages them to get as drunk as possible as quickly as possible so it'll last for whatever event they are going to later.

One only has to think about any movie about college or high school partying to invariably remember it containing at least one scene in which you have a bunch of students cheering on someone to the chorus chant of "chug ... chug ... chug ... chug!"

This is the nature of college drinking. You don't ONLY drink a few beers to just get a good buzz going. You often want to either outdrink a friend, enemy, or just prove to yourself that you can hold as much alcohol as anyone else.

As a young person, the irony of the fact that young people typically want to drink more is that because of their youth, they often don't feel the effects as strongly or as long as someone who is older. Many times, one can be extremely intoxicated at a young age and not demonstrate the same appearance of drunkenness as someone older.

Also, we all know how much easier it was to bounce back from a hard night drinking when we were younger. These two natural responses of our bodies in our youth increase the chances that we will drink more at one time and more often because we don't experience the type of negative effects that would deter us or help regulate our consumption.

This can be incredibly damaging to the brain long term. Increasingly, more studies are coming out that show binge drinking at a young age can cause short-term and perhaps even permanent damage to one's brain.

Some people have considered the 21-year-old drinking age limit as being arbitrary, but there is solid scientific research[44] to support this because any heavy binge drinking at any age much earlier than this could lead to some long-term brain development problems that may not be easy to reverse.

A recent study[45] published in *Frontiers in Behavioral Neuroscience* showed that binge drinking altered the resting brain of college students and may have led to cognitive issues.

In the study, students who reported binge drinking in the last 30 days displayed higher measurement of an activity known as beta and theta oscillations in the right temporal lobe and bilateral occipital cortex brain regions. In layman's terms, this means that students who binge drink had more difficulty understanding complex information when these regions in their brain were stimulated due to the effect of the excessive alcohol consumption.

In another study,[46] this hypothesis was extrapolated over a two-year period to see what could be the possible immediate long-term results on continuing to exhibit this behavior. In this study, two groups of students were measured for the baseline of their gray matter at an average age of 18.5. They were divided into two distinct groups of light-to-abstinent drinkers and heavy drinkers.

At the end of this two-year study, their gray matter was measured again and both groups appeared to have lost a fair amount over the two-year period, but the heavy drinking group lost significantly more. Specifically, this loss was way more widespread and larger across a number of different important development regions, including the very important frontal lobe.

The frontal lobe is often associated with higher-order executive functions, emotional regulation, integration of novel stimuli, and cognitive flexibility. Adults who drink heavily have been found to have smaller frontal lobes than those who don't, while adolescents who drink large amounts are way more susceptible to being negatively affected[47] in this region of their brain.

The damage that alcohol can do to your brain at such a young age is scary when one thinks that it could potentially be irreversible and make it much more challenging to be successful at various endeavors in the future.

If you think about getting a job out of college and all the work that can entail from a learning perspective, then the fear of the brain not producing to an optimal level can be overwhelming when one's future can be tied so much to this.

To make the connection to our earlier story, let's go back to the example of AC (alcohol-conscious) Scott versus Drinking Scott in college. Drinking Scott found it much more difficult to remember spatial concepts in his physics class, and the large amount of information that he was supposed to remember in his organic chemistry class was beyond anything that an alcohol-soaked brain could comprehend.

There is a reason that some students study all day and still find it very difficult to retain information, while others can put in the same amount of time and tend to have the ability to retain so much more information.

This has to do with the damage alcohol does to the hippocampus and your brain's ability to retain information. As a freshman, you may be able to keep up with the studies because you are just starting to experience college drinking life and are still a bit new to it.

However, as time progresses and you become more accustomed to nights of drinking large amounts of alcohol and hanging with the "homies," the damage to your frontal lobes and prefrontal cortex begins to take shape.

Not only will this make it harder for you to retain information, but it will often make it more difficult for you to make better decisions than you did in the past. Your frontal lobes affect your decision-making and long-term thinking, so whereas in the past, you would choose not to drink on a Tuesday night because you have an exam the next day, you don't think it's as bad of a decision this time around.

It's these "little" decisions that can have such an impact on our college career and, subsequently, life as we graduate from college that no one tells us about when we're cracking another can of Bud Ice and drinking until the sun comes up the next day.

College is so important because it often lays the foundation for the rest of your life. However, if you did fall into this trap (like I did) and found yourself partaking in what many would consider the usual life of college, there is still a very real chance of you recovering in the future, so there's no need to beat yourself up or fret at all.

We will discuss why and how in later chapters, but for now this chapter is primarily for education and awareness purposes and to perhaps warn those who haven't started yet (high school or early college students). It can also lay the context for parents to share this information with their kids to prevent them from doing so in the future to increase their chances of success.

As we continue on this educational part of the journey, let's now take a look at how we can't blame it all on college. The reality is we were indoctrinated with the concept of drinking alcohol well before we stepped on any college campus, as well as long after we've graduated from something that we are surrounded by every single day.

CHAPTER THREE

Drinking in the "Real World"

"It is our choices, Harry, that show what we truly are,
far more than our abilities."

—J.K. ROWLING,
HARRY POTTER AND THE CHAMBER OF SECRETS

Nobody graduates from college to get a job in which we will be mediocre the majority of the time.

When we get that first job out of college, many of us are super excited about our future and what lies ahead. The opportunity to grow with a company and make a name for ourselves is a driving force for many, as the thought of becoming Director or VP one day can be exciting.

Everyone understands there will probably be a bit of office politics involved, and building relationships with the right people will probably be important in the long run.

What surprises a lot of people, however, is the importance of the office happy hour as it relates to the possibility of a fruitful career at many companies.

While your college courses may have given you a good idea of how to present yourself in meetings or compose an email to send to your boss about a particular subject, there are no classes on what the correct ratio of alcohol to water should be at the office happy hour every Friday, or how many fireball shots is too many at the company's national meeting.

Therefore, many individuals new to the workforce are left to figure out the world of Ketel One and Patrón on their own, and many of them, unfortunately, don't figure it out until it may be too late.

SARAH AND SUSAN

Sarah and Susan both started at CS Marketing right out of college. They didn't know each other, but quickly hit it off because they started on the same day and were working on many of the same projects.

Both enjoyed the camaraderie of the office as there seemed to be a true family in which everyone wanted to help the other person and they often did things outside of the office together.

One of the favorite office pastimes was the random afternoon happy hour that would take place whenever a group of people decided that it was a stressful day, and the best way to deal with that was to go to a bar and drink together.

Both Sarah and Susan loved this part of the job and felt that it was one of the things that made them like working there. As time progressed, however, Sarah started to notice that many of the people who were always trying to strike up these happy hours maybe one or two times per week weren't really the individuals who she would've considered the highly respected of the office.

True, some of them were the best sales people they had who did a good job of schmoozing their clients to sign up for large campaigns that usually led to big deals for the office and commissions for them, but as she did an assessment of the people who she felt were putting in the creative work for the office and thinking through things like strategy and campaign direction, it was more the individuals who didn't attend all the happy hours that were the ones she felt fell into this group.

She also noticed that many of the senior managers and directors never were at any of these impromptu gatherings and, if they were, they rarely drank anything, if at all.

As she began to assess what she wanted for her career and where she wanted to go in the next 3-5 years, she wondered if spending too much time at these events was hurting more than helping her career aspirations.

She had already had more than one episode in which she had gotten to the office much later than her usual 7:00 a.m. arrival time because she was still recovering from the night before. She even had to call out "sick" a few times because of staying up too late and not being able to muscle through it the next day.

Also, there were many days in which she was actually at the office and was so recovering from a hangover from the night before that she knew she was not giving the job the 100% that she promised herself every day.

Therefore, Sarah thought that perhaps she should pass on some of the happy hours and instead focus more on putting in hours each day to be successful. She very much wanted to be in a managerial role in 3-5 years and felt that learning different aspects of the job and emulating what the senior managers did now was probably the best way to go to be successful.

Therefore, Sarah regulated herself to only do the Friday happy hours every other week and passed entirely on the Fridays in which she had a late project that she wanted to finish or when she wanted to wake up early on Saturday to get a few projects done around the house or for work.

Susan, on the other hand, saw nothing wrong with the happy hours at all. In fact, she truly felt like this was the best part of the job, in which she was able to party and work with people that she truly liked.

Sure, there were times she had to call out of work because they decided to go to another place after the happy hour was over, but this was all part of building relationships, wasn't it? The meeting after the meeting and all that?

How was she supposed to truly get to know people if she put a governor on the time she was spending with them? You don't usually get to hear the story of how someone was working on their third marriage between the hours of 9-5.

Typically, the happy hour day was Friday afternoon when everyone felt that they had earned it from a hard day of work, but occasionally someone would throw in a Wine-down Wednesday for a middle-of-the-week "break." There was also the sporadic "Friday Eve" Thursday night out that seemed to happen more and more often, just with a smaller group of people.

Combine that with the Monday, congrats-on-making-it-through-the-beginning-of-the-week drink, and you really only had Tuesday as the day that you could unequivocally say there wasn't a very good chance of some group of people getting together to celebrate the day.

Susan wasn't stupid, or an alcoholic, so she made sure that she never went out more than two nights per week, but you just never knew what two nights they were going to be. Friday was usually a staple, with the other day purely being decided by how she was feeling on that particular day of the week.

When Susan and Sarah both started, they were the bright-eyed newbies in the office and dedicated to showing they were there to work. For that reason, they both decided to get to the office every day at 7:00 a.m., even though the workday didn't start until 8:00 a.m. and many people didn't arrive until about 15 minutes before the first meeting of the day at 9:00 a.m.

As time progressed, however, and Susan and Sarah started to get more and more ingrained into the daily routines of the jobs, their habits started to go different ways.

Because Susan saw the happy hours as one of the best parts of the job, she was a frequent attendee and spent a lot of time getting to know her co-workers at the bars and various after-hours that they would attend.

This translated into Susan becoming part of the "in" crowd much faster than Sarah did and she was known as someone who could party with the best of them. Sarah built a few relationships with some of her co-workers outside of the office, but she was becoming more well-known for her hardcore work ethic and focus in the office.

Many times, when some of her co-workers would leave the office at 5:00 p.m. or 5:30 p.m. to hit up the local happy hour spot, Sarah would stay in the office until 7:00 p.m. or even 8:00 p.m. putting the finishing touches on a project or working on the framework of a new one.

Susan stopped coming in at 7:00 a.m. with Sarah about halfway through their first year, so now it was only Sarah by herself, often opening up the office and beginning the day ahead of everyone else. Typically, the only other people who showed up to work that early were VP's and Directors, and many of them were starting to notice Sarah by herself in the office working when no one else was there.

There was one Director, in particular, who took notice of this and started striking up a conversation with Sarah each morning and, over time, they started to develop a relationship. She became an unofficial mentor to Sarah, and they started to get lunch from time to time and discuss where Sarah wanted to take her future.

Eighteen months into the job, Sarah was up for a potential promotion to a Sr. Marketing Analyst because the Director had coached her on how to go about discussing a plan to get her direct manager to approve of to make this a possibility.

Her manager approved the promotion and Sarah was given a $10k bump in salary immediately. Two years later, she was promoted into a managerial role based on continual superb performance and high work ethic. Four years after that, she was asked to step into the role as a Sr. Manager, and then Director three years later.

This had her in the role as a Director at the age of 32, and she was proud of the growth she had made in her career.

Susan didn't quite have the same luck. She continued to work in the same position for two years without a promotion, as much of her work was at or below satisfactory level. She felt it wasn't because of *anything that she was doing, however, and instantly blamed it on her direct boss not liking her for some reason.*

Therefore, she left this job and looked for another marketing position in which she felt she would be treated more fairly. Upon arriving at another great marketing firm, she looked for the happy hour crowd immediately and jumped in to enjoy the weekly festivities and even pioneered the group going out on Mondays, as it was not something they did before she arrived.

She continued to party 2-3 times during the week and got to the office right at 9:00 a.m., or a little after some days. After another 2.5 years, she once again didn't feel her work was being respected, and it was time for her to move on to another company that would give her the opportunity for growth that she needed.

She worked for three different companies over the next five years and got steady pay bumps as she moved around, but none of them would promote her to a managerial position because she was a poor example to the other junior analysts and her work was average at best.

When Sarah and Susan met for coffee the next time, Susan could not believe Sarah was still with the same company that had treated Susan so badly, but had to admit she was a bit jealous of the success she had there and the stability of it all.

Sarah, on the other hand, could not believe that Susan had already had five jobs in a 10-year time span and still had no real direction in her career. She felt lucky that she had found a company that she could stick with for some time to grow and develop.

As the two ladies looked at each other, it was amazing to see how far they had both gone in different directions, when they both started on the same path so many years ago.

For two employees who started out with such promising careers, what caused such a dramatic change in their directions?

The Office Happy Hour

In the US today, alcohol and the workplace go together like peanut butter and jelly.

One would think that in an environment in which professionalism and decorum are expected by all the majority of the time, to encourage behavior that decreases one's professionalism, e.g. taking shots of tequila at 5:00 p.m., would be shunned. However, anyone who has ever stepped foot into any office happy hour knows this is most certainly not the case.

Happy hours seemed to have been created specifically for the workplace, as it would seem somewhat weird for someone to sit at home all day and then say they were going to a happy hour. Funny enough, however, the creation of the happy hour is not tied to work at all.

The origin of happy hour is a bit jumbled, but many people believe you can trace its origin back to the Navy in 1914[48] when the USS *Arkansas* created what was referred to as the "Happy Hour Social." These events were created to stave off boredom among the sailors and included things like boxing matches and target practice.

Fast forward to Prohibition, and the time of merriness and joy on a navy ship was adopted by those who were forced to drink in secret at home or at speakeasies before going out to the restaurant of choice since it was prohibited.

Often, this would be a quick session that involved drinking as much as you could in a short period of time, so you could enjoy the buzz during the rest of the dinner at the restaurant later.

One can only imagine that during this time, it somewhat resembled the happy hour of today, as you had people from different parts of life coalescing to talk about their day and get as good a buzz as possible in a short amount of time.

After Prohibition ended, restaurants wanted to get in on the action, and they started using the term to attract patrons to their locations to get cheap alcohol and food. As the popularity of happy hours increased, the battle between different locations began to heat up and establishments were offering great deals to compete with each other.

So much so that some states actually began banning happy hours because of a spike in alcohol-related incidents connected with individuals drinking large amounts of alcohol in a short amount of time. In fact, happy hours are still considered illegal[49] in a number of states!

For many companies, the concept of the happy hour is what allows their employees to truly bond with each other. What better way to speed up a relationship than to throw a bunch of margaritas and tequila shots in the midst?

Individuals who hate each other at the office often find out that they are best friends when it comes to their ability to throw back drinks with the best of them and consume nachos at an ungodly rate.

For some companies, this is not only encouraged but expected as part of their company culture to help build connections between employees. It has also been a focal point of networking events for years, in which individuals are typically a bit nervous to meet new people and could use a little help to grease the social skids.

This has not only been a point of expectation for some companies but has become somewhat a point of differentiation and attraction for others. At one point, it was expected for up and coming startups[50] to have some type of alcohol served in the building or the office itself if it was going to attract the best employees.

The once praised and later embattled company, WeWork, made it a point to include free beer and wine[51] at many of its locations so the young, talented minds of the future didn't even have to leave the location to enjoy the spirits of the day after a long day of work.

Alcohol has become a very important part of a lot of things we do related to work.

It seems weird that we would associate something so strict and orderly as work to a drug that often has people doing things that could make them question whether they have a job the next day. *Did you really tell Mark from finance that you would have his babies?*

There seems to be such a fine line as it relates to the role alcohol plays in the workplace that many people believe you can't do true business without it. Throughout the world, there are different rules related to how work and play integrate to actually get business done and alcohol typically will have a role in the play part.

In Australia, for example, it is customary to attend the designated happy hours after work and enjoy a customary "shout,"[52] in which it is expected of you to buy the group a round. It is accepted, and somewhat expected, for things to get a little rowdy as the event progresses.

In China, the drinking of alcohol, and specifically something known as Baijiu, the national drink of China, is very important in the scope of doing business.[53] Often a meal will involve making many toasts with the drink, in order of highest rank to least, and your ability to consume it can even make or break a deal.

In France, the consumption of wine, as you would imagine, is big in the business culture. It is customary to drink one or two glasses at lunch and it can last well into the afternoon as individuals are getting to know each other to build a business relationship. It has been said to NEVER refuse wine, even if you're not drinking it, as this can be seen as an insult to your host.

These are just three examples of how countries have put such an emphasis on alcohol in the business world that it could even hurt your ability to be successful in the long run.

Some may not admit it, but there are sects in American culture that are very similar in that if you don't drink under certain circumstances, it could possibly hurt your career. Many individuals value drinking as somewhat of a relationship-builder with the people they do business with.

This is especially important in the world of sales, where one is often expected to "wine and dine" their customers to win as much business as possible. When one is given a corporate credit card with a very high limit and told to use it to "win" business, the lines can get a bit blurry in regard to what you can and cannot do.

As a salesperson who has lived in this world for over 15 years, I can tell you that some people will expect you to drink with them to begin to break down those walls and build a relationship so they feel they can trust you. When I first started selling, it was one of the things I really enjoyed about the job.

Therefore, if you are someone who doesn't drink that much, it could appear that you are at somewhat of a disadvantage compared with your competition and their ability to drink with your customers to build that relationship with them.

One then has to figure out different creative ways to continue to build relationships with customers without feeling like she/he has to drink large amounts of alcohol. This, in itself, is the reason many people don't feel that abstaining from drinking is truly an option they can explore as they work to build their career.

Drinking and Driving

When you talk about the warnings of workplace happy hours, the fear of the damage that drinking and driving can cause are not too far behind.

In today's world of Uber and Lyft, the concept of driving when you're clearly too inebriated to operate a vehicle should be something of the past, but there are still those who make this decision every day, putting themselves, as well as the lives of everyone on the road, at risk.

The statistics related to DUI driving in America are staggering. Even with so many rideshare apps making it easy to prevent, every day 32 people die from a drunk-driving crash. That's one person every 45 minutes.[54]

While it is clear that the number of deaths were coming down (in 2019, we saw the lowest number of deaths since 1982 with 10,142[55]), they have gone up recently with a 14% increase in 2020. The reality is that all of these deaths could've been prevented and forever changed the lives of those involved in them.

What we see when we dive into the numbers is that age and gender play a bit of a role in the risk related to people who are involved in DUI's. While many people will probably make the wise long-term decision to not drive when they have the means to order a rideshare app and get their car the next day, this is not the decision made by some younger individuals.

Individuals between the ages of 21-34 make up 52%[56] of all drunk-driving fatalities in the US each year, with 80% of those being males.

There could be many different reasons for this, but the connection between happy hours and drunk driving charges is something that has been explored in various studies and the data suggests there are some connections[57] based on age and sex. Those who are more price-conscious (i.e. broke) tend to drink more when drinks are reduced and/or provided for free.

I think back to my immediate post-college days in Raleigh, NC, and drinking at Pantana Bob's (is that place still there?) on their dollar nights on Tuesday and Saturday. Basically, with $20, you could drink all you wanted all night, and we often did.

Now, take that same situation and involve a successful co-worker buying drinks for the "newbies" in the office at a bar to talk shop and build a relationship, and you could have a similar situation: someone may drink more than they should because they don't have to pay for it.

While this may not always be the case, the reality is that some individuals are not quite able to regulate their drinking in a healthy manner and when they are put in situations where they don't have to worry about actually paying for how much they consume, it could be disastrous if not monitored accordingly.

When we're older and can afford a $30 Uber/Lyft drive home and then another $30 ride back to get our car the next day, not a big deal. However, when you're new in your career and may only have $100 in your bank account for the week, that $60 is a very big deal and is the reason that many young people still drive when they know they shouldn't.

Workplace happy hours are the cause of these situations way more than most companies would probably care to admit and this culture needs to be examined more thoroughly to recognize the damage that so many are exposed to because of it.

The Dangers of Workplace Alcohol

John said "WHAT" to the boss???

We have all either been in the middle of such an episode, or perhaps just been a witness to one in which a co-worker forgot that the office happy hour or after-hours event was still considered a "work" function and got a little loosey-goosey, as they say, with some of their fellow co-workers.

Whenever there is a workplace event, there is typically a fear of that one person not quite understanding that you can't treat work events the same way you would treat a typical night on the town.

This usually leads to someone saying or doing something that some people might find offensive, which could lead to creating a very awkward and tense situation for those involved. Workplace drinking is typically acceptable for many companies, but most HR departments encourage them to put strict guidelines on the type of alcohol served as well as the volume, e.g., no liquor and two drink maximum.

The companies that don't have strict limits (typically sales organization) and that see drinking as a way to build camaraderie and personal relationships, you have to be careful to understand where the line is to ensure you don't go overboard and risk doing something that could damage your career permanently.

The annals of workplace history are littered with stories of promising young up-and-comers as well as seasoned veterans who ruined a promising or storied career by doing or saying something at an office happy hour that they could never recover from.

DAN AND DAVID

Dan and David had both been working at a sales company for a little over a year.

Dan was hired right out of college with a degree in business, and he always knew sales was the way he wanted to go. David had graduated from college about four years before Dan with a Sociology degree. He got a job as a middle school social studies teacher because he minored in history.

David quit teaching after only two years, however, and began waiting tables full-time. He wandered around for a few years trying to figure out what he wanted to do and then stumbled upon the opportunity with the sales company through one of his restaurant patrons. They thought he had a personality that would make for a good salesperson.

Once he got the job at the new sales company, he was instantly surprised at how much the company seemed a lot like his job waiting tables, as it was highly encouraged to drink at happy hours in the afternoon to build office unity.

It wasn't that David had an issue with drinking, but he wanted to get away from waiting tables because he felt many people there just drank way too much and were going nowhere in life. He thought get-ting a corporate ("real") job would get him away from that. Now, he was finding that was not the case and was somewhat shocked by it.

Dan, on the other hand, was rather elated with how much drinking was encouraged. Having been in a fraternity in college, he felt like the party was still going on in the corporate world and now the company he worked for would pay for the time. Sounds like he hit the jackpot!

Dan was a constant at happy hours and enjoyed the chance to get to party with many of his co-workers. They hired a number of people that were right out of college, so Dan often found himself very attracted to some of his co-workers and just enjoyed the team environment of them all working and being able to go out together.

His co-workers loved him for this reason, and Dan was seen as a favorite among many of them. This allowed him to build personal relationships that helped him in the workplace, as many people would give him advice about his career during these outings.

Dan was a rising star. He had a number of more senior sales-people who were backing him and a few who mentored him to help him learn the tricks of the trade in the sales environment. He started hanging out with these individuals on the weekends and eventually found himself in the "good old boys club" by doing so.

David was more reserved than Dan when it came to drinking on the job. Having been in the restaurant business for so long, he had seen some horror stories of what too much drinking could lead to and how it could leave people in very bad situations.

He often would not get anything to drink at all, or would just get a club soda or diet drink to have something in his hands during this time. As time progressed, however, he realized that most people drank as much as they desired at these events, and he was being teased a fair amount for not drinking more.

Finally, one night, tired of being the oddball out, he decided to let his hair down and drink more than he usually would. Believe it or not, he had one of the best nights ever with his co-workers. He got the chance to bond with a few people that he thought didn't like him and discovered it was only because they felt he was a little too uptight.

This continued for some time, as David became more of a regular at happy hours and started to be seen more as one of the "boys" than he was before.

One night when David was out with some co-workers, he drank a bit more than usual, and he couldn't quite remember how he got home. He was relieved the next day when one of his co-workers let him know that they ordered him an Uber because he was more than a few shots deep, and they wanted to make sure he got home safely.

As he heard the story of some things that he said and did, he was horrified because he had no recollection of this whatsoever.

Many people found it funny, but he had seen this play out numerous times with his co-workers at the restaurant. It was always funny until someone did something that led to a fight or got someone arrested.

For this reason, he decided he would go back to being conservative during office happy hours, as he just didn't want to risk saying or doing something that could ultimately hurt his career.

Fast forward ten years, and he and Dan are both managers with their company now. David didn't move up quite as fast as Dan because Dan had done a great job of building better relationships with higher level mentors for being known as a fun guy to hang out with and get to know.

Dan was considered a Senior Manager, while David was promoted into the manager position only three years ago. Both had been married for five years now and were overall at a stable place within the company.

Recently, however, David had been hearing that Dan was having some issues at home with his wife and that perhaps it was spilling over into this work world.

The only reason David was aware of this was Dan was apparently telling more than a few people about this at the office happy hours whenever they took place. Some people were becoming concerned, as Dan was becoming more relaxed and open each time they went out.

There were more than a few instances in which individuals said they had to make sure Dan got home okay because he appeared to be incoherent by the end of the night. When the news that he was being put on HR suspension broke, David wondered if Dan had done something at a happy hour that put his career in jeopardy.

Unfortunately, as it turned out, this was exactly what had happened, as the details of the incident began to circulate among the office. It was being alleged that Dan made a very aggressive pass at one of the young interns and may have even physically accosted her when she turned him down. This created a bit of a scene in which he had to be removed from the establishment. He threatened to fight the workers at the bar and ultimately the police were called, and he was hauled off to jail.

The company didn't immediately fire him since he has been with the company for so long, and they felt an investigation needed to take place first. After three months, his indefinite leave was made permanent, as the investigation was complete, and it was clear that Dan was guilty of all the things of which he was accused. David met up with him during the investigation, and they discussed how things got so out of hand for him.

Dan said he did remember some of the stuff that he was being accused of and that he thought at the time that it was a little risqué, but he felt it was merited. From what he could remember, the young woman had been flirting with him, so he couldn't understand why she was acting so innocent afterward.

Dan thought about where this left him in his career, however. He wasn't sure where he would go from here.

David empathized and suggested that he needed to look at his alcohol consumption as a possible problem, as he had been able to control it in the past, but he had noticed how it had gotten a bit out of hand over the past few years.

Dan agreed, but he wasn't sure how it had gotten so out of hand. He didn't consider himself an alcoholic and always felt his drinking was recreational, so how could it have damaged his career in such a manner and possibly ruined his life? He admitted that as he got older, he was drinking more frequently and in a greater volume than he had in the past.

This was one of the things that he and his wife had argued about so many times, as he had a tendency to say and do things while he was drinking that would lead to a major argument and would cause rifts in their relationship.

He even admitted to David that he had cheated on his wife a few times, and felt that alcohol was a big reason for why this happened in the first place.

As he sat with David and thought about where he was in his life, Dan wondered, When did alcohol stop becoming something that he could control and drink as he desired and, instead, now seemed to control him more than anything?

This change didn't happen overnight. What Dan experienced is part of the extreme danger of alcohol for many who see it as a companion and friend for so long only to find out it becomes a master later in their lives.

Let's explore how in the next chapter.

CHAPTER FOUR

Weird Science 101

"99% is a bitch; 100% is a breeze."

— JACK CANFIELD

How does alcohol shift from being fun and recreational to a problem? Many people find themselves in the same confusing situation as Dan, wondering how something they used to enjoy with no issues suddenly plays a central role in their worst moments.

I don't think anyone starts drinking with the thought that it could possibly ruin their lives. Therefore, the question becomes: How do individuals who have a good life and do their best to keep their drinking in control sometimes find themselves drinking way more than they know they should and struggling to cut back or stop? How can someone who only started drinking after college in their mid-twenties find themselves needing to drink every night just to take the "edge" off the day?

Much of this relates to how alcohol naturally affects our bodies and the ways we are physiologically wired that make us susceptible to its dangers. We're told by the marketing geniuses of the alcohol industry that as long as you "drink responsibly," i.e., in moderation, the dangers of becoming addicted to alcohol are low or nonexistent.

This is absolutely not true. Due to our natural survival instincts and biological predispositions, everyone is at risk of becoming addicted to alcohol if they dare to drink it on a consistent basis. In this chapter, we'll explore the science behind alcohol's addictiveness and the risks for everyone.

Actually, the most dangerous thing about alcohol is that it often gives little to no warning at all before it might be too late.

CHRIS AND VICTOR

Chris and Victor were both consultant leaders in their respective organizations. They had started roughly fifteen years ago right out of college and had worked hard to get to where they were today.

Chris was the top consultant in his division and was known for always having the ability to close a difficult deal with his schmoozing and willingness to make sure that all of his clients were shown an exceptionally good time whenever he was out with them.

He would consistently take his clients to the best restaurants in town and get very nice seats and suites at some of the major sporting events in the city. He liked to party and have a good time with his clients and did not shy away from the fact that this was part of the reason he was able to win as many deals as he did.

Victor was similar to Chris in that he also enjoyed taking his clients out for nights on the town and enjoyed having a very large expense account for all it was worth. As they both rounded their 37th year on the planet, they were very thankful for where they were in life and how blessed they had been up to that point.

They were both Directors in their current companies, leading groups of consultants, teaching them how to be great at the job and how to win business for the company. They were seen as "rising stars" with a bright future ahead of them.

During this time, each of them started to notice that the hangovers they used to recover from so quickly were becoming increasingly more and more difficult to recover from as time progressed. They wondered if it was time to cut back on the late-night partying and weekend binges to give their bodies a break.

Separately, Chris and Victor decided that perhaps it was time to stop drinking quite as much as they did in the past and look at different ways to interact with their clients to win business and keep their careers going strong.

As they started down this path, they both recognized that it was more difficult than they originally thought it would be. They were both trying to regulate themselves to only one day per week on Friday or Saturday, and it seemed like it was not going to be easy.

The first week, neither one managed to make it the entire week without drinking, and by Thursday, they both broke down and had to go out and do something to let off some "steam" because it was a tough week.

The following Monday was so aggressive that Chris felt he had no choice but to drink and Victor ended up breaking his oath to not drink until the weekend by Tuesday of that same week. This seesaw battle of commitment and recommitment took place for about a month until both of them felt they had had enough and knew they needed to make a change.

Chris decided that clearly alcohol was too much a part of his life to just let it go, and he needed to figure out some better way to just cope with it instead of trying to drink only once per week. Therefore, he decided he was just going to continue to drink, but in moderation. This meant he would only allow himself to drink 2-3 nights per week and to make sure that he never did it back-to-back nights to give his body a rest, unless he was on vacation.

Victor, on the other hand, was a bit concerned that he couldn't even regulate himself to one day per week and was disappointed in himself, as he had always been successful in almost anything else he tried in the past. He felt he needed to prove that he could abstain from drinking for at least three months to ensure alcohol did not have as much power over him as it appeared to have.

Those three months of not drinking were extremely difficult. Victor thought about drinking almost every day and had to battle himself to not do it. He knew that he had to at least prove to himself that he could make it this long or he would be worried that he had a serious issue.

The first weekend was much harder than he expected, as he could not remember the last Friday and Saturday that he had not had an alcoholic beverage of some kind. He wasn't able to do anything with his friends because he just feared they would either pick on him too much and make him drink or would really think that he had a problem that they needed to worry about.

He felt it was best to just act like he already had plans for the weekend and not try to go out with anyone. He stayed in the house with his boyfriend, and they watched movies together, something they hadn't done in some time. He found that they liked the quiet 1-on-1 time with just each other and felt it would be something he would do even when he went back to drinking again.

Once the second week was over, he felt things were a little easier, and he didn't think about it as much. He would get a little twinge from time to time (especially on the weekends), but he had resolved to make it three months, and he felt he needed to do so regardless.

After about the third week, he started to notice that he was sleeping a lot better than he had in a long time, and he felt as if his thinking was way clearer than at any other time in his adult life. He started to be able to process things much faster than he had before and had way more energy than he could remember having in the past.

Since he wasn't out drinking late all the time like he was before, he would go to bed early and wake up early to hit the gym. He started working out three times a week in the morning and eating better since he cut out all the late night UberEats orders that was the usual ritual once he got home from his drinking nights out.

After about two months, he was down 15 pounds and started to think that maybe he should abstain a bit longer to see where it got him. Once he was a week away from three months, he decided to see if he could do it up to six months, as he was down 20 pounds and felt if he could lose 20 more pounds, he would be golden.

As three months turned into six months, Victor was in the best shape of his life and felt better than he had in quite some time. His sleep was insanely better and consistent. His energy level was through the roof, and he felt, mentally, he was sharper than he could remember in some time.

Therefore, he decided that this was just too good to risk losing right now, and he was going to go for one year and THEN decide if he wanted to go back.

Five years later, Victor has still not had a drink and experienced some major growth as a result of that decision, personally and professionally.

He was still in amazing shape and felt like he was in his late twenties as opposed to early forties. He was promoted to VP for his strong work ethic and ability to drive results with the team with his strategic thinking and ability to see around corners. He was also very well-liked as a very personable person who always had an encouraging word for others and never seemed to cause any major issues.

For Chris, the next five years were starkly different.

No matter how hard he tried, he was not able to regulate himself to only drinking 2-3 nights per week. Three nights turned into five nights that eventually turned into every day. By the time Chris was coming up on his 42nd birthday, he couldn't remember a day when he didn't have a drink.

Life wasn't quite as enjoyable anymore, either, as the little things that used to bring him joy didn't excite him at all for some reason. He got in a fight with one of his co-workers at a happy hour in which he drank a bit too much four years ago and was forever labeled as someone who was probably too much of a risk for a higher-level role.

He was seen as competent in his current role, but was not viewed as someone who was a high-level thinker or could look at things from more than just an X's and O's perspective. Therefore, he felt he had hit his ceiling at work and found himself somewhat depressed because of it.

This caused him to drink even more, as he felt he could do his current job as a Director with little to no effort and found no joy in doing it anymore. This led him to question almost everything about his life, and he wondered if he was even happy.

He started to feel unhappy with all aspects of his personal life, even his marriage, and continued to use drinking to cope with it. His wife questioned how much he drank, which led to arguments and even more unhappiness that drove him to only want to drink more.

By the end of the five-year span, he and his wife were separated and on the verge of getting a divorce. His wife said she could no longer live in his world of unhappiness and alcohol. She chided him for drinking every day, but he didn't know what else to do because nothing else made him happy.

If he didn't drink, he feared he would have no joy at all, as his days seem to have no meaning and were pointless.

As he moved into a bare one-bedroom apartment with no furniture, he sat down on one of his moving boxes and wondered silently how he could have let it get this bad?

Is Alcohol a Drug?

This question has puzzled me for some time.

In school, we are warned about drugs and alcohol, but they are always considered separate. We are warned to NEVER do drugs and to ONLY drink alcohol in moderation. From that direction, it would make sense that one would consider alcohol not as bad or as dangerous as "drugs," but is that true?

The reality is alcohol *is* a drug. Regardless of the term "drugs and alcohol" being coined in the lexicon of everyday speech, scientifically, alcohol is a type of drug based on its characteristics.

According to Merriam-Webster,[58] the definition of "drug" is rather straightforward: A substance other than food intended to affect the structure or function of the body.

According to this definition, coffee is one of the most widely consumed drugs in the world.

However, as we all know, there are really two different definitions for a drug (according to Webster, actually four, but the last two are a bit unrelated to how the word is used in everyday society).

This first definition can often refer to anything that changes the way our mind and body work and is also related to the medications and vitamins that many people take to improve their lives and prevent some illness from occurring.

The second definition, however, is more in line with the purposes of this book: something, and often an illegal substance, that causes addiction, habituation, or a marked change in consciousness.

This is the group of drugs that we are referring to when people reference the war on drugs or "say no to drugs." This is what the infamous DEA (Drug Enforcement Agency) spends millions of dollars of resources on each year - to prevent individuals from becoming hooked on them and to catch and imprison the individuals who are selling them illegally.

It's confusing, however, when one considers this and then looks at the specific five category scheduling system[59] by which the DEA identifies the different groups of drugs, only to see that alcohol is not considered in any of these designations. This detailed system breaks down all the different types of drugs and their dangers, and yet alcohol does not fall into any of its expansive categories.

And while some will point out that the DEA's job is to enforce things that are illegal, it has to be noted that Adderall, Ambien, and even Robitussin AC (I'm not making this up . . . check for yourself) are included in this list, so that can't be the only criteria.

From the various designations, it appears the opportunity for potential addiction and abuse are the top identifiers of what falls into each schedule, as the lower the numbers on the schedule, the more addictive and dangerous it appears to be considered.

Schedule I drugs are those that are considered "drugs, substances, or chemicals" that have "no currently accepted medical use and a high potential for abuse." Examples include heroin, LSD, marijuana, and ecstasy.

This continues all the way down to schedule V, the "least" dangerous, with no sign of alcohol being mentioned in any capacity. It does seem rather odd that this would be the case, as when you dive into the science behind alcohol and how it creates the need for itself over time, one can argue that it is the most dangerous and insidious of all the drugs.

The Science of Alcohol

When I started the Medium publication, *AINYF (Alcohol is NOT Your Friend)*, one of my first endeavors was debunking how "safe" alcohol is. One of the first articles I wrote that got a lot of response from readers was focused on explaining why this line of thinking was false.

While drinking every day may be a sign that alcohol has moved from a casual occurrence to a potential problem, there are many warning signs before this that could allude to drinking being a problem.

To understand why alcohol has this effect on us, you must dive into the science of what happens every time our bodies and minds are exposed to alcohol.

The moment that most people realize that alcohol has more of a stronghold on them than they desire is often the moment when they begin to fear that maybe they have a problem with drinking. And while there are a few warning signs that could've given individuals cause for concern before this moment, the natural way that one gets to this point often makes it very challenging to recognize them. Alcohol tends to move you very subtly from "like" to "want" to "must."

I LIKE to Drink

When we first begin drinking, similar to our earlier friends, Mitchell and Mason, in college, alcohol is something that we typically enjoy because it seems to do all the things that we were promised it would do growing up.

It helps us loosen up in tense situations and be less shy than we normally would be in front of individuals that we don't know. In the college setting, in which part of what makes it amazing is how many first-time experiences one will be exposed to, this appears to be exactly the type of help a scared 18- or 19-year-old would want.

Officially, alcohol is considered a depressant, but this seems to contradict many people's experiences, because it seems to give people more energy and "get the partying going" when things are a little stale at a function.

If this is the case, then why would alcohol be considered a depressant, and why don't we see people getting depressed after drinking?

The answer lies in the difference between the way we visually perceive alcohol's effects and how alcohol is truly affecting us from a psychological and physiological perspective.

When we first start drinking, our body experiences a major dopamine spike that is quite unnatural compared to the level of dopamine to which our brain is generally familiar. To lay the proper context, dopamine is known by many as the "feel good" drug.

Any time you experience something pleasurable or enjoyable, your body creates a dopamine spike[60] that rushes to your brain and allows you to enjoy this moment. When you eat your favorite dessert, your brain gets a dopamine spike. When you hug a loved one, you get a dopamine spike. When you get an A on that test that you worked so hard for, you get a dopamine spike.

Pretty much anything that creates a feeling of pleasure and excitement in you generally gives you a dopamine spike that rushes to your brain.

There is nothing wrong with this at all, and, in fact, this is primarily one of the ways in which we, as a species, have been able to survive for all of these years. But we will get into that later. For now, what you need to know is that the general concept of dopamine is good because it helps us understand what is good for us versus what is bad.

The problem with the dopamine spike that is created by alcohol, and most other drugs, is that it is artificially high[61] from what our body naturally creates from our day-to-day normal experiences. This heightened dopamine creation confuses our body and it has to respond, and therein lies the initial issue with alcohol.

When your brain receives such an artificially high spike from dopamine, it releases a large number of endorphins throughout your body. We are all familiar with the concept of endorphins, as anything that gives us this feeling naturally is typically seen as a positive thing.

What most people don't realize, however, is that endorphins are also known as peptide hormones, whose sole purpose is to reduce stress and pain.[62] They are similar to opioids in that they make you feel good and can produce a feeling of euphoria. Even the word *endorphin* takes its second part from the word morphine, which is an opioid pain reliever.

When this large number of endorphins is released in your body as a result of alcohol consumption, the body's equilibrium is thrown off, and it needs to try to get back in balance as quickly as possible. To do so, it then releases another opioid peptide to counterbalance the effects of the endorphins to get you back to homeostasis.

These chemicals are known as dynorphins[63] and they are released in a large amount to get an individual back to a position of neutrality when the current state is spiked due to the effects of the alcohol. Typically, this release takes place about 20-30 minutes after the dopamine spike takes place.

This is part of the reason that often individuals feel they need to continue drinking to keep their "buzz" as opposed to staying continually drunk with little or no effort. The brain works hard to try to get the body back to that baseline quickly by releasing a much larger amount of dynorphins as compared to endorphins.

This creates the constant battle of "chasing the high" for individuals, as they have to keep drinking to keep that buzz going as long as dynorphins are being created.

As the night wears on and an individual gets to a point in which they are not going to drink anymore, the large amount of dynorphins is typically still in their body and continues to work on them in an attempt to bring them back down from the extreme artificial high.

This, coupled with the amount of sugar that some consume in their mixed drinks, as well as the natural phenomenon known as the rebound effect,[64] is part of the reason that many people often wake up at that 2:00 a.m. or 3:00 a.m. "witching hour" and feel a bit depressed and lonely. Even though the person has stopped drinking hours ago, the dynorphins are still doing their job in an attempt to bring you back down to homeostasis. The dynorphins are still present even though there is no further consumption of alcohol for which they were initially needed.

This is the continuous cycle that many people experience as alcohol is such a normal, everyday part of their lives. The ups and downs of the endorphin/dynorphin regulation is a constant seesaw battle in which we drink to feel good and experience pleasure, and our body wants to keep us safe by not overdoing it.

As with most things with our bodies, it has the amazing ability to adapt to what happens consistently in an attempt to keep us safe, and this is where the second progression of our relationship with alcohol can take a turn.

I WANT to Drink

When we experience the endorphin/dynorphin battle initially, it will not seem to be anything special. Most people take no notice of it whatsoever, as most people see the "coming down" of their high as the natural progression of the alcohol's effects wearing off, not realizing that our bodies are actively fighting against us getting too excited from alcohol's excessive dopamine spike.

However, as we begin to make drinking a normal and consistent part of our lives, our bodies begin to adapt in an attempt to actually keep us alive.

While dopamine is known by most people as the feel-good drug, as shared earlier, it is also well known scientifically as the learning drug. In fact, dopamine and the endorphin spike associated with it is part of the reason we have been able to survive as a species for so long. It is through the combination of the dopamine and endorphin recognition that we receive when we do something that we like that we typically figure out what is good for us versus what isn't.

If you go back to prehistoric times, this was one of the only ways that our ancestors would be able to understand what was something they should do versus something that they shouldn't. Eat an apple? They would get a dopamine spike from enjoying the taste of it and instantly associate it with a good thing. Therefore, subconsciously the dopamine received would help sear into our ancestor's brain where and when they found the tasty fruit.

With no way to write anything down or record it on video, our ancestors had to rely on their associative memories to make sure they could remember when they found something that was pleasurable, so they could come back to it again and again and share it with their family.

This learning technique is how our ancestors knew what areas were safe versus which ones could potentially cause damage because of negative experiences. The positive dopamine would have a strong effect on the traverser and she/he might only consciously remember the taste and the look of the new piece of fruit, but their brain would also remind them of all the smells, sounds, and anything else associated with them discovering this new item.

Their brain wanted to ensure they didn't forget it and made sure they knew how to get back to it when needed. This feature of the brain is what happens when our brain associates certain people, places, or even times as "triggers" that result in creating a desire for the potential item that could give the dopamine.

This is very similar to the concept of Pavlov's dog[65] in which the dog began to salivate at the ring of the bell without the food being presented because its mind had made the association between the two variables. Ringing of the bell = food, and food = saliva. Therefore, ringing of the bell = saliva.

In the same way, when our bodies receive alcohol regularly, our brain is taught to expect and desire that dopamine hit at regular intervals to maintain homeostasis.

For those who are not aware, homeostasis[66] is the body's way of ensuring that it is firing on all cylinders and operating properly. The easiest way to explain this is that our body has an average temperature of 98.6 degrees Fahrenheit. Whenever we get too far above this, our body sweats to cool us back down. When we get too far below it, our body begins to shiver to heat us back up.

It's the body's natural way of maintaining its chemical balance, because if any one thing is off for too long, it can dramatically affect a number of other things that will create a debilitating cycle of your body trying to "fix" itself to get back to its normal state.

Once you have been drinking for a number of years and specifically at the same time during the day, your body begins to adapt to this realization and makes decisions based on what it thinks will keep you the most safe (in a state of homeostasis) in the long run.

Therefore, if you begin to drink every other day at 5:00 p.m. because that is your regular schedule to keep your drinking "moderate," your body will begin to think that this is a pattern that you will continue for some time. Over time, your body will then begin to expect that alcohol is coming most days at 5:00 p.m.

Instead of trying to figure out what days you are going to drink versus what days you aren't, your body just begins to expect alcohol to come every day at 5:00 p.m. For this reason, instead of waiting for the alcohol to come and then releasing the dynorphins to counterbalance it, your body decides that it should just get in front of it and release the dynorphins ahead of time.

When the dynorphins are released without any endorphins present to level them, your mood will then go below your homeostasis level because your body is expecting you to drink soon. This dropping of your mood is part of what happens when you find yourself wanting to drink on the days you don't normally drink.

Now, instead of drinking because you like alcohol and it makes you feel good, you find yourself wanting to drink because you don't feel particularly happy at the moment, and you want something to make you feel at least not depressed or sad. Now, your body thinks it needs the alcohol to raise it back to homeostasis.

It cannot be stated enough how important this change is in regard to your drinking motivation. This is where things become VERY dangerous as it relates to someone ultimately developing a serious problem and dependency on alcohol.

The difference between drinking to be happy versus drinking to NOT be sad is immense, and this is the turn that takes place in individuals when their relationship with alcohol begins to find its footing on a very slippery slope.

This change doesn't take place overnight, but it can be accelerated by individuals who drink heavily consistently over a period of time. For most people who don't consider themselves overly "heavy" drinkers, this may happen over a 15 to19-year time frame. For some who may have a history of alcoholism in their family and, subsequently, are more predisposed to it, this may only take 3-5 years of heavy drinking. For those who aren't predisposed but drink heavily, this could take 8-10 years.

From studies, it appears the younger one is when she/he starts drinking,[67] the less time it takes for your brain to think it needs alcohol to get you to a homeostatic state.

This is the reason that many people begin experiencing some issues with drinking in the mid-thirties to early forties, as one's tolerance has increased with time, and the likelihood that one's drinking habits have increased with it is very good.

Some people say alcoholism seems to sneak up on you. No one thinks they are going to become an alcoholic when they start drinking. Most people feel they are very much in control and can stop/cut back whenever they desire.

What occurs, however, is that slowly over time, as the endorphin and dynorphin cycle continues, your body gets so used to drinking each day that it just isn't something that you LIKE to do, but it becomes something that you WANT to do now to get back to that all-important baseline. As your dynorphins are released preemptively each day, you will find yourself feeling more and more in need of that afternoon drink at 5:00 p.m.

It happens so subtly that it's almost imperceptible over time and, one day, you just wake up and realize that you can't remember the last day that you didn't have a drink of some kind. You will get to the point that drinking 4-5 days will seem normal, and your 2-3 days off will feel more abnormal than the days that you drink.

You will begin to feel a bit "off" on the days that you don't drink, and that would be the indicator of the rising of the third and most dangerous step in this journey.

I MUST Drink

When you begin to drink more days than not and your body seems to crave alcohol on a consistent basis, the dangerous third phase has begun. At this point, it may be too late for you to stop drinking alcohol unless you get some type of help to do so.

At this stage in your journey, your body has become so used to the release of the dynorphins and expecting the artificial alcohol spike each day, that it will not only begin to release the dynorphins early, but it will become so used to getting the artificial dopamine spike from alcohol to create endorphins that it will actually lose its natural ability to create them without it.

This is similar to anything in your body that you create artificially instead of allowing the body to go through its natural processes to do so. If you do this long and consistently enough, your body's ability to create this protein on its own will decrease and eventually become completely dormant because it hasn't been needed for some time.

It's somewhat similar to the warnings for men not to take Viagra if you don't need it. It seems AMAZING initially because your body is overwhelmed with this new thing that makes it function much better than it did when it wasn't present in the body. However, as you keep using it, your body begins to get used to it and anticipate it as a necessary part of the sex process.

Because your body knows the drug is coming and will help with the creation of the erection needed for sex, it will then slowly lose its own ability to create the erection without the pill being present. And I'm sure anyone can see how this would turn into a rather sad and "droopy" situation for any young guy out there.

Similarly, with alcohol, your body can get so used to the use of alcohol to release endorphins and create the "feel good" emotion in the body that it will slowly lose its ability to create that same feeling without alcohol being present. What this means is that the things that used to excite you and make you feel good in the past—e.g., sex, hugging a loved one, good food—will not have the same effect on you anymore.

Just like any muscle that isn't used for a long time, your endorphin-creating part of your brain will atrophy over time. Your body will no longer create the same level of adrenaline and endorphin rush that it had before because it will have lost its ability to do so without the added help of alcohol to artificially produce it for you.

This is what happens when individuals start to feel that they are depressed without alcohol bringing them up in some way. With the consistent release of dynorphins to preempt the expected artificial increase of endorphins to your system, you are already going to feel down and a bit depressed.

And with the depletion of your body's ability to naturally create endorphins from regular everyday activities, you will then NEED alcohol as one of the only things that can give you a feeling of normalcy or homeostasis. This is one of the reasons those who drink consistently eventually get to the place in which they don't want to do anything other than drink.

It's not that they desire to just drink all of the time to waste their lives. It's because their bodies have been so rewired from alcohol over such a long period of time that they no longer physiologically have the ability to truly enjoy anything other than alcohol.

It's part of the reason why when we were younger, we had the ability to enjoy almost anything and it truly brought us excitement that we can somewhat remember. With things like the joy of getting a new toy or going to a place that we have never been before, there was a palpable and tangible sense of happiness that was very real.

As alcohol rewires our bodies' ability to just enjoy little things to create a heightened endorphin spike, we may find ourselves unable to enjoy very many things WITHOUT the presence of alcohol to heighten it. That's also part of the reason, as we age, so many activities that we should be able to enjoy without alcohol still manage to include it, e.g., baby showers, kid's birthdays, sporting events, etc.

We have been so wired to couple alcohol with a good time that it becomes hard to have that same childlike feeling of joy and excitement at things that should genuinely create this feeling for us.

The good news is that, with enough separation from alcohol, it is possible to regain that childlike feeling and a focus on truly enjoying all the little things that life has to offer. More about *how* we can do that later, but for now, let's dive into why we were put at a great disadvantage from birth with the social indoctrination we receive of needing alcohol for our lives, and how Hollywood has played such a large role in perpetuating this lie to us every single day.

CHAPTER FIVE

"But Mom, Hollywood Says Everyone's Doing It"

"Until you realize how easy it is for your mind to be manipulated,
you remain the puppet of someone else's game."

—EVITA OCHEL

In the movie *Focus*, Nicky, played by Will Smith (PCRS or Pre-Chris Rock Slap), has been on a losing streak with gambling during a football game. In a last-ditch effort to win back money, he challenges the character Liyuan, played by BD Wong,[68] to pick a random player's number on the field. For two million dollars, Nicky suggests that he'll guess the number Liyuan picks. Liyuan won't agree, suspicious of some kind of manipulation on Nicky's part. To sweeten the deal even more for Liyuan, Nicky then offers that his girlfriend, Jess, played by Margot Robbie, could guess the right number instead.

This sounds like a crazy plan. Nicky has been known to have too much confidence in his luck in the past, but now they think he has completely lost his mind, as the odds are astronomically not in his favor.

Liyuan confidently accepts the bet and picks his number. Then Jess reluctantly scans the field with binoculars. Eventually, her eye lands on number 55. She says the number with a feeling of confidence for some reason. She is correct. Liyuan is so impressed that Nicky got it correct, that he doesn't actually care that he just lost two million dollars, calling Nicky his hero.

So how did Will Smith's character pull off this unbelievable feat, and what does it have to do with the alcohol industry?

Spoiler alert: If you haven't already seen the film, you may want to stop reading right now, go watch it, and finish this afterwards.

How did he do it? It has to do with the concept of priming.

Priming is a psychological effect in which exposure to one specific stimulus affects our response to a different but still somewhat related stimulus. For example, Wikipedia describes that the word *nurse* is recognized more quickly following the word *doctor* than the word *bread*.

In the movie *Focus*, Nicky knew this meeting was going to take place, and he orchestrated what appeared to be a random and unlikely bet because he knew Liyuan would take it. In preparation for this bet, he had been subconsciously priming BD Wong's character by exposing him to the number 55 all over the place the entire day.

He first did this visually. Everywhere Liyuan went that day, the number 55 was in the background all around him. It was not direct enough for him to notice, but close enough that there was no way for him to miss it. He did this audibly by having a song repeat the word "woo, woo, woo," which is the number 55 in Liyuan's native language. Lastly, the cab driver who picked Liyuan up was one of the players on the field who was actually wearing the number 55 that day. How Nicky orchestrated this last trick is beyond the average person's resources or capabilities, but it's a movie, so what are you going to do?

When Liyuan looked on the field and saw that somewhat familiar face, coupled with all the visual and audio priming that took place that day, he felt he was instinctively choosing that number as intuition, not realizing that he had been encouraged to do that almost the entire day.

You may not consciously realize it, but we are primed to accept that alcohol is what we are "supposed" to do as soon as we get to the legal age of 21. The subtle message we receive is, "No drinking before 21, but if you want to live a happy and exciting life afterward, then you NEED alcohol in your life to do so."

We see this messaging more blatantly in the numerous television and magazine ads that we are exposed to, but nowhere is it more subtle or effective than in the priming that we all receive from Hollywood through the movies and shows we watch every day.

DAWN

Dawn was about as smart as you can be. She always got straight A's in school and excelled at a number of different areas outside of class as well. She was an excellent basketball player and captain of her high school debate team.

When she had the chance to go to college, she wanted to get away from her hometown of Raleigh, NC, but she didn't want to go so far that it would take too long to get back home. She visited a number of different schools in North Carolina and just wasn't quite sure how to make up her mind.

She visited a number of different places, but when she arrived at the University of Georgia in Athens, GA, it instantly felt like she belonged. She looked at the huge college football stadium and the decor of all the sorority and fraternity houses lined up on Greek row, and she instantly felt a kinship there.

She shared this with her parents, and they were reluctant at first because of the enormous cost of out-of-state tuition, but decided they could make it work if she got some partial loans and scholarships to pay for it.

To say that Dawn's time at UGA was exciting would be an under-statement. She instantly joined a sorority her first year in college and moved into her sorority's sponsored house her sophomore year. She partied her way through her sophomore year and pretty much had to repeat it the following year. Two years later, she was still more than 40 credits shy of graduating and would have to do a 5th year, if not a 6th, to finally get her degree.

This caused numerous arguments between her and her parents, as her scholarship had been taken away her sophomore year, and they had been footing the bill since then. They had constant argu-ments about what she was doing with her time, and whether putting so much time into her sorority was a good idea for her future.

Dawn could not understand why her parents were so against her having the full college experience. She was just living out her dream of what college was supposed to be. Having fun with her friends, throwing parties from week to week, and traveling to different campuses from time to time.

Did her parents not want her to live the fun life that she had dreamed of since she was a little girl? They told her they would pay for her up to her fourth year of college, but after that, she would have to take out loans in her own name. She was upset about this being the case, but just decided this is the sacrifice you have to make to live the life you want.

As she stumbled into her senior year as a 6th year student and many of her previous friends had already graduated, she began to regret her decisions. She wondered how she had gotten so far off the path of success that she felt she was destined for coming out of high school. She had so much fun at UGA and really enjoyed her time there, but she questioned if she maybe had too much fun and how much this was going to affect her life going forward.

As a leading member of her sorority, she was in charge of throwing a number of parties and had developed a pretty strong tolerance for alcohol during her time there. This had, of course, set her back in her studies, but she was living the college dream, right?

She was living the life that she had always imagined and was doing the things that she always wanted to do, so why was she now feeling like maybe she had wasted the past six years of her life and was so far off the path of where she thought she would be at this time?

She was 24 years old and still in college and didn't have a whole lot to show for it.

What Dawn didn't realize is that her perception of who she should be in college and what she wanted was not completely her choice, as it was subconsciously created for her over many years of watching shows and ads that planted her desires to help her get to the point where she was today.

The Manipulation of the Media

While many people distrust the media today because of the perception of fake news and the intentional manipulation of individuals' political views, what we don't quite realize is that we have been shaped and molded by what we see on television for about as long as the medium itself has existed.

From the very beginning of television, the power of its ability to influence the hearts and minds of those who watched it has been recognized. In fact, many concerned Americans in the 1950s worried that television would entirely destroy the family-centered values that were prized at that time.

Researchers expressed concern that television could potentially give kids nightmares, and then in the late 1960s, there began to be growing concern about the possible connection between youth violence and what kids were exposed to on television.[69] Many believed that kids would emulate the on-screen violence of shows and movies they saw at home.

While these things were researched and considered possible issues that needed to be addressed, no one was thinking about the profound effect that *commercials* were having, not only on the youth, but on American society as a whole.

The consistent effect of advertising is not just relegated to television, but that is the one that seems to have the greatest effect. In today's society, it is the most dangerous medium because it is the most subtle and insidious. Its effects are very similar to alcohol in that they do not affect you immediately. If they did, you would have more cause for concern and notice it enough to work to fight against it.

However, commercials often seem completely benign and non-consequential. Most people don't think of themselves as weak enough to allow a commercial to influence their desires or decision to do something. And that is exactly how they would like for you to think.

If advertising did not work, there is no way that television stations and companies would spend billions (approximately $296 billion in

2021[70]) on this each and every year. It's the reason why companies like Facebook (now Meta) and Google were able to turn their company's ability to obtain individuals' attention to a viable business that is almost guaranteed to generate billions of dollars of revenue each year.

When we watch television ads, we are cognizant of the attempt to sell us something. The very definition of the word is based on promoting something to create a sale. The bottom line is that the creator of the ad would like for you to spend your money in some way to consume whatever product or service they are offering. There are a number of ways that advertisers accomplish this, as focus and technique have gotten more sophisticated over time. In the past, advertisers were very straightforward in saying, "If you do this, then you'll get that" through the ad. Some of the older Axe Body Spray commercials used this technique very well. The repeating of the phrase "I want your bod" comes to mind.

This technique is still used today, but it is much more subtle in promising something for your purchase. This is usually presented through some type of simple scenario that involves the purchase of some item or service meeting a basic human need or providing some symbolism involving the meeting of that need. Emotion is a large part of this, as companies have found that most people are willing to buy if they are stirred to certain types of strong emotions (desire, regret, happiness) when seeing certain ads and connecting said emotion or the alleviation of it with the purchase of the product.

This more subtle type of advertising is prevalent throughout our lives every day. Advertisements for the alcohol industry encourage us to drink "responsibly" to enjoy nights of fun out and to become the "Captain" of our lives. Corona has somewhat become the master of this, as their messaging has positioned them to be almost synonymous with vacations and "living the good life."

While these advertisements are highly effective, especially when we're very young and curious about the way the world works, they are not anywhere near as effective as another medium. This method is more subtle and yet much more effective when it comes to manipulating us: shows and movies.

Manipulation Through Storytelling

We often don't think about any type of social engineering or advertising taking place during a movie or show, as we are more focused on the storyline and the plight of the main characters. However, it is this assumption that makes the influence of movies and shows on our decision-making so ingenious.

Let's go back to traditional advertising to explain it in a bit more detail.

One of the ways advertising works is to do something called "referencing"[71] in which they present a lifestyle that is ideal and attractive to the consumer and often don't go into the negative consequences of living said lifestyle, based on all factors involved.

One example of this is from the well-known comedy *Friends*, in which Rachel and Monica share a very large apartment in Manhattan (where the average rent is now $4,072) with Rachel often working as a waitress and Monica as a chef.

While they do explain in the first episode how Monica was gifted this amazing apartment from her grandmother, it still doesn't take into account the exorbitant cost of day-to-day living that would present certain challenges during some bouts of unemployment or very low-paying jobs (Rachel was a waitress for two seasons).

Instead, the show presents an ideal lifestyle that would make someone think if they get to Manhattan, they could aspire to live such a nice lifestyle without a lot of sacrifice as well.

We often see the same ideals played out with alcohol. Many times, we will see either positive or even neutral alcohol consumption on shows and in movies. In this manner, you often see the main character indulging in alcohol as much as they desire, with little to no negative consequences demonstrated in the moment or later.

Many times, shows will have the character perform some physical or mental feat that the average person would not be capable of while under the influence. Have you ever watched an episode of *Scandal* to see Oliva Pope sit down to read a 30-page deposition with a glass of wine?

I know that it is possible for many people to only have one glass of wine or alcohol in general and not feel tempted to drink a second one. However, the reason they are able to do so is likely because they do not drink alcohol on a consistent basis and, therefore, have not developed the psychological and physiological cravings we discussed in the previous chapters.

Anyone who watches *Scandal* would know that Olivia Pope's consumption of wine seems to be a bit more than casual, as she and Annalise Keating from *How to Get Away With Murder* seem to share the same habit of using alcohol as their "go-to" in times of stress . . . and there are LOTS of times of stress in a Shonda Rhimes drama.

For the purpose of fully looking at this from all angles and playing devil's advocate, let's say that Olivia is someone who can drink one glass of wine and not desire to have another one easily.

This would lead one to believe that she is what most would consider a "lightweight" as it relates to drinking. We've all seen those individuals who often are able to get a very light buzz off of one drink because they don't drink that often. Therefore, that one glass would have a strong effect, altering this individual's ability to think and act normally, as the natural depressant effects of alcohol take place.

It's unlikely that lightweights would feel they are at their best with even just one glass of wine, or that they would have the high level of mental acuity needed to digest difficult information in a manner that allows one to retain it for proper recall or analysis. And while some may argue from recent studies[72] and the history of some of the best writers of all time, such as Ernest Hemingway, that alcohol helps the creative process, the reality is that the mental work required to create something new through writing is much different from that needed to thoughtfully and thoroughly read something for critical analysis.

For those who drink so much that one glass of wine would probably not have much of an effect at all (which appears to be the case for Olivia's character in *Scandal)*, one glass of wine probably would not do much and that individual would be fine as it relates to having a clear and sound mind for which to pursue work.

However, heavier drinkers would experience a catch-22 situation. Since they have built up such a tolerance to alcohol and can maintain their mental abilities despite drinking one glass of wine, the chances that they would not then crave another glass are very low, based on the physiological and psychological development that had to have taken place for this to be a reality.

To put it more simply, the fact that one glass doesn't affect them makes it highly likely they are going to crave a second glass very soon.

This is one of the reasons that when I used to drink, I would never try to drink and do anything mentally challenging or important at the same time. My tolerance was relatively high compared to others, and one glass of alcohol would not hurt me in the slightest, but because I had developed that psychological and physiological pull that made me want more after only having one, I knew that I could not drink that one drink without risking being mentally unfocused, because my mind would be telling me to have another.

This is the side of drinking that movies almost never show. They always make it seem as if you can do *both*, as opposed to it typically being a decision you need to make to ensure you are able to complete whatever task you are attempting to the best of your ability.

Hollywood often presents a world in which you can drink with little to no consequences and the negative effect of having made the decision to drink almost never truly is presented in the manner that it would probably play out in real life.

Hollywood wants you to believe that when you drink, there are no negative repercussions. You never see how crappy their presentation turns out the next day because they didn't prepare as seriously as they should have or how they missed some important aspect of a crime scene as a detective because they were trying to get over their hangover.

No. Instead, Olivia Pope is always on point and seems to have digested everything to the nth degree, never missing a beat.

Often, the speed with which Hollywood shows a character having recovered from a hangover is beyond comical, when one thinks about it. Robert Downey's Jr.'s portrayal of Sherlock Holmes is a great example of this, in which Sherlock drinks incessantly yet is always ready to fight and deduct with the utmost precision and wit.

This is also very prevalent in crime and cop shows similar to Sherlock, in which the main detective has a drinking problem, e.g., Jessica Jones[73] or Strike,[74] and they are able to bounce back the next day with the greatest of speed.

If there is any semblance of a hangover, it is often a quick scene in which the character is popping a few pain relievers the next morning, but they are still at work that day at the top of their game, ready to figure out whatever murder occurred last night. There are very few instances of characters calling out of work to actually recover or even missing work because of something stupid they did while drinking that put them in some legal trouble of their own.

Movies and shows also don't tend to acknowledge how impaired one's mental capabilities can become when one drinks on a consistent basis. Instead, you still see the characters have the same mental clarity regardless of alcohol consumption that often makes them the smartest person in the room.

The connection between Hollywood and its influence in persuading individuals to use certain types of dangerous products has been recognized for decades. In a speech to his marketing division in 1983, Hamish Maxwell, the president of Philip Morris International, said, "I do feel heartened at the increasing number of occasions when I go to a movie and see a pack of cigarettes in the hands of the leading lady." Maxwell continued, "We must continue to exploit new opportunities to get cigarettes on screen and into the hands of smokers."

While in 1970, smoking was banned from advertising on television and paying actors to use their products on the big screen (from 1979–1983, Sylvester Stallone actually had a contract that he had to smoke in his movie to receive royalties from one tobacco company up to the tune of $300,000), alcohol was not, and alcohol manufacturers still make the most of this opportunity, as they make up 1.5% of all advertisements on television and 7% of all ads during sports programming.[75]

One study performed in 2015[76] pointed out that alcohol use in movies definitely has an impact on whether adolescents decided to try alcohol in the future, as subjects who were exposed to high alcohol use in movies were 1.2 times more likely than those who were not and 1.7 times (almost twice as much) more likely to binge drink. They were also 2.4 more times to drink weekly and 2 times more likely to have had alcohol-related difficulties in the past (e.g., alcohol-related problems, drinking in hazardous situations, police problems, issues related to school, etc.).

In another study done internationally, there was a connection between European adolescents being exposed to alcohol through movies and subsequent risky behavior in the future. In this study,[77] it was discovered that students who were exposed to alcohol through movies were twice as likely (127% greater) to try alcohol as a result of seeing those movies and three times more likely (225% greater) to engage in binge drinking as a result of said exposure.

The interesting part about many of these studies is that they are almost exclusively focused on those below the age of 18, while ignoring the effects of movies on the acceptance and potential continual abuse of alcohol by adults as they age. While it can be argued that many of our views of alcohol and behaviors in regard to what is acceptable related to it begins when we are young, we cannot deny that our continual desire to drink and include alcohol in almost all aspects of our lives is still influenced by the things we watch on television as we age.

The alcohol industry executives seem to recognize this, as the depiction of alcohol use in movies has increased dramatically over the past years. It is believed that this has taken the form of native advertising in movies, in which a character is shown drinking a particular brand of alcohol without explicitly drawing attention to it.

This type of advertising is very subtle but still effective in influencing the viewer to have a favorable view of the brand if the character appears to have a positive experience while consuming it. This type of subtle advertising of alcohol has increased dramatically over time.

A study was done in 1996[78] and then repeated again in 2017 to quantify the depiction of alcohol brands (something that would seem to indicate this was not just an accident) in the top 100 films of the year, and there was a 96% increase of this reality.

In this study, researchers found that 80% of movies have some type of alcohol depiction throughout the movie, including even G and PG rated movies. Many of these depictions are of positive experiences that involve camaraderie or some type of party environment that would make the viewer desire to partake in a similar activity.

Taking into consideration the results of the previously shared study that demonstrates the negative impact such portrayals can have on youth viewers, there can be no denial that such things don't affect adults as well. You first have to take into account simply that if we are all adults, then it is a fact that we were once adolescents and similarly exposed to the same type of subconscious advertisement of alcohol to which these studies refer.

All of us have been influenced by these depictions in the past and our current view on the acceptability of consistent alcohol consumption has been shaped by these things, whether we're consciously aware of it or not.

From research, it has been proven that creating exposure to new and different views can change a person's perspective on a number of things. For example, through film, it has been proven that individuals have changed their view of gender-based beliefs,[79] as well as views on ethnic stereotypes.[80] Films have also created more empathy for individuals with various mental disorders[81] as well as those in the gay[82] and transgender[83] community.

Movies and television have such a tremendous effect on shaping almost every aspect of how we look at the world today and to not recognize that alcohol falls into this category would seem that we are turning a blind eye to reality.

Much of what we've been taught about alcohol has been through commercial mediums in some shape, form, or fashion—and now that we know how easy it is to manipulate these mediums, we have to question our almost religious acceptance of alcohol as a necessary part of our lives.

Have we really stopped to question what our lives would be like without it, and if there is any opportunity for us to create a different world for ourselves if we adopted this view?

Is alcohol really a necessary and fun part of our lives, or have we just made it so? What would a bachelor's party be without alcohol to spruce it up? How would we get all those endless memories from our nights in college and our wedding day without it?

What could you possibly have to gain by stopping drinking that can in any way make it worth it?

I'm glad you asked, my friend.

The answer is very simple, and if you are willing to consider it, your life will be forever changed for the better.

Let's discuss in detail, as we move to the next chapter and section of how this decision can be the beginning of a life that you may have never imagined.

PART II

What Do You Have
To Gain By Becoming
Alcohol-Conscious?

CHAPTER SIX

Everything!
The Concept of the Inverted Triangle

"Give me a place to stand and with a lever,
I will move the whole world."

—ARCHIMEDES

T he quote above by the ancient Greek mathematician, Archimedes, demonstrates the power of having the right amount of focus on the right things.

To accomplish our goals, we are sometimes faced with the decision to work harder or smarter. While working harder will always have its place in the historical context of all human achievement, working smarter has always been the decision that has allowed many people to achieve things they may have previously not thought possible. Working smarter can be pretty much boiled down to identifying and stopping those things that are hindering one's progress and instead focusing the majority, if not all, of our energy on those things that will give us the biggest ROI on our time and energy.

Alcohol is one of the major factors that prevents us from working smarter. To truly understand how alcohol can negatively affect someone's ability to maximize their potential, let me introduce a concept that I created called the Inverted Triangle.

The Inverted Triangle (see below) is the structure of success for all of our lives. If we can identify the base and overcome our deficiency there, we can see cascading success in almost all the different areas of our lives. In all transparency, this symbol was also associated with the classification of Jews at Nazi concentration camps[84] in the past, so I want to acknowledge that truth for the reader. However, for this explanation, it is a visual representation of the one thing in life that can be holding you back from accomplishing all the things you desire in life.

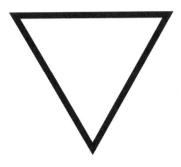

How does it work?

The top, dual-angled side of the triangle represents all the things that you want to accomplish in life, laid out in a pattern of three rows demonstrating the most difficult accomplishments on the top row, with the less difficult achievements in the two rows below them.

Underneath the top three rows are the habits that one needs to do consistently to achieve the goals on the top. Below is what my Inverted Triangle looks like as I work to accomplish a number of different things in life.

There are a number of different types of daily activities that will go into my being successful in my endeavors, and these things will generally require a level of commitment and consistency from me to actualize the effects that I desire.

At the base of the triangle is the one thing that I was able to identify as the biggest lever for what could possibly hold me back from achieving these things. It is the one thing that, if I'm truly honest with myself, I knew was keeping me from stepping up my game to do all the things I knew I was capable of.

Depending on your goals, you will have a number of different inverted triangles that will focus on a number of different aspects of your life. Many of them will often boil down to one thing as the main culprit.

For me, the base of my Inverted Triangles always boiled down to one thing: alcohol.

I knew that for me to have a chance to exhibit the characteristics and habits that would get me anywhere close to reaching the three highest levels of success in my triangle, I had to be willing to give up alcohol first.

For many, it is the negative gift that keeps on giving. Often, it doesn't cause just one negative thing to happen in life, but creates a series of negative consequences that build upon themselves over time. These events make it difficult for anyone to stay committed to one single path for any amount of time and ultimately is the reason why many feel they have underachieved in life.

To understand the positive aspects of overcoming the base of your inverted triangle, you must first understand the negative aspects of it and recognize how it makes it almost impossible to achieve all of the things you desire with something so negative holding you back all the time.

SHAREIF

Shareif was a brand-new schoolteacher who enjoyed reading and teaching English at Green Hope High School in Cary, NC. He woke up early most mornings and spent hours on the weekend reading and researching all the information he could to make his lesson plans exciting for his students.

He would work out most mornings before school around 5:00 a.m. and ate pretty healthy across the board.

As his first year wore on, however, he noticed that there was a group of young teachers who always got together on Tuesday and Friday afternoons after school at a local bar in town and talked about a number of different things. These newer teachers were right out of college or were single, unmarried teachers who didn't have kids or other responsibilities waiting for them at home. These afternoons would consist of each member sharing their favorite funny story of the week so far, while consuming their favorite alcoholic beverage of choice.

Being new, Shareif felt compelled to join them since he didn't know anyone in town and soon found himself really looking forward to the Tuesday and Friday "Post Work Review," as they called it.

When he first started attending these meetings, he wouldn't stay too long, as they would meet around 4:30 p.m., and he would try to be gone by 5:30 or 6:00 so he could make it home at a decent time to maybe get some work in before bed. Since this was his first year, he always felt compelled to prepare for the next day's lesson the night before to make sure he didn't forget anything the next day.

While he enjoyed the camaraderie of getting to know the new teachers, he didn't like how much the teachers seemed to only complain about the students during this time and didn't want to allow it to jade his perspective if possible. Sure, the students weren't perfect, but they were kids after all and were only doing what kids did. He was generally pretty positive and felt kids lived up to the expectations that teachers place on them. Also, they were only the products of their parents' parenting, so it was hard to blame them completely for their own behavior.

However, since he didn't have a lot of other friends in the local area at the time, he felt he didn't have much of a choice and decided to keep hanging out there to kill time but not to let their negativity rub off on him.

As the second half of the year wore on, however, he found that he was starting to enjoy the company of his fellow teachers more and more and didn't have the same desire to get home early for prep as he did before.

While the pull was still somewhat there in the back of his head to get home early to prepare for the next day's lesson, his desire to make friends at the school and drink another round of drinks seemed to be much stronger now.

Therefore, 6:00 p.m. started to look more like 7:00, which eventually turned into 8:00. By the time he was leaving at 8:00, he had just enough time to make it home and get something to eat to soak up the alcohol he had been consuming for over three hours to make sure he woke up in the morning sober and not be hungover for his classes the next day.

He used to wake up at 5:00 a.m. to work out each day before school, but on the Wednesday after the Tuesday night Review, there was a better chance of Michael Jordan not taking something disrespectful personally in basketball than him waking up early to work out.

On Friday nights, he would extend his time out to 11:00 p.m. or even midnight, and didn't wake up the next day until around 10:00 a.m. or even later. This changed his weekend schedule from waking up early on Saturday, working out, and then reviewing the lesson plans from the previous week to improve them, to his not having the energy or desire to do any of it.

Instead, when he did finally wake up on Saturday, he would gather some strength to begin getting some work done by 3:00 p.m. or 4:00, but usually, shortly after, he was getting calls from his fellow teacher friends around 6:00 to see if he wanted to meet for another night on the town.

At first, he would always pass on these nights, as drinking two nights in a row was something he was not used to. He never did it in college, and he didn't think that his liver could take it. Also, he felt he needed Sunday to at least do a quick review of the previous week and spend time creating future lesson plans. He was very industrious with his efforts in pre-planning lessons and was typically 4–6 weeks ahead of the students in having a general sense of what he was going to do and how he was going to do it. He knew drinking two nights in a row would make it hard, if not impossible, for him to do this on Sunday.

As time progressed, however, and the Tuesday and Friday night routine became a staple of his week, he found that he was even starting to look forward to the Saturday night follow-up. He found that his body began making him feel that he could bounce back relatively quickly on Saturday and by the time 6:00 p.m. came around, he began to get a little itch to go out and have another fun night with his friends. Why not? It was the weekend, after all.

Just as he had previously been meticulous about planning his lesson plans accordingly and prepping before each week and class, he learned that if he ate certain things and monitored his drinking accordingly, he could maximize his time to drink without feeling like he was doing too much damage to his liver because he didn't want to feel like complete sh*t the next day.

Pretty soon, however, he would wake up later than he wanted on Sunday (having missed another work out) and then would be scrambling to try to review the previous week and plan for future weeks. This ultimately turned into him forgetting the review altogether and just focusing on making sure he was prepared for the upcoming week.

Since he was so pressed for time, he didn't have the ability to look as far ahead with future planning as he had in the past and went from being 4–6 weeks ahead to just being prepared week to week.

He also started to make a number of mistakes in his lesson plans, which sometimes had him trying to figure out what to give students to kill time, as he had not prepared properly with his backups in case an assignment didn't go the way he had planned.

In the past, he would have a number of possible avenues to go, as he anticipated his ideas not always panning out as planned. However, since he was not spending the time preparing for lessons and having contingencies for the unexpected, he was often left trying to improvise, which made him look highly unprepared and disheveled.

He also found himself starting to share a little bit in the negativity of the other teachers and was much more irritable and less patient with his students than he had been in the past. Whereas before, he would laugh something off and find time to grab a student after class to better understand a comment or something they said or did in class, he now found himself much too tired and focused on his own head feeling better than to care enough to follow up on these episodes as much anymore.

His overall health was also taking a bit of a hit during this time. He had gained a fair amount of weight over the past six months since he no longer was waking up early to work out as he did in the past. He definitely didn't work out on Wednesday, Saturday, or Sunday mornings because he was just too hungover from the night before and found it increasingly difficult to even wake up on the days that he wasn't drinking, since he still needed to catch up on sleep from the previous nights.

Whereas in the past, he would spend his open, planning period grading papers and getting himself set up for a class a few weeks down the road, he was now using it to get an extra hour of sleep in when he could because he was generally just so tired.

Where he had received amazing scores from all of his students and teachers his first semester teaching, he now received below-average scores his second semester. As he finished his year review, the principal didn't try to make him feel too bad, as he said scores can fluctuate greatly between semesters based on the group of students you get.

Shareif thanked him for his sentiment, but left knowing exactly what had changed from when he first started teaching back in the fall to where things stood now. As he left the principal's office, thinking *about his career and the commitment he made to himself to be the best teacher possible, he knew what he had to do if he wanted to truly live up to that promise.*

As you can imagine, the determining factor was how much he was drinking. He came to the conclusion that hanging out and drinking with the other teachers and complaining about how terrible their jobs were was not really helping him in any capacity. Therefore, he decided that the Tuesday and Friday nights on the town were not the best use of his time, and it was time to recommit himself to what he knew he needed to do to be the quality of teacher that he had always set out to be.

He stopped going to the happy hours altogether and was able to get back on his regular workout and sleep routine as he had in the past. He started getting seven or more hours of sleep every night again and began feeling much better in the morning.

He went back to working out every morning and found his energy level coming back as he began to shed the weight from his waist. Since he was waking up early again on the weekends, he started to come up with some pretty creative ideas for his lesson plans and was getting excited about delivering them to the class to see their faces and watch how they responded to learning something in a different way.

Overall, his passion for the job started to return and he began to feel the same excitement that he had felt that first day over a year ago. He began to realize that drinking alcohol and hanging out with friends was fun, but it was often in direct competition with the things that he needed to do to be successful on a consistent basis.

Once he gave up alcohol and focused his time and energy back on his schoolwork, he began to immediately see the results that he desired again. He was able to give up this ONE thing, and it made all the difference in the world.

The Inverted Triangle

As shared above, the Inverted Triangle's base is the one thing in your life that, if you're able to give it up, you'll see a number of great results from doing so. Giving up this one thing is the foundation on which you can build the version of yourself that you so desire. The flip side to this is if you're not willing to sacrifice this one thing but still try to adopt all the other habits and activities that are on the top of your triangle, any success that you might see will not last because the foundation will not be strong enough to hold it over an extended period of time.

Let's say you want to lose 20 pounds, go back to school to get your MBA, and get promoted at work. Those goals will be at the upper portion of your Inverted Triangle. You can try to accomplish all of them without giving up alcohol, but it will be incredibly difficult to balance everything on the limited foundation you have.

We often don't realize how limiting alcohol can be in our lives. The decision to drink begets other bad decisions that don't make it easier for you to stay committed to the behaviors needed to accomplish difficult goals. Similar to Shareif above, when one is hungover from drinking the night before, it can be extremely challenging for one to become motivated to do the necessary work to accomplish different tasks the following day.

So let's say that the goal is to wake up Saturday morning, hit the gym, work on a work-related project for two hours, and then spend the next 4–6 hours studying for the GMAT for your B-school application. If you don't go out drinking Friday night, then this could potentially be a breeze to accomplish.

However, if you find yourself enticed by the 4:30 p.m. text message to meet the crew out at your usual favorite bar to get the weekend started early, you may find it very difficult to wake up the next morning after a long night on the town.

Similar to Shareif, instead of waking up early Saturday morning, you may find yourself sleeping in until 11:00 a.m. and then moping around until around 1:00 p.m. to get something done.

This will still give you a fair amount of time to get work done, but you find yourself a bit more distracted than usual because your brain is still covered in an alcohol fog from the night before. Also, your focus isn't helped by the fact the young lady that you met last night is texting you, asking if you're interested in coming out with her and her crew tonight.

Whereas before, you had planned to study until 10:00 p.m. and then get a good night's rest, instead you find yourself cutting studying early at 7:00 p.m. and then going out to meet this new group of people.

It is a wash, rinse, and repeat scenario in which you don't get anywhere near as much stuff done on Sunday as you had committed to earlier and you hate yourself on Monday on your way to work, not having done anything related to the work project, either.

Project this cycle out for the next six months until you eventually say that getting your MBA is a dumb idea since you just don't have the "time" and getting promoted will happen when it "should," but you're not going to waste your life away and use your weekends working toward it. YOLO and all that, right?

This is exactly what escapes most people as they evaluate why others are so successful in their lives, yet they themselves aren't. They think that others are lucky and are given more opportunities than them, when the reality is that others have just discovered what liabilities lie at the bases of their Inverted Triangle, and they've decided to not allow them to control their lives.

How Do You Find Kryptonite?

If you are reading this book (and honestly, this is probably true for many people), the base of your triangle is probably giving up alcohol, but it can be many other things. For some, it's video games. For others, it's their sexual desires or even television.

Most people intrinsically know what it is for them because as they read this paragraph, their mind already created an image or gave a little whisper of something that they have been questioning for some time. Naturally, we all have a sense of it because it's the one thing that we know is somewhat of a guilty pleasure. We have already questioned ourselves about it in the past and recognize that we may have an unhealthy relationship with it at times, but we just find it a bit difficult to give up.

And it's because it is somewhat difficult for us to give up that it is imperative that we absolutely do so for our future to be as bright as we desire. We'll discuss how to give it up later in the book, but for now, it's important to recognize what it is and know that you can no longer have it in your life if you are going to achieve the things you desire.

The question to ask yourself is, "Is the pleasure you're experiencing from doing the things you desire better than the regret you have from constantly realizing that you're not living up to your ability and the life you truly desire?"

Now that we've established that giving up alcohol can give you EVERYTHING back in life, let's look at some of the more specific immediate advantages of giving it up in more detail.

CHAPTER SEVEN

Show Me the Money!

"Not wasting money is the best way to save money."

—MOKOKOMA MOKHONOANA

Probably about 1.5 million dollars.

I was doing the math, looking at my W2s since I turned 19, and I estimated that I probably made nearly 1.5 million dollars over the 19 years that I was drinking. Immediately, I started thinking, "What did I *do* with all of that???"

It is almost hard to explain how much money I probably actually wasted as a result of drinking. Being in a fortunate situation in which I made a fair amount of money from my previous sales job, I would sometimes spend money like I was Lil Wayne in a Miami strip club, "making it rain."

While I wasn't paying any strippers' car notes or condo bills, and they definitely weren't referring to me as Buffalo (you would have to research Lil Wayne's lyrics to get that reference), spending money typically looked like me meeting people that I didn't know and buying them drink after drink because the alcohol put me in a great *sharing* mood. As you can imagine, even going out just one night per week could become a rather pricey weekly expense.

This leads us to the fact that one of the biggest benefits of stopping drinking is the immense amount of money you can save by no longer doing so. It seems pretty straightforward, but the actual total amount is more nuanced than just the literal money that you can add or subtract.

KARMEN

Karmen enjoyed a night out with her friends as much as anyone. It wasn't something to which she gave much thought, as she made really good money and was never in a situation where she had to watch how much she was spending when she was out.

As a successful sales rep with her company, she typically brought in anywhere from $180–210k each year, so money was not that big of a deal to her. As she continued to excel in her job, and her earnings increased, she began to spend more and more money out on the town. This would also continue when she traveled out of town with family and friends.

By the time she got to about 42, she started to look at her bank account and realized that she should've done a much better job of saving money over the years, as she had nowhere near the nest egg she thought she should've had by that time.

Sure, she had been smart enough to not waste all of her money on partying and had a few nice things to show for her hard work over the years, like a nice house and car to go along with it. However, when she looked at how much money she had saved for retirement, she realized she was sorely lacking.

She thought back to her drinking days from the past and realized that this had a lot to do with her small nest egg and why she hadn't saved anywhere near as much money as she should've over that time. She had lived life to the fullest and truly enjoyed it, but she hadn't spent the time to invest in a number of things that could've made a difference for her future.

She was more concerned with planning the next trip that she was going to take with the girls instead of analyzing the next stock or cryptocurrency that was going to blow up. As she thought about it in more detail, this wasn't the only thing that had held her back from making as much money as possible.

Not only had she not spent the time to understand the next potential financially beneficial trend, but she also had not put as much time into actual work as she probably could've. Since she would hit the happy hour at least once a week and every weekend, she found herself getting to the office a little later a few days a week, as well as being completely incapacitated on the weekends.

How was she supposed to find more time to work when she barely had enough time as it was to get everything done during the week? She knew that some of her co-workers were putting in time on the weekends to get ahead, but she didn't see that as something she was willing to do. Her weekends were her own, and she didn't think it was fair to think that she would have to spend her own personal time to just get ahead in her career.

Now, as she turned the corner on her 42nd birthday, she was wondering if perhaps she had made the wrong decision. She had a little bit of money in the bank, but nothing compared to how much she thought she would have at this time in her life. She wasn't sure what she needed to do differently going forward, but something needed to change.

How much money do you lose because of alcohol?

It's hard to put a definite number around this, but there are a few ways to assess how different your life could be financially if you just cut out something as simple as alcohol from your life.

The Literal Financial Cost

You only have to spend one weekend in Miami to know the financial cost of adding alcohol to your bill can drastically change the full price of any outing for any given night. The first time I experienced this was in 2009 when the cost of a Heineken and Red Bull was $21, and it was crazy to think that at only four rounds, I was basically at $100 for the night once you add in a tip. And that was in 2009!

The true cost of alcohol adds up very quickly over the course of a night out or a trip. Let's look at how it impacts the average person's finances when they make it a consistent part of their life and usual routine.

First, there is the actual amount that you spend each week when you go out. Of course, the amount varies from person to person, but I'll use myself as a barometer to give a sense of how this can add up tremendously without realizing it.

The average night out for me would be anywhere from $50 on the low end to $150 on the high end. Sometimes, it could exceed $150 if I was out with the homies and there was a group of girls that I wanted to impress, but for the most part $150 would be the upper limit.

With that being said, let's use $100 as the average of what a night out would cost. I would typically go out every Saturday and at least two other times during the week, whether it was on a Friday or Sunday to double up the weekend experience, or one other night in the middle of the week to just break the monotony.

So on average, I would be looking at about $300 per week. Extrapolate this to the month, and we would be looking at around $1200 per month. Easily, $1200 is the mortgage on a small townhome in Atlanta. Yearly, that cost would come in at about $14,400. That amount could have easily been spent on a number of other things that could've helped build my financial portfolio instead, like real estate or stocks.

While this amount is large enough to make one easily see the benefits of quitting, there's also the cost of doing something stupid while under the influence that could turn into a large, ongoing monetary expense, such as causing an accident or getting a DUI. As someone who experienced this firsthand, I can tell you that the cost of getting a DUI is high—and not just financially.

For one, there is the time frame in which you are on probation and are not supposed to leave the city without permission from your probation officer. This can be extremely inconvenient for a number of reasons, but if there is a work event in which you are required to leave the city, it could hurt your career if your probation officer doesn't allow you to go.

I found myself in this exact situation in 2015, when I was supposed to go to Canada for a work trip shortly after being arrested and charged with reckless driving. My probation officer was not open to my making the trip, and I don't even know if Canada would've let me in with their strict immigration policy[85] that restricts entry based on certain criminal infractions.

I ultimately had to miss the work trip because of this. Luckily, I had a great boss who was also a personal mentor and friend, so I was able to be completely straight up with him about it. He kept it between just us two, and it did not adversely affect my career, but everyone might not be this fortunate.

On top of that, there is the cost of the actual lawyer to make sure you don't get a harsh sentence and the fines/fees that come on top of that. For me, once you added together the full cost of the fines and monthly probation fees, the total cost was about $10,000 when it was all said and done.

The Opportunity Cost

Outside of not being able to do things at your current job, a DUI may limit your future employment opportunities as well, as there are some companies that will not hire someone who has a DUI on their record. You may be forced to stay in a job that you hate only because you're worried about whether you're going to pass the background check of a different company.

Overall, the biggest opportunity cost that many people just don't think about is the amount of time that they spend drinking or recovering from a night of drinking that they in turn can't dedicate to getting better at their current job or working on a side hustle that will allow them to succeed in a new endeavor.

As alluded to in Karmen's story, when you are preoccupied with having as much fun as possible and drinking as much as you can with your friends, you often don't have a lot of time on the weekends to do anything else. It is this time that is spent hanging out with the homies or the crew that truly ends up costing more than anything else.

There is a universal truth that I discovered some years ago that I started using in my interviews and conversations with the younger generations to help them understand how to think about work/life balance in regard to their future success and ability to be monetarily successful at a job. It goes, "The amount of time you spend outside of your paid time doing and getting better at the job for which you're paid will be in direct positive correlation to the amount of money people will eventually be willing to pay to do that exact same job."

Therefore, if you are the type of person who is never willing to work on the weekends or when you're not being paid for it, then you are impairing your ability to earn exponentially more in the future. The amount of time that you could be using to focus on ways to improve your ability at work or to work on a project that relates directly to work is huge, and if you don't understand the true loss that comes from this, the cost can become extremely high. Of course, there must be a balance here to prevent burnout and protect psychological health, but if you are willing to put in only a few extra hours to improve your craft and get better at your job, it can go a long way.

Think about the cost you are paying by being mediocre at work. When you go out and drink hard the night before a workday or don't allow yourself the energy and time to go above and beyond the call of duty on the weekend, you are decreasing your chances of being recognized and promoted.

Who knows ... being at the top of your game on a random Wednesday corporate meeting to bring up a novel idea that saves the company tons of money or dramatically improves efficiency in an area in which the company was struggling could be exactly what is needed to get you on the radar as someone with good ideas and a great work ethic.

It's these *small* opportunities that can lead to huge results in the future if taken advantage of. And even if you are currently in a position in which you are producing great results, how much higher could you take your game if you are willing to keep your mind clear and able to produce results at an even higher clip than before.

One promotion could lead to another promotion that could lead you to somewhere you never even expected. By being careful to not drink too much and always giving yourself the chance to put your best foot forward, you are putting the gods on your side, and making sure you don't miss out on an opportunity that could forever change your career.

The Health Cost

While the literal financial cost can easily be calculated and seen in our bank accounts, and the opportunity cost is probably impossible to truly understand, there is another cost that we can identify over time, which may be the scariest and generally takes the longest to take effect.

This is the health cost.

Drinking can not only shorten our lives in a number of ways, but it can also drastically reduce the quality of our lives as we age.

Just as the alcohol industry has used Hollywood and advertising to make you believe that drinking is a normal part of everyday life, they have also done a quite masterful job of using the media to report stories that drinking is good for you and helps your health in the long term, when the evidence supporting this idea is shaky and prejudicial at best.

There is no shortage of stories that suggest drinking a certain amount of alcohol (usually red wine) is good for you and that to live longer, drinking should be a daily part of your life. To the alcohol industry's defense, this is not always their doing, as writers are pressured to create stories that will sell and get the reader to click through. And who wouldn't want to read a story that confirms their desire to do something that gives them immense pleasure is good for them?

Therefore, whenever a new study comes out that in some way suggests the consumption of alcohol can lead to positive health benefits, writers are apt to put their own slant on it because they know it will be a winner with their readers.

Over the years, the reported ways that alcohol can *help* has varied dramatically. Some studies have suggested that drinking alcohol in moderate consumption can decrease your risk of heart attack,[86] stroke, or hardened arteries by anywhere from 20% to 30%. The belief is this takes place because alcohol has a tendency to increase your HDL levels. This is the "good" cholesterol that absorbs it and carries it back to your liver, thus flushing it from your body.

Other studies have attributed a 33% to 41% decrease in the chances of getting kidney stones[87] as a result of drinking. They attribute this to alcohol's ability to make us pee more often, thus cleaning out our bladder more often and reducing the chance of the accumulation of the crystal stones that would eventually turn into kidney stones.

There is also the study[88] that found that women who had a drink or two have reported more sexual desire and satisfaction than those who had no drinks at all, while men saw a slight increase in testosterone as a result of one or two drinks.

What all three of these studies have in common, however, is that the reported "benefit" of consuming alcohol to achieve the suggested results quickly go from positive to negative as soon as one crosses the two-drink threshold.

For heart attacks, as soon as you drink more than the recommended maximum of two glasses of wine per day, your chances of heart disease increase dramatically[89] rather than decrease due to alcohol. With kidney stones, due to the dehydration caused by alcohol,[90] anything more than two drinks actually *increases* the chances of them occurring. And lastly, both men and women all over the world have experienced the negative arousal effects of having too much to drink, known as erectile dysfunction for men and female sexual arousal/interest disorder for women.

Suggesting that drinking actually helps you rather than hurts you health-wise is like suggesting that smoking is good for you because it helps you reduce your weight (which is true,[91] BTW). While this may be true, the chances of your getting lung cancer will outweigh any benefit you might get from not being overweight. The thought process is just flawed logic at best, along with being one hell of a diet plan to try to sell to anyone.

A recent scientific study has shown that ANY amount of drinking[92] is dangerous long term to the health of your brain. This study assessed the medical records of 25,000 participants, with an average age of 54 years old.

The researchers started with the premise that moderate alcohol consumption is harmless to brain health. What they found, however, is that any amount of alcohol consumption leads to a decrease in white and gray brain matter. White matter is how the brain communicates with the rest of the body, while gray matter is where the processing of this communication takes place. As you can imagine, anything that decreases the effectiveness of those parts of our brain can have disastrous effects over time on how the rest of our body functions.

Another longitudinal study[93] took place in over 195 countries from 1995 to 2016. In this study, scientists looked at a number of different factors related to alcohol consumption and also came to the conclusion that no amount of drinking was safe in the long term. The study showed that drinking led to 2.8 million deaths in 2016 and was the leading risk factor for deaths worldwide, accounting for 10% of deaths between the ages of 15 to 49. Whereas in the past, the number considered safe was anywhere from one to two drinks, depending on your sex, this new study said that, compared to non-drinkers, people who drank at least one unit of alcohol per day saw a .5% increase in developing 23 health-related diseases,[94] including tuberculosis and breast cancer.

These diseases can add up tremendously over time, as the cost of healthcare for preventable issues easily costs the world trillions. In the US alone, a study conducted in 2016[95] found that 27% of all healthcare was caused by preventable diseases.

To give you a sense of the staggering size of this number, the US spent $3.8 trillion dollars on healthcare in 2019, which would make 27% of that about $730.4 billion annually. Outside of the next 19th richest countries in the world, this amount is more than the next 117 countries spent on all of healthcare *combined*.

As you dig into these numbers to understand the specific cost of alcohol, the picture begins to become clearer. The total annual health costs related to only alcohol-related problems comes to about $22.5 billion per year and the cost associated with all aspects of alcohol-related issues, e.g., court cases, car damage, etc., ranges in the $175.9 billion range.

As you age, the cost of your yearly medical expenses[96] increase with time and change with age groups. As you can probably imagine, the lowest amount you will ever pay will take place in your adolescent years, from 5–17 at around $1,921 per year. As you pass from the adolescent stage into adulthood, the cost goes up slightly to $2,985 annually, but remains there up until the age of 44.

At 45, we begin to see a doubling of cost to $6,406 annually. Later, it almost doubles again at 65 to reach an average of $11,316 every year. While this cost may not seem like much at the moment, the amount associated with treating alcohol-related diseases can be much more than this annually with time.

As we continue to age, the effect of alcohol on our body is different from what it was when we were younger. As we age, the enzyme that generally breaks down alcohol in our bodies, alcohol dehydrogenase[97] (or ADH), declines and increases our sensitivity to alcohol. Simply, what this means is that we can get drunk faster. This could lead to a number of negative consequences, from falling or otherwise hurting ourselves in our advanced age.

Alcohol has a much stronger negative effect on various diseases as we age and puts us at risk of increased medical bills as a result of this. Diabetes, high blood pressure, congestive heart failure and many others[98] are highly exacerbated by alcohol and the resulting medical bills can increase exorbitantly.

Despite the various health benefits that some have espoused related to drinking, the reality is that the numerous negative health consequences that could result from it far outweigh any positive benefits that one might see. Overall, including alcohol as a significant part of your life at any age will lead to much higher cost in a number of different ways and affect your life significantly.

The costs may not always be apparent, but they will be there and will add up over time. The question then becomes: How much are you willing to pay over the course of your life for the "good times" it seems to give you? And the true reality is that it's stealing way more than just money.

CHAPTER EIGHT

Tiiiiiiime Is on Your Side . . . Yes, It Is

"If you love life, don't waste your time
because time is what it's made of."

—BRUCE LEE

Monday | Tuesday | Groundhog's Day

Every time I think about how alcohol so subtly steals our most precious resource in life, time, I hear in my head the refrain of the song sung by the villain in Denzel Washington's 1998 thriller, *Fallen.*[99]

In it, Denzel's character is a cop chasing a supernatural serial killer that has developed the ability to jump into other people's bodies, and it's through the possessed individual's singing of this one line from this song by the Rolling Stones that Denzel is able to identify into whom the killer has jumped.

I think of this because alcohol is similarly a villain in many of our lives, as it tells us every day when we consistently do the same things over and over again without making any real progress because of it. You can waste all the money in the world and always have the chance to get it back, but no one has figured out how to get time back.

We have a number of different resources at our disposal as we live. We often think of money as being the most important, but the reality is that we can always get more money if we are smart enough and apply ourselves correctly.

However, the one thing that is finite for all of us is how much time we have on this earth. When we are young, we like to think that we have all the time in the world and will be able to do everything we want in the future, but at some point, time will run out and our ability to achieve our goals will be hampered by our age in some respects.

Therefore, to truly take advantage of our opportunity to do all the things we desire in life, there has to be some sense of urgency to take advantage of our youth and do as much as we can as quickly as we can to be successful.

While there are a lot of people who have achieved significant things later in life, the chances of an individual doing that without first putting in the work at a younger age are not very good. Therefore, while money is a great resource that is stolen from us by drinking alcohol, time is a much greater resource that we can reclaim if we make the decision to no longer allow alcohol to be a part of our lives.

LEATON

Leaton had been working at his software tech company as a software engineer for the past 10 years. He had done reasonably well, as he had received a few promotions during his time there, but not at the clip of some of his peers.

In 10 years, he had two promotions and had received a few bumps in pay as a result of it, but his counterpart, Bailey, had been promoted four times and was on her way to becoming a Director. He could not quite understand what she was doing differently, as they both had started in the same department and appeared to produce similar quality levels of work.

For whatever reason, Bailey just seemed to be able to get more work done than he could, and Leaton couldn't quite understand why. He felt that he was putting hours upon hours of time in each week and would try to get a little work in on the weekends when possible, but there were only so many hours in a day.

As he looked at the end of the year in 2018, he questioned what he could do differently to possibly improve his life and change his output. He felt he was really putting in lots of hours at work, but the one area in which he knew he could cut back a bit was his drinking. It wasn't that he drank all the time, but he did realize that whenever he went out with his friends on the weekends, he would pretty much be useless that Sunday, and it took him about half a day to get going on Monday.

He did this every weekend because he figured that he needed to have more of a work-life balance, but as he finished his 10th year at his company, he felt that maybe it was time for a change to see if it would make much of a difference.

Therefore, he decided to completely give up drinking for three months to see how that would affect his productivity at work. As the three months were coming to an end next week, the only thing he could think about was how much this decision had done absolute wonders for his work productivity.

He had no idea how much time he was wasting on drinking until he stopped doing it for a substantial length of time. What he recognized was that by not drinking on the weekends, he had so much more time to do things than he would've even imagined. Surprisingly, he also had significantly more energy during the weekdays, as he had no idea how the hangover of a Saturday night outing or "Sunday Funday" continued to affect him well beyond half the day on Monday but also well into the week.

He found himself waking up on Monday morning actually excited to go to work every week and saw this translate into his producing much better quality of code than he ever had in the past. His mind began to work at a much faster and efficient pace than it had in the past. As before, he would make a number of mistakes associated with code and the QA engineers would catch them, but now he was catching his own mistakes much faster and therefore had more time to focus on why he was making the mistakes in the first place.

This helped him improve his own process of coding that he found extremely helpful in making him a much more efficient programmer. He then began sharing this process with a few of his peers. When his manager realized that the entire team's productivity and efficiency had improved dramatically as a result of Leaton's coaching and development of others, he instantly started giving him more responsibilities as he recognized Leaton could provide more benefit to the team than just as an individual contributor.

While Leaton only initially considered giving up drinking for three months, he saw so much success in that time frame that he figured he had to go a while longer to see where it could take him.

Three months turned into three years and Leaton could hardly believe the success he experienced.

He received two promotions in that time span—one to manager and the other to senior manager. He did so well in his new roles that he was on a short list of individuals being considered for a newly created Director position that was very much in line with many of the strengths he had exhibited over the past three years.

What he recognized was that during his time of sobriety, he had discovered an impressive ability to identify inefficiencies and wasted efforts in processes that helped the company save tons of money as it related to duplicate work and operational costs.

He was consistently asked to join projects and committees to help identify where there may be opportunities for improvement, and now they were looking at a Director to head up a new group created just for that reason across the entire software landscape, and his name was one that was very highly regarded.

The reason Leaton had been so successful in this endeavor is that he had recognized how much time he used to waste doing things that were not productive to his future. When he was drinking, he always thought that he just didn't have enough time in the day and week to get things done.

Now that he stopped, he all of a sudden found all of this free time that he had no idea he had before, and it made all the difference in the world.

Now, on the weekends, instead of having to nurse a hangover to recover from a Friday night out, he was up at 5:00 a.m. on Saturday and reviewing his week to see where the opportunities may lie for him to produce at a better clip.

He was up early reviewing his code from the past week, picking out any bugs before it was sent to QA and then identifying new ways

to make the code even more efficient for the next round of develop-
ment. He was able to spend more time thinking about HOW he was
doing his job instead of just doing it, and this allowed him to improve
his effectiveness in so many ways.

Overall, the time that he used to spend drinking, recovering from
a hangover, or just being lazy in general turned into him putting that
energy and time into figuring out how to get better at his job every
single day.

The Imperceptible, Compound Time Suck of Alcohol

Alcohol appears harmless while you're doing it, and you generally feel that there won't be any lasting long-term effects on your life. You spend time in the Uber traveling from place to place and enjoy the time out with your friends at the bars/clubs, but that is probably the majority of where one would think that most of the time goes.

However, what many people don't recognize is that the actual time spent going to or engaging in the act of drinking alcohol is not, by any means, the majority of the time that is consumed as a result of it.

Tons of time are wasted as a result of alcohol's aftereffects, but the majority of people don't ever really realize it. The way alcohol eats up our time is so subtle and all-encompassing that often it is seen as a natural part of our lives, not realizing that without alcohol, we would be able to accomplish so much more.

We often think of our decision to drink as being in a vacuum in which we only have to contend with the consequences of that one sin-gular decision. However, this couldn't be further from the truth, as each decision that we make will, in some way, affect future decisions either positively or negatively. With alcohol, the effects will almost always be negative. Alcohol creates a debilitating cycle of consequences that can have a long-range impact in unforeseen ways.

As shared earlier, when we are asked to go out on a Friday night, the outcome of that one decision is like a domino effect for consequential decisions related to it. By making this decision to drink instead of staying in, we don't study for a test that is coming up Monday. By not studying for that test, we fail and don't pass a course that we need to graduate college. Then, by not graduating on time, we have to spend an extra semester in college. Having to take this extra semester discourages us so much that we decide we just need to take a "quick" break instead and will come back the following semester to finish up. Four years later, that break is still going. This ONE decision affected our life in a number of different ways.

Now, I admit this example is overdramatic, but there are a number of things that are greatly affected when we decide to drink that are related to more than just the alcohol at hand.

Drinking, most days, creates a world in which we spend an exorbitant amount of time doing repetitive and mundane things that provide no true value for the betterment of our lives. However, since we're drinking, we somehow see them as fun and worth the consistent repetition.

Many people, when they drink, are typically traversing the same or similar types of establishments and have a consistent routine that makes them feel comfortable and safe. They don't desire or truly have the capacity to do much thinking other than to execute this consistent pattern of events due to their already inebriated and impaired state. The flip side of this is that when we try to do that same or similar activity without alcohol involved, e.g., watching a sporting event or just hanging out at the house all day, it just doesn't seem as much fun. Most people just don't recognize how repetitive and unproductive so many activities are when they are doing them with alcohol because alcohol just makes the time pass quickly and it appears that something fun is happening.

The other side of this coin is that the concept of opportunity cost doesn't really come into play until individuals stop drinking and they realize all the things they could've been spending their time on rather than drinking. In fact, when you first stop drinking, it will almost seem like there is so much time in a day that you aren't really sure what to do with it. Believe it or not, most people will sit at home bored and wondering what they were doing with all that time before. When going out to the bar and wasting countless hours upon hours isn't an option anymore, you'll find yourself surprised at how much additional time you'll have in a day, week, month. This time could be used in so many more productive ways.

Not only do you get the additional time tradeoff from not spending all day and night in Ubers and bars around the town, but when you don't drink, you also don't have to worry about being hungover the next morning and trying to recover the next day. If you live more of a Friday night party life, with a night of heavy weekend drinking, you might not get into bed until around 2:00 a.m. and not wake up until 10:00 a.m. the next day. This would create a slow start for any subsequent Saturday morning.

This, in turn, creates a cycle in which most people don't get going the following day until after they have had lunch, and if the night was REALLY heavy, this could easily bleed into the afternoon. And if you're anything like me, and the sun begins to dip below the horizon to transform the day from afternoon to evening, you are beginning to think about how much fun you had last night and how cool it would be to do it all again. This then creates a desire (some might say a need) to begin drinking again right around the dinner time frame, and then you end up doing it all over again on Saturday night.

Many times, that Sunday hangover might be a bit worse than the Saturday one since it's coming on the heels of back-to-back outings. Therefore, if you didn't get much done on Saturday, there's a very good chance you're not going to do much better that Sunday.

By the time you get your bearings about you around 3:00 or 4:00 p.m., you are thinking about how you have to go to bed in about 6 or 7 hours and then have to possibly go to work the next day having not accomplished a whole lot unless you can muster up the energy to shake the hangover spiderwebs out of your head and get to work in the next few hours . . . which is usually about a 50/50 proposition.

This vicious cycle continues most weekends, as you always wonder why you can't get as much done as some of your co-workers, and, therefore, are not considered one of the top performers in the office. This, subsequently, holds you back from getting promoted or growing your career, which keeps you in the same place in life, wondering what you're missing that others have.

Time is such a great commodity that most people would agree it should not be wasted, but when we are living in a world in which our actions are often dictated by our alcohol use, then we just do not think about how precious every second is.

For many of us, the time spent going out with a number of our friends doing the same type of things over and over again are good uses of our time, and perhaps this is true to some extent, as life is much about memories and moments that you'll never forget.

However, as we look to mature in age and accomplish a number of more complicated things than just paying our bills every month, this type of lifestyle can eventually leave us with a bunch of fun memories, but not much else to show for it.

It took Leaton some time to recognize this, but once he did, it made all the difference in the world.

CHAPTER NINE

Alcohol and Fitness
Are NOT BFFs

"Almost anything can be preserved in alcohol,
except health, happiness, and money."

—MARY WILSON LITTLE

Finding a succinct quote that effectively establishes the negative relationship between alcohol and fitness was much harder than I expected, even with how clearly opposed the two endeavors are to each other.

In fact, when I was searching for quotes for this chapter, I got the exact opposite of what I was looking for. Instead of finding quotes and images of how stopping drinking can take one's fitness to new heights, I found inspirational quotes added over pictures of people drinking that actually encourages drinking more. I will admit, however, some of them are pretty hilarious and worth a view for a chuckle. Just google "alcohol and fitness quotes" to see what I'm talking about.

For me, fitness has always been important. At the age of 25, I started working out with a fitness instructor at my local gym because I wanted to date her. I didn't fall in love with my instructor, but I did fall in love with the gym and have had a 20-plus year relationship that has defined who I am in many ways.

It is for this reason that I also started AINYF Fitness, a lifestyle fitness company focused on helping people create the bodies and lives of their dreams by controlling their relationship with alcohol. For some people, this could mean moderating their drinking considerably, while for most, it means giving it up entirely.

The end result is a lifestyle that doesn't involve alcohol as a considerable player in any way and allows people the opportunity to get in the best shape of their lives. The difference this can make in one's fitness is tremendous.

DARLENE

Darlene had tried to get in better shape a few times in the past, but she just couldn't figure out why she couldn't stick with it. She wasn't sure exactly what she needed to do differently, but she knew that trying to do the same thing over and over wasn't going to get her the results she was looking for.

She had tried a number of different things in the past, and they had continued to put her on a seesaw when it came to her weight. She didn't think she was in the worst shape ever, but she knew that she needed to get a handle on her ever-expanding waistline and weight before it was too late.

Since college, it seemed that she had consistently put on 5 pounds every year and now she was sitting at 50 pounds over what she used to be only 10 years ago. At 32, she felt pretty terrible at times and didn't think she looked much better.

She had tried a number of different diets in the past, and some of them helped but none of them stuck long term. She tried the Tim Ferris diet, the Atkin's diet, and the keto diet. You name it . . . she'd tried it.

They would all typically work for a week or two, as she was excited about the thought that this new diet was the "answer," and her life was going to be completely different. She would stay pretty disciplined and focused on following the rules of engagement initially to a T, as she felt she needed to do so to have any chance at success.

She always felt that she was making some progress, but it was difficult for her to stay as disciplined as she hoped she would. She would diet and work out consistently for a week or two and then something would happen that would distract her from staying committed. This could be her friends inviting her out for a drink or a party that was taking place at someone's house.

Inevitably, she found herself drinking alcohol of some kind and then throwing her diet completely out the window. She would be out with friends and enjoying a night on the town and someone would suggest that they have pizza to finish the night or swing by Taco Bell for a fourth meal to soak up all the alcohol they just drank.

Even though she knew this was terrible for her diet and she had told herself before that she would not succumb to eating things that would set her back in any capacity, when she was drinking, she found it very hard to stick to this initial decision. When she was inebriated, she did not find it easy to say no to certain things. She was not quite in the same mindset as when she was sober. Therefore, all the willpower and discipline she had before she began to drink went completely out the window as the alcohol began to be her voice of reason and influence.

For some time, Darlene kept thinking about how this vicious cycle seemed to put her on a hamster wheel with fitness. She would get inspired and start making some good progress, but it would only last a week or two before she was back to her old habits. She thought through what she should do differently, and she kept coming back to the same suggestion.

What if she gave up alcohol?

She had been thinking about it for some time, but had no idea how she would do it. Alcohol was a very intricate part of her life. She couldn't remember the last time she didn't have a drink at least once a week since she had started drinking at the age of 18.

In the back of her head, she knew that it was the thing that was the common denominator in all the poor eating and exercise decisions she had made in the past. Whenever she had gotten off the path in the past, it was in some way related to her going out and drinking with her friends and making a series of bad decisions as a result of it.

She sat there thinking to herself how drastically that might change her life and maybe even who she was as a person, and questioned if she would really have the ability to make such a monumental decision.

She thought about it and asked, what if she only gave up alcohol for a quarter to see where it led her? Ninety days was a long time, but she didn't think she could really see any major results in only a month. Besides, she knew a lot of people who did Dry January or Sober July all the time, and they never really seemed to make any significant life changes.

Therefore, she felt she needed a longer time frame that would allow her to truly see if this could be the catalyst for her to finally stop going back and forth seesawing on diets and truly become the person that she always thought she could become.

The first week was absolute hell, as she was used to drinking every other day, if not every day, at that point. To not drink anything at all seemed like torture, and she just didn't know how she was going to cope. She was used to coming home and grabbing a glass of wine each time she had a tough day at work, and that seemed to be happening more and more frequently now.

She was an accountant at a telecommunications company, and they were gearing up for an audit that was taking place in three months. They were well ahead of it, but that didn't mean that there still wasn't a lot of pressure to make sure they had all the right materials and information to get it right the first time. She had to double and triple check all the documents they were gathering to make sure nothing was missing because the work it would take to find a document after going through the initial discovery mission could be enormous. Therefore, it had to be done right the first time, and there was a fair amount of mental anguish and stress associated with it.

Not drinking that first week did not take any of that mental anguish away. She had done a little bit of research about what could help prevent cravings and make quitting a little bit easier, and she had read a number of articles that said exercise was a key driver. This worked out well because she needed something to help alleviate her stress from the audit, and she knew exercise could be a good release from stress.

Therefore, she just replaced all the days she would traditionally drink each week (Sunday, Tuesday, Thursday, and Saturday) with exercise in the afternoon to see if that made up for it. During the week, she got to the gym most days right at 6:00 p.m. and worked out until 6:30 p.m. On the weekends, she would get there a bit earlier, at 5:00, and still do her 30-minute routine.

As she got closer to 5:00 p.m. each day, the cravings were strong—but she had to admit that she did feel better after working out. After her workout, she was more hungry than anything, even though she had to admit that having a glass of wine did often sound like the perfect thing to quench her thirst for some reason. She fought this craving every time and got some food instead and instantly felt better, because that was what her body really needed after such a strenuous workout.

The second week, surprisingly, was a little easier, as she started to notice some things that encouraged her to keep going. She began to get the best sleep of her life and could only attribute it to not drinking. She found herself insanely tired by 10:00 p.m. (she used to stay up until at least 11:00 p.m., if not midnight) and would sleep the entire night through until her alarm went off at 5:00 a.m. with no issues.

She had been doing research and had read that getting better sleep was one of the benefits of abstaining from drinking. She also learned that sleep was very important to exercise and fitness, as it keeps your satiety glands in control and, naturally, gives you more energy at the gym.

She was experiencing both of these effects, as she was more satisfied with the food she ate and wasn't craving all the bad stuff that she did in the past. She found she was always ready to work out hard after a great night of sleep.

The improvement that she started to see was slow, but she recognized that it was taking place. The first week, she didn't lose any weight and was struggling with the alcohol cravings. By the second week, she felt a little better as she started to sleep through the night with no issues and found herself waking up with much more energy and excitement for the day.

She managed to lose 2 pounds the second week and just felt overall healthier and more in control of what she wanted to do each day. By the third week, she was starting to really see how this could change her life for the better, as she started to actually look forward to waking up each morning and working out.

So much so that she actually decided to push her workouts to 45 minutes instead of only 30 and added a few extra days during the week to see how much of a difference that would make with her weight loss. She wasn't eating particularly great, but she wasn't scarfing down pizza at 1:30 a.m. anymore, either.

The food she was eating wasn't overly healthy, and she found herself eating a lot more sugar than she had in the past (she had read that increased sugar consumption was another initial side effect of giving up alcohol), but she just had so much more energy that she felt she could work it off.

She started working out six days per week, with Sunday being her only day off, and began to see the weight loss increase dramatically. She went from losing only 1 to 2 pounds per week to consistently cutting down around 3 pounds per week.

By the end of the second month, she found herself down 20 pounds and felt like a brand-new person. Two total months without drinking, and she was beginning to feel more alive than she had in a very long time. She had more energy than she could remember having anytime recently and was getting amazing sleep.

She was making great progress, but knew she could do better if she was more disciplined with what she was putting in her body and decided to start doing a bit more research to figure out what she should be eating.

In the past, she wouldn't have had any free time to spend researching diet decisions, but since she was not going out and *drinking two to three nights per week or on the weekend, she had so much free time that she wasn't 100% sure what to do with it.*

From her research, she learned of a number of different health mistakes she was making and began to implement the new strategies immediately. By the end of the third month, she was down 35 pounds and could not believe that she was actually doing what she could never do in the past.

She looked in the mirror at her much slimmer self and thought, Why had it taken her so long to finally realize that alcohol was the thing holding her fitness back for all of these years? As she put on her sneakers to head to the gym for another early morning workout, she realized her life had completely changed with that one decision.

Fitness and Alcohol

While some people would like to always associate alcohol with the celebratory world of sports, there is a difference between the drinking habits of those who watch the sports in the confines of their home couches and those who actually put in the heavy work and sweat to play the sport.

When it comes to health, there are few things that impede one's advancement or maintenance of a healthy lifestyle the way alcohol does. There's a reason this is the first question your doctor asks you after he asks whether you smoke. You know there is a line between what is considered a right answer versus the wrong one. If you answer that you only drink "occasionally" or "socially," your doctor will just give the cursory reminder to make sure it doesn't go more than that. If you tell them how much you really drink (a full six pack every night), they will probably tell you that this is not a sustainable pattern and could lead to long-term health implications.

When it comes to one's health, there is a direct inverse correlation to how much alcohol one consumes daily and how healthy someone would be considered by their doctor. Many doctors will not tell you to blatantly stop drinking, however, unless you have a major issue that would require you to do so.

When we think about the adverse effects that alcohol can have on our health, much of the focus is put on several recognized health concerns. Not only is alcohol associated with a number of different diseases related to your liver,[100] it is also the second biggest risk factor for cancer[101] after smoking and is directly related to an increase in the risk for a number of diseases related to your lungs[102] and heart.[103] However, what many people don't think about is how much their ability to exercise and eat right is hampered by all the consistent bad habits that are created as a result of our drinking. Most people won't die in a car crash from a drunk driving accident or be told by their doctor that if they don't stop drinking their liver will fail them.

Only a small minority of individuals will ever experience that. However, most people will find that alcohol is one of the many things that keeps them from realizing their potential for getting in the best shape of their lives.

When it comes to everyday fitness and all of the obstacles that can keep us from executing the daily habits that we all know we should— such as eating right, running consistently, drinking enough water— alcohol will typically make it much harder for someone to stay focused and committed to these things long term.

For example, someone can have a pretty good run of waking up each morning and hitting the gym at 5:00 a.m. for a new workout routine that will create a new body for them. They have no issues staying committed for the first week, as they don't usually drink during the week and therefore don't have a hangover to contend with.

However, Saturday comes, and as they get a little wild with their friends that night, they find themselves not going to sleep until Sunday morning at 3:00 a.m. This makes for a very sluggish Sunday, and by the time Monday rolls around the next morning, there is no way they can find the energy to pull themselves out of their recovering slumber early.

They decide to skip that Monday, which then makes it easier to skip Tuesday, then Wednesday, and so forth and so on.

The negative effects of alcohol make it almost impossible for us to lose weight consistently, as they can be somewhat insidious in how they affect our bodies and make it difficult for us to stick to our commitments and goals.

Not only does it physiologically slow down our metabolism[104] from a scientific standpoint, the chances of us staying consistently on our diet and workout regimen when our motivation and willpower have been stolen from us by alcohol is highly unlikely.

One of the most important things for someone who would like to have a high level of fitness success is consistency and routine. When one embarks on a journey to get into great shape, working out is not something the body is going to scream for you to come back to every day.

For that reason, your mind will try to find any reason possible for you not to inflict this pain upon yourself and instead pamper you with things that will drive consistent dopamine to your body. As shared in earlier chapters, this is why your body enjoys alcohol so much, as the high dopamine spike that your body receives as a result of it makes it want more and more.

When it comes to exercise, your body isn't getting quite the same type of dopamine spike and, instead sometimes, is afraid of what is coming next because there can be some pain associated with working out. Therefore, if you don't build up consistent routines to put your mind and body in programmed mode, you will find it easy to talk yourself out of working out that morning or afternoon.

Whenever there is too much variability in one's life, specifically around the time exercise is supposed to take place, it greatly decreases our chances that we will stay committed to the plan at hand and follow through with our commitments to stay the course.

Alcohol is the harbinger of variability and novelty, and this is why some people like it so much. You can go to the same place a thousand times and feel like it's different every time if you're drunk. Alcohol has the ability to turn the nominal and boring into something quite a bit more exciting, hence the reason it is so hard to turn down.

The negative side of this is that whenever we do partake in such an event, the likelihood that we will still work out afterwards is very unlikely. Alcohol can turn "I'm just going out to have one drink with a friend" into "Where am I and who is this lying next to me?"

Although this might be great for a story night with the crew the next time you all get together, this may not be the best thing for your workout and diet program, since if you can't remember who you went to bed with that night, there's a good chance you also may have eaten something that didn't fit within your macro count as well.

With alcohol, one bad decision leads to a course of other bad decisions, and when it comes to fitness, our long-term success is typically based on the connectivity and consistency of our compounded decisions.

There are some who are great at being able to balance both (like pro athletes) and drinking alcohol does not affect their ability to be great at sports. And while this is impressive, I would argue that the very best athletes keep strict regulations on how much and when they drink alcohol, as there is no way it would not interfere with their ability to perform within a game.

Tom Brady would be the perfect example of this. While the debated GOAT of all sports doesn't profess to abstaining from alcohol completely, he greatly limits it to the point that most people would consider his lifestyle as sober.[105]

It is impossible for one to be at one's best physically and mentally and partake in such things consistently. This is true of individuals who have the best equipment in the world, the best personal trainers, and the best dieticians—so how much truer do you think it is for you?

Alcohol and fitness mix together like oil and water, with alcohol being the nasty oil that always rises to the top.

CHAPTER TEN

Like a Fine Wine

"It is not how old you are, but how you are old."

—JULES RENARD

For many people, growing old is one of the scariest things about living.

When we're younger, we can't wait to age and "grow up," as it seems every year goes by at a snail's pace. Then when we reach a certain age, it seems the years begin to fly by like a rocket and we look back, thinking, "Where did all the time go?"

Our body starts to experience aches and pains in places that it never did before. Our memory isn't quite as sharp as it was in the past and overall we start to recognize that we are not living in the years of our youth anymore. A good indicator of this is when you hear a new artist on television or the radio and think, "Is that what they're calling *music* now?"

As it relates to alcohol, this realization can come with another stark truth that we must be ready to recognize and accept if we are going to have any semblance of aging gracefully and holding on to all of our mental and physical faculties for as long as possible.

This truth?

You have to stop drinking by 40.

While I personally advocate that people should stop earlier if they can, I do acknowledge that there is a place for alcohol in people's lives up to a certain point. I have never been one to push complete abstinence, as I believe there is a time in your life in which alcohol can help with experiencing things that you never would've done otherwise.

However, as we age, the tradeoffs that we are making with each drink become more costly every single day.

MICHELLE

Michelle walked back down the hallway and began to question what just happened a minute ago.

She was walking through her speech and her talking points and just couldn't understand how she had let a key piece of her three-point plan fall from her memory. She had worked on her talking points with her staff numerous times.

They had role-played what her opponent was going to say over and over ad nauseam, to the point that she felt perhaps she was overpreparing. Therefore, why when the rubber hit the road, and she was in the heat of the debate, had she found it challenging to remember all the different options her team had given her in regard to responses?

The main point of embarrassment, and what will no doubt be played on television screens over and over tonight as a representation of why many early commentators were declaring her opponent the winner before it was over, was when she was trying to make a three-point rebuttal to her opponent's healthcare plan and couldn't remember her third point.

As she kept searching for her last point, because it was completely clear that she intended to share three reasons from the very beginning (she started the statement with, "There are three reasons that statement you made is false"), the embarrassment seemed to increase exponentially with every second that passed while she couldn't recall it.

What was even more embarrassing was that it was the best of her three points, which is why she saved it for last, so she didn't want to just let it go. She tried everything in her power to remember it, as she continued to look through her notes. The discomfort and awkwardness of the moment was palpable, as the moderator finally said they needed to move on to the next point because the time was up.

As she sat in the back of her town car riding home, her mind began racing around the various other things she had been having trouble with the past few years or so. When she had celebrated her 48th birthday and simultaneously used it to announce her candidacy for Congress, one of her friends had joked that she was close to being the big 5-0 and over the hill.

They both laughed heartily at this but two years later, now that she had just eclipsed this number, she found herself becoming fearful of the potential foreshadowing of that moment. The last two years had been somewhat of a nightmare for her. During that time, she had found things that she used to take for granted disappearing or becoming extremely difficult for her, and she couldn't understand why.

She had always had the ability to remember people's names and things about them to make them feel special. She seemed to have a knack to know the right thing to say in whatever situation and could remember key details of financial figures with no issues at all.

This was something that used to come so naturally to her when she presented at conferences or in meetings with her former company as a VP, but lately, this was just not the case.

She had trouble remembering names of people that she was meeting and found herself afraid to meet anyone for the second time for fear of not being able to remember their name and being expected to do so. This was her third debate performance, and they had, unfortunately, gotten worse each time.

In previous debates, she had trouble remembering a number of key points that caused her to miss many opportunities to score points with the voters and drive home the messaging that her campaign had worked so hard on. This was the first time, however, that she made such a recognizable and embarrassing error that would no doubt be the dagger in her campaign.

As she sat in the back of her town car and poured herself a glass of white zinfandel to take her mind off of her miserable performance, *she paused right before she was going to take a sip and looked at the glass.*

It reminded her of something her wife said three weeks ago about a friend of hers who was also having trouble with their memory when it had been so great in the past. They said that they stopped drinking a year earlier on the recommendation of their doctor from an enzyme chemical abnormality that was causing them to get extremely sick because their liver could no longer metabolize the acetaldehyde from the alcohol at a fast enough rate to not potentially poison their body.

One amazing byproduct of this decision is that they all of a sudden felt like their memory began to improve dramatically over the past year. Whereas before, they would chalk up forgetting someone's name or not remembering a detail from a previous conversation to their advanced age (they were closer to the 60 mark at 58 years old), they now found their ability to recall things much better without anywhere near as much effort as they used to exert.

Michelle's mind raced on this possibility as she looked at the glass of bubbly still sitting in her hand, and decided that perhaps she should take a break from alcohol for a while to see where it might lead her.

Four years later...

Michelle sat in the back of her town car riding home with her wife, on cloud nine after her victory party for having been officially declared the winner of the seat in Congress that she had run for and so embarrassingly lost only four years prior.

In that race, due to her terrible performances in the debates and inability to truly connect with the voters, she barely registered 10% of the votes and came in a dismal fourth. She had decided not to run again when the opportunity came two years later, but decided to continue to work on herself to grow in a number of areas before putting her hat in the ring again this time around.

That fateful decision that she made four years ago to see what life would be like without alcohol proved to be exactly what she needed to take her political career and life to the next level.

During her two years running for office the first time, she had not only had a significant memory and brain lapse, but she had put on a fair amount of weight. This was doubly due to the added stress she was handling with performing so poorly in a number of different arenas, as well as the difficulty she was having trying to find time to work out at all.

After her decision to take a break from alcohol, she found herself more inclined to do whatever she could to make time to work out. Whereas in the past, she might wake up with a bit of a headache or brain fog from drinking and find a way to talk herself out of working out, now that she wasn't experiencing that, she found she was always able to squeeze in 30 minutes at least once a day if she tried.

She began to drop weight steadily because of her new commitment to working out daily and also began to eat better to complement it. Without the allure of the drunken-hungries encouraging her to get pizza or tikka masala on any given night, she found a good salad or grilled chicken meal was just as good when she was sober.

Also, as she began to see the benefits of a much-improved memory and ability to learn and retain new things based on her break from alcohol, she started researching other potential things that she should be doing to protect her memory as well. This led her to eating more whole, organic foods, as well as making sleep a top priority in her life.

She eventually dropped 40 pounds and looked like a brand-new person when she jumped back on the campaign trail two years later to give it another go. Instead of running immediately for that year's House of Representatives seat, however, she decided to spend the upcoming two years visiting various towns, talking to residents about what was important to them, and continuing to build the very best version of herself possible to prepare for another run.

When she put her hat back in the ring officially four years later, she was almost four years removed from her last ever alcoholic drink and felt like a brand-new candidate. She held her wife's hand and reminisced on that solemn car ride of defeat four years earlier and how that one spur-of-the-moment decision had made this current, much happier car ride of victory possible.

The problem with alcohol and aging

This saying may be somewhat tongue in cheek, but I think most people would definitely agree with the statement that no one sets out to become an alcoholic. Many times, individuals become accustomed to drinking alcohol at a certain pace when they are younger, keeping in mind not to drink every day or go overboard too many times to keep themselves in check.

Alcohol becomes part of their life as something they do socially from time to time with friends or when they go on vacations. They don't consider themselves as having any particular problem with it, as it doesn't appear to have been interfering with their ability to be successful in life or their career.

They don't have any DUI's, don't have any relationships that have been damaged dramatically from their drinking, and they generally feel they are in overall solid physical shape. Therefore, they don't think of their drinking as a "problem" and probably find very little reason to monitor it or cut it out at all as they get older.

They have been able to handle it when they were younger without any major issues or situations, so why would things change as they age?

The funny thing about the answer to this question is they are correct; nothing about the alcohol has changed at all. However, it's because of the changes that we go through as human beings that the decision to continue to drink it on a consistent basis as we age puts not only our long-term physical and mental health in danger, but also our immediate health in a number of different ways.

While we've already shared how the effects of alcohol are damaging to your brain and body based on consistent consumption above the recommended minimum, we have yet to dive into the explanation of how all of these effects are dramatically intensified as we get older.

Let's do that now.

The myths of the "normal" drinker and of alcohol being good for you

Often, the argument that you hear from people is that alcohol is considered healthy as long as you drink it in moderation. There have even been a few articles recently[106] that have professed you should NOT start drinking until you reach a certain age to reap the benefits they believe come with it.

The funny thing about this is that all of these articles still recommend staying within the suggested guidelines by the CDC[107] and not go overboard. This number is pretty well known, as it typically is two alcoholic drinks per day for men and one alcoholic drink per day for women.

Seems pretty harmless, right?

One or two drinks per night is probably the amount that most people would consider a "normal" drinker would be able to have. You have just enough to provide positive benefits to your heart and then stop without any desire to keep drinking past that.

The stat that is not shared about this recommended amount, however, is that if you only drink one alcoholic drink per night over the course of seven days, this amount would put you in the top 30th percentile[108] of ALL alcohol consumers in the world. If you gave yourself the freedom to have one more drink per night, since it's still within the recommended CDC guidelines, you'll then be right on the cusp of moving into the 20th percentile that sits at an average of 15.28 drinks per week.

This proves there is no true concept of a "normal" drinker, as this amount squarely puts one in the Pareto Principle realm of being in that small 20% that consumes the larger 80%.

The other idea that needs to be addressed and debunked is that often repeated belief that drinking this amount of alcohol each day should be considered healthy because it comes with a number of health benefits. While these beliefs have been espoused by previous studies and reporters[109] who love to write about things that will get people to click on their articles, modern science is beginning to debunk whether this is a possibility at all.

More and more studies are coming out that espouse NO amount of alcohol is healthy[110] for you long term, as any health benefits are severely outweighed by the additional health risks that one exposes themselves to when they make this decision.

What they found is that any health benefits that had been touted in the past for the heart were heavily outweighed by the increased risk of potentially developing cancer and other alcohol-related diseases as a result of drinking even a moderate amount. The report clearly states in summation, "Our results show that the safest level of drinking is none."

Alcohol and your body

As we age, we know that our bodies are not quite as resilient in a number of different ways. Our knees hurt for no good reason. We can't make any sudden moves without the risk of pulling something. And the thought of running fast for any reason other than because something is chasing you sounds like an idea out of a horror novel.

One of the other ways that we know our body is not what it used to be is how it reacts to alcohol as we age. While it may sound desirable to those who are in college now and would like to save as much money as possible, as you age, you generally feel the effects of alcohol much faster than before.

Our overall body composition is much different from what it was when we were in college or shortly after. During that time, our body was probably close to or at its peak physical fitness. This is one of the first ways that alcohol changes in how it interacts with our body.

When you're younger, you are typically much slimmer, with a leaner body mass index and muscle density. Now that you've aged a bit, your muscle density is probably much less than in years past. This decreased muscle density allows alcohol to hit you much faster and simultaneously makes it much more difficult for you to realize it.

The second reason relates to how our body decreases its natural ability to regulate our temperature from exercise and movement[111] in the same manner it did when we were younger. While this seems completely unrelated, the truth is our body doesn't naturally regulate our internal temperature as well from heat and exercise, so we lose water at a much quicker rate than our younger days.

This decrease in water accumulation and saturation in our bodies leads to alcohol having a much faster and stronger effect on us when we drink as we age. It has been well documented that alcohol has a number of different effects on the body that can prove dangerous for older adults who continue to drink at the same clip that they did when they were younger.

In a study[112] conducted by University of Florida professor Sara Jo Nixon, researchers tested the response rate and cognitive functions of two groups of drinkers to analyze how our bodies change their responses to alcohol over time.

In the study, Nixon recruited 42 men and women aged 50 to 74 and 26 men and women aged 25 to 35. She had each of them drink either alcohol or a placebo that should've allowed them to reach the same blood alcohol level across the board to duplicate the amount (40 mg/100 ml) most people would drink in the average social setting.

Afterward, they were asked to take a cognitive and visual-motor coordination test called the Trail Making Test. In this test, participants were asked to connect a series of numbered letters and dots as fast as they could. This would demonstrate their ability to think strategically, plan ahead, and move from one thought to the next quickly. Each person took the test twice. Once, 25 minutes after drinking and then a second time 75 minutes after drinking.

The results were conclusive: The older adults did significantly worse than their younger counterparts. There was a full five-second difference between their reaction times, which could easily mean the difference between a car accident or not.

Also, qualitatively, most of the older drinkers said they felt fine and not impaired at all, even though the results of the tests showed that the alcohol had definitely taken effect.

What this means is that the level of drunkenness that you may have felt at five to six drinks in the past can now be achieved with only two or three drinks, and you won't even realize it. The scary thing about this level of intoxication is two-fold:

One, it can take someone who was a novice and social drinker, careful not to allow themselves to become drunk each night, over the edge to the realm of becoming inebriated more consistently. This could, with time, eventually lead to the natural flow of desire to dependence that can overtake anyone who drinks to intoxication on a consistent basis.

Two, when you can get drunk so quickly without realizing, it can lead to a number of dangerous situations in which you might attempt to drink as much as you did in the past without understanding the change in how your body reacts to it. This mistake could result in you getting way more drunk than you had planned and, in turn, become a series of embarrassing situations that you regret.

I often think back to the David Hasselhoff hamburger incident[113] in 2007. He had probably drunk way more than he had on any other given night in the past, but with his advanced age, the alcohol had a much stronger effect than it had when he was younger, resulting in him reaching a level of inebriation that was embarrassing and resulted in the "incident."

How often has this happened to individuals who didn't realize that alcohol was sneaking up on them so quickly, and the next thing they know they are in the back of a police car for doing something that they shouldn't have but often can't even remember?

The second way our body changes its relationship to alcohol relates to our liver and its ability to metabolize it. We recognize the effects of this change when we wake up in the morning after a night of drinking and know that our hangovers are much worse now than they were when we were younger.

When we were younger, it seemed like we could go on a binger all weekend and still wake up in our dorm with no major issues, other than a slight headache, to be able to make our 10:00 a.m. Monday morning class. As we age, however, any "night on the town" that involves extensive drinking can easily turn into a one or two-day recovery period, trying to get our head and body back to baseline.

While the natural response is that this is just one of those things that happens when one begins to get "old," the more scientific reason behind this relates to your body's decreased ability to metabolize alcohol with the same speed and efficiency as it did when we were younger.

The liver is an important part of our physical health in a number of ways. It is one of the most complex organs in the body and serves a number of functions that are directly related to our overall health and ability to actually live. Some of its major functions include aiding food digestion, regulating blood sugar and cholesterol levels, helping to fight infection and disease, and, of course, filtering toxins from the blood.

It is this last one that relates to its importance in the metabolizing of alcohol for your body. The entire process is a bit complex and there are numerous steps involved that must go right each time to keep you protected from the poisonous effects of alcohol to keep you alive. The entire process consists of your body changing the dangerous poisonous form of alcohol from different chemical versions to different chemical versions until it finally becomes a version that can exit your body without danger.

First, there is the initial breaking down of the alcohol by an enzyme in your liver that turns it into alcohol dehydrogenase (ADH). ADH eventually breaks down to become a substance known as acetaldehyde. Acetaldehyde is then broken down by another enzyme, aldehyde dehydrogenase (ALDH), to become acetate. Acetate is then metabolized to eventually leave our body as carbon dioxide and water.

The problem with this entire process typically falls on the creation of acetaldehyde. Acetaldehyde[114] is an organic compound that falls into the category known as aldehydes[115] that occur naturally in nature. This substance, while short-lived during the entire metabolic process, is highly dangerous to our bodies, as it is a known carcinogen that has been linked to numerous mutations and adductions[116] related to cancer formation in the liver.

Our body is highly efficient at reducing our exposure to this dangerous chemical when we are young by quickly metabolizing it and changing it into the harmless combination of carbon and water that eventually leaves our bodies. However, as we age and we experience the wear and tear on our organs with time, it loses its ability to function as quickly and efficiently as before.

This, in turn, causes the process to work more slowly and less efficiently, exposing the liver to the dangerous carcinogenic effects of the acetaldehyde. This is one of the reasons as you age, you are more at risk for certain types of cancers and diseases, as the body is just not as able to process and fight against various chemicals and germs as well as it could in previous years.

Couple this with the fact that if you were a heavy drinker when you were younger, there is a good chance that the liver has already been damaged from your excessive drinking. This means that even though our livers naturally don't work as efficiently when we age, if we are someone who drank heavily in our younger years, they could already work at a much less efficient clip than someone who didn't.

How this occurs relates to our body's natural rate of metabolizing alcohol. It typically takes the body one hour to process one alcoholic beverage. This is part of the reason that it is recommended to only have one or two drinks at any given time, as this is the rate at which your body can safely metabolize the alcohol to not put you at risk of damage from the acetaldehyde remaining in your liver.

What actually occurs when you drink more than this amount in an hour is that the remains seep out of your liver and go into your bloodstream. This alcohol and acetaldehyde in your bloodstream[117] start to affect your heart and brain, which is what actually creates the effect of the intoxication. So while the feeling of euphoria and dopamine release from alcohol feels great, it is actually the byproduct of our liver not being able to metabolize the alcohol quickly enough to prevent it from potentially causing harmful effects to our body.

The more you drink, the slower your body is able to metabolize the alcohol, which, in turn, begins to allow more acetaldehyde to remain in the liver for longer. When this gets to a dangerous level in one night of drinking, this becomes alcohol poisoning because the body can no longer metabolize the alcohol at a fast enough rate[118] versus the rate you are ingesting it to prevent it from killing you.

As this buildup occurs through chronic alcohol abuse, this can eventually lead to a number of dangerous health effects,[119] such as the scarring of the liver (cirrhosis), alcohol hepatitis, and cellular mutation that could lead to cancer. However, what is perhaps as scary is that even if these conditions don't fully form to become recognizable health conditions by your doctor, consistent excessive drinking can still do major damage to the effectiveness of your liver over time due to the accumulated effects of acetaldehyde staying in your system for much longer than it should.

What this means is that while you should be concerned about your liver's natural decrease in effectiveness as you age putting you at risk for the above and other diseases, if you drank consistently when you were younger, there's a good chance that it's even MORE compromised and damaged than you may realize.

This truth then makes quitting when you reach the age of 40 even more important, as it puts you at greater risk than someone who may have drunk more moderately or not at all when they were younger.

The second reason this age should be considered the end of alcohol in one's life to age gracefully relates back to our story about Michelle, her campaign, and what many people take for granted until they can no longer count on it to be there for them.

Alcohol and the brain

Our memory is so precious.

One of the greatest fears I've always had as I became an adult and watched various movies of how family dynamics change over time was about who took care of whom. Initially, it was the parents who were responsible for the kids and everything related to their well-being, but as they aged and the effects of aging became more apparent, this relationship changed to the kids soon becoming the caretaker of the parents.

When I would watch these shows and see the parents not sure where they were at times or lose the ability to remember the names and faces of their loved ones, it frightened me. It seemed like it would cause such drama in someone's life when they couldn't trust their own memory and brain to give them the information they need when they needed it.

Enter the relationship between alcohol and the brain.

There is no doubt that drinking heavily impairs our ability to think and remember things in the short term, as blackouts are periods of time in which our mind loses the ability to transfer our short-term memories to long-term storage.

This is part of the reason that you sometimes seem to remember bits and pieces of what happened the night before but can't quite put the entire story together. This is something referred to as "fragmentary blackouts"[120] or a brownout. This is different from the more advanced and more dangerous version of blackouts known as "en bloc,"[121] blackouts in which you can't remember absolutely anything for an extended period of time.

The problem with both of these occurrences is that they put undue stress on your brain and specifically on your hippocampus. While there are parts of your brain that are able to develop a tolerance to alcohol and respond to it accordingly, the hippocampus is not one of those parts. One of its primary functions is to create and store memories for your long-term retrieval when needed.

When you experience a fragmentary or en bloc blackout, the hippocampus is prevented from creating a memory that you can recall easily. In terms of the fragmentary blackout, individuals are often able to recall some of their memories that were created during the course of an episode with some prompting from others who were there.

However, in terms of a complete "en bloc" blackout, the individual cannot recall anything regardless of how many clues or information they receive from someone there. You could even show someone a video recording of them holding an entire conversation with someone else, and they may not be able to recall it.

To understand the possible effects of blackouts and alcohol on our long-term memory, we first must establish a model of memory formation that outlines the process of how this occurs. One of the most widely adopted models is known as the modal model of memory[122] created by Richard Atkinson and Richard Shiffrin in 1968. This model states that your memory is formed in several stages that take place through gateways that are opened or closed due to a number of different factors such as time, motivation, arousal, and true understanding of material.

This starts with sensory memory, which is our recognition of something based on our senses. It is then moved to our short-term memory for our retrieval for later if prompted. After some time and assessment of some of the other factors listed above, it is then moved to our long-term memory for later recall as needed.

The effects of alcohol on short-term memory have been recorded in a number of different studies that show there can be a range of different effects depending on the quantity of alcohol consumed and the time period in which it was done. Some of these impacts were things such as a participant's ability to recall various items[123] from a list in a timely manner. With alcohol impairment, the speed at which they were able to do so was reduced dramatically.

Another big lesson from these studies is that those who have been under the influence of heavy drinking are more susceptible to what are called "intrusion errors."[124] Intrusion errors occur when the participant produces information that is not related to the task. This means that participants mistakenly "remember" different details of a story or items from a list that were not originally there.

And while the two significant effects above might be enough cause for concern for anyone who drinks consistently, perhaps the most damaging effects of alcohol on our memory relates to its ability to slow, hinder, or completely eliminate the efficient transfer of much of the information in our short-term memory to our long-term memory for our access if needed later.

This impact is directly related to alcohol's effect on our hippocampus over time. The importance of the hippocampus to our memory and learning cannot be understated. Some people refer to it as our inner hard drive. It is at the center of the formation of new memories, learning, and emotional memories.

Many of our new memories are formed in the hippocampus based on the sensory connection that we described above in the modal model of memory. These memories do not automatically become long-term memories, however, as memories stay here for some time until the brain has gone through the necessary channels of repetitive exposure, awareness of need for recall, and emotional long-term impact to decide if this is something that should move from the short-term memory storage location to our long-term memory location.

The effects of alcohol on the hippocampus's ability to function properly have been documented in numerous studies,[125] but the gist of the effects show that alcohol impairs a number of different functions that allow the hippocampus to transfer short-term memories to long-term memories when you're drinking heavily. This is part of the reason that during blackouts or brownouts, we are not able to recall exactly what happened unless prompted by someone who can help.

The further we get away from the blackout episode, the less chance we will have of remembering exactly what happened since only certain portions, if any, are able to make it from our short-term memory in that moment to our long-term memory for future recall.

What does this mean for learning and your memory long term?

Over time, this consistent impairment of your brain's ability to transfer short-term memory over to long-term memory can eventually decrease your brain's ability to do so when you're not drinking. This, in turn, will make it easier for you to forget things that you already know, as well as harder to learn new things which you are trying to remember.

In a study[126] published in *Alcoholism: Clinical & Experimental Research*, researchers discovered that those who drank heavily typically reported 25–30% more memory-related issues than someone who only drank a little or not at all. Many of these things related to tasks that we would often refer to as prospective memory,[127] or day-to-day tasks that we should be working on autopilot to complete. Some examples of this are forgetting to send a birthday card to a loved one to arrive on time, forgetting what you were going to say in the middle of a sentence, or forgetting where regularly used household items are kept.

In terms of learning new things and having the ability to recall specific details when needed, this is related to our explicit memory[128] ability, a function that is directly damaged by alcohol in the hippocampus. This is the part of our memory that helps us remember names we've just learned or pull specific information related to dates and key talking points that we would need to remember for a speech.

In Michelle's case, it was the part of her memory that would help her with her fundraising activities, political debates, and speeches. While many of the studies[129] that show a direct link between cognitive decline and aging have test subjects in their 60s and 70s, they also show that increased oxidative stress and neuroinflammation in the hippocampus in younger subjects can have the same effects.[130]

Couple this with recent studies[131] that show the possibility of this natural cognitive decline can begin as early as 45, and the consistent effects of alcohol to alter the function of our hippocampus could potentially put those who drink consistently at much higher risk of experiencing these effects much sooner than necessary.

Therefore, if you are someone who drinks rather consistently 2–3 times per week, you are putting yourself at risk of decreasing your brain's ability to function at an optimal level as you age. While this might happen naturally anyway to many people as a result of aging, the damage that we can do to our hippocampus due to drinking can speed up these effects alarmingly.

In Michelle's case, it greatly limited her ability to remember things at the depth and efficiency that she needed to be successful in her campaign events and at debates. While Michelle was not what one would consider a heavy drinker by any means, she was a consistent one.

This type of consistency can be detrimental to one's ability to age gracefully, as losing one's memory and finding it challenging to learn new things (teach an old dog new tricks) is one of the first things you hear about individuals who are stereotyped as too old to be able to keep up with the demands of an ever-changing and dynamic world.

The great thing about this, however, is there is always the ability to bounce back from the effects of alcohol on our memory and reclaim our previous ability to learn and remember things with ease. Just like Michelle was able to improve her memory dramatically by giving up alcohol and focusing on learning the material she needed to improve her abilities as a candidate, you can do so as well. You can retain and even improve your memory and learning abilities by practicing the numerous positive strategies[132] that will do so, with limiting or giving up alcohol as one of those main strategies.

Now that we've covered how becoming alcohol-conscious will help you age gracefully to create a dynamic future, let's talk about how by doing so, you'll also increase the chances of finding that special someone who will be able to age gracefully with you.

CHAPTER ELEVEN

What Love Has To Do With It

"Drinking makes such fools of people, and people are such
fools to begin with, that it's compounding a felony."

—Robert Benchley

Relationships and alcohol.

Some people will think back to their previous relationships and feel like the two go hand in hand.

For those who may have grown up with some anxiety, like me, the concept of going up and talking to someone of the opposite sex was extremely terrifying and one of the scariest things that one could do in life.

As a 9- or 10-year-old with a crush on the prettiest girl in school, there was no way that I saw myself going to talk to her by any stretch of the imagination without some major encouragement by my friends or some divine sign from God that our love was meant to be. While I'm sure that I probably got a fair amount of encouragement from my friends and perhaps thought that God was talking to me every now and then when I was younger, as I aged, this type of motivation didn't quite have the same effect. I was not quite as naive or easily influenced by others as time went on.

By the time I reached 18, I was still pretty shy and did not see a lot of things helping me in the way of getting over this and being able to find the love of my life.

Enter the magic elixir of alcohol and all of my problems appeared to be no more.

Not that I wasn't still a bit anxious and unsure of myself at times when approaching the opposite sex, but I instantly felt more confident and really "just didn't give a f*ck" as much as I did when I wasn't drinking.

And as weird as it always sounds, by not caring so much about how girls saw me, I was in a much better position than I was when I cared more.

When I was drinking, I had no boundaries or fears, and typically would go up to just about anyone that I thought was attractive and say what I thought might work to get them to find some interest in me. Of course, this didn't work all the time, but it worked just enough (probably close to 50%) that I knew it was working and created a pretty fun life over the 19 years I was drinking.

Fast forward to my time of sobriety, and I had an epiphany about myself, my love life, and how much better a position I was in to succeed now that alcohol was no longer part of my life.

MY STORY

Growing up without a dad wasn't anything that I considered negative for much of my life, except in two specific ways.

In fact, living in a household without a male presence seemed to have more positives than negatives in my opinion, as when I saw dads portrayed in a lot of households on television, they generally were the ones who were doing the cheating or the beating on the wives or kids.

My life with my mom and siblings was good, and even though we didn't have anywhere near all the money I wished we had, we were generally happy because my mom was easygoing and we could pretty much do whatever we wanted.

As I got older, however, and grew from a young adolescent to young teenager, the two deficiencies that I had to overcome from not having a father began to rear their ugly heads more and more, and I had to figure out what I was going to do about them.

The first issue was how to fight. If you are never shown exactly what to do in a fight, how are you supposed to figure out what works and what doesn't without going through it? And while sometimes you have to literally get the bumps and bruises to learn how to effectively do something, I would have preferred to have a sense of what to do before actually having to participate in one.

Step in my older cousin, who had definitely had his share of fights in the past and now I had someone to turn to for advice and direction. He taught me that if I ever got into a fight, the first thing I should do was fake a kick to my opponent's leg and when they naturally reacted to try to block it, jump in and swing a right hook to knock them out.

I've only been in one real fight in my life, and that was the technique I used to knock my opponent to the ground and come out on top.

Check on that front.

Now, the other issue was not so easy to solve, since I couldn't rely on having one simple move in my repertoire that would always work. Also, it wasn't so simple that I would only have to learn it one time to "win." I knew it would probably be a lifelong process, which some guys who even had fathers growing up never truly figured out because their dads may not have figured it out, either:

How to talk to women.

It's not that I didn't know how to talk to women in general. I wasn't overly shy or anything like that. I did have a fair number of girlfriends growing up. It's just that I didn't have that ability that we would all see in movies of that guy who could go up to about any girl and get her to like him instantly.

If a girl already liked me or thought I was cute, there wasn't much more I needed to do. I just had to be careful not to mess it up. That wasn't what I was interested in, however, as that was a bit too easy.

I wanted to be the guy who could go up to any girl and say just the right things to make them laugh, see how confident I was, and be so intrigued by me that they had to give me a shot to get to know them better. This was always the mental image that came to mind as I started attending parties in college at all the various dorms.

My issue was that I just didn't know what to say. When I was in class, and we were talking about some subject at which I was adept, I would have no issues explaining to them what they may not have known.

This worked on certain girls who were interested in those things, but as with life, we always want what doesn't come easiest, so as I sat at parties and looked at the most attractive girls there, I wasn't quite sure what to say.

Enter alcohol into the mix, and my life was forever changed.

As with most situations, it wasn't that alcohol helped me say all the right things or do the right things, but it just gave me the confidence not to care as much. Not caring seems to go a long way when it comes to being funny and intriguing, and alcohol was just the thing to give me this attitude.

Over my four years in college, I can say that alcohol helped me in a number of ways when it came to relationships and having some amazing times. As I graduated school and moved into the real world, these good times continued, as the parties moved from the dorms into the cities in which I lived.

I continued to have amazing times on the town and mounds of fun for the most part, but I will tell you that, as I matured, the concept of settling down seemed to elude me for some reason. There were probably a number of reasons, but one was definitely related to my love of alcohol and how I felt it created a world in which I really didn't have to take any relationship seriously.

Overall, I found myself in relationship after relationship with different women, but very few of them were in any way serious. This was mostly because I was just too focused on having a good time and experiencing a number of different things that life had to offer.

When I met my now wife, then girlfriend, I was still very much in a YOLO phase of my life. We were in this phase together, honestly, and typically had a very good time going out and enjoying the sights and sounds that cities had to offer.

We loved to go out and party consistently at different bars, whether they were local to Atlanta or in some new city that we'd never been to before. This allowed us to have loads of fun during the time because of alcohol, but it was also alcohol that caused one of the biggest arguments that we had ever had that made us break up for six months.

During those six months, I continued to live my life, and she continued to live hers, but luckily we recognized that we truly belonged together and reunited. Once we got back together, we went right back to our routine of drinking and partying and enjoying life.

And while we were having a great time, we did have a few bumps and arguments along the way that were (once again) caused by some drunken episode of one of us drinking too much and not doing something we were supposed to, or doing something we probably weren't supposed to do.

Funny enough, the reason we decided to stop drinking altogether really had nothing to do with our relationship at all, because we felt it was pretty much fine, but I must say that I think our relationship has seen the greatest benefit from the decision as opposed to anything else.

Whereas before, we enjoyed partying together and traveling to different cities and different bars as a couple, this was pretty much all we did. While this made for easy planning in regard to what we were going to do when we went to various cities, it didn't allow us to truly grow as a couple and really get to know each other better and develop our relationship.

Now that we've given up alcohol, our lives are much more focused on understanding what each of us needs to do to become the best partner to the other and to ensure that we are also putting our best foot forward to make the other feel special.

This doesn't mean that we never have disagreements and don't get upset with each other from time to time, but when these times happen now, we are able to talk through it like civilized adults since there is no alcohol involved to fuel any anger. This has made all the difference in the world, as we've looked to create a life that involves patience, learning, and love.

With alcohol in the picture, we were just focused on fun and excitement with each other. Now, we are more in tune with understanding what the other person needs in the relationship to be whole and feel loved, and we have the mental/emotional capacity and ability to work toward that goal each day.

Alcohol's Negative Effects on Relationships

While alcohol is great for getting over one's fear of talking to women, and can even help with creating some "exciting" situations that probably wouldn't have happened without it, alcohol typically fails in truly giving someone the mental and emotional maturity they need to create a serious and thriving relationship.

This was the case for me, as alcohol did help me begin to feel pretty comfortable in my own skin around the opposite sex, but there were some major drawbacks as I looked to maturity and thought about the idea of "settling down."

The problem was that regardless of how much I tried to focus on my relationships and stay committed to one person, I would eventually find myself not able to maintain the correct mindset to do so for very long.

When I thought about relationships, I generally thought about sacrifices and being willing to put that person before yourself in a number of ways. However, as I saw relationship after relationship not work out, I realized that this was just not a characteristic that I felt I had overall.

For whatever reason, making that commitment was just not something that I was willing to do at the moment, and I could never quite put my finger on it until I understood the hold that alcohol had on me and how much more difficult it made it for me to stay committed to what it took to be successful in romantic relationships.

When I was drinking, I just did not have the emotional maturity that it took to be in a serious relationship. I didn't realize it then, but now that I've been alcohol-conscious for such a long time, it is clearly apparent to me.

There were three main ways that alcohol immediately damaged my ability to find and keep long-term love, and I venture to say that this is true for most people. You might say to yourself, "That's absurd. How can alcohol have that much power?" Or "Only three parts? That's not that big of a deal."

The reality is that not only does alcohol definitely affect these three parts of any relationship, I would venture to say that these are three of the *most* important aspects of our lives as it relates to relationships.

Let's discuss them all in detail.

How You Find and Choose a Partner

Taking it back to my college age example, this is where much of it starts. I am pretty confident now, but I was your typical 19-year-old college teenager, not quite sure of myself and uncomfortable in situations where I had little to no experience.

This is normal for most kids that age and I did what a lot of my peers were doing at the time. Instead of facing my discomfort head-on and trying to get better at navigating awkward situations, I took the easy way out and drank alcohol to overcome it.

I often say, the most dangerous thing about alcohol and its effects on our lives is that it actually works so well. It did exactly what I wanted it to do, and I was able to overcome all of the fears and inhibitions that would've kept me in a scared corner had I not developed the ability to overcome it myself.

Ten years later, I was a 29-year-old adult still using alcohol to loosen myself up around the opposite sex, as I still never learned how to do the tough work of being myself and getting through that uncomfortable stage of needing alcohol as a crutch. This would typically lead me to make two distinct mistakes in choosing the type of women that I would get into a relationship with.

The first mistake involved how I would find these women and the type of dates that I was committed to always going on.

Because I knew I was not quite comfortable being myself without alcohol, I would always suggest that the first date be at some type of bar to drink. This is typically the way that I would meet women anyway (at local bars), so to try to deviate from this place of excitement seemed to go against common good sense. I was so stuck on this method that if someone had an issue with our first date being at some type of restaurant or bar, I would usually label them a fuddy-duddy and decide not to go on another date with them.

Now that I'm much older and more mature, I cringe to think of the number of amazing women that I may have missed out on because of this mindset back then. They weren't saying that they wouldn't date me because I did drink, while I completely excluded them as a possibility because they didn't drink to the level that I did.

While I admit this was a bit extreme and probably not duplicated by everybody, mistake #2 is probably something that most individuals do all the time and just not realize it at all.

This is the reason that so many people are in relationships with people that they absolutely can't stand, where they wake up one day and ask, "How did I get here and why am I with this person?" You'll look at a number of different things about that individual and say we are not truly compatible at all, so why have we been together for x number of years?

The problem likely had to do with one characteristic that you both shared and something that is almost stronger than any differences between individuals. That is the desire to have fun and enjoy life.

While this may sound absurd, if you think about it, it will truly make sense.

When we're younger, we enjoy the sights and sounds of just exploring the city and having fun. At that age, we typically look for one of two things when we're "falling in love" with someone—someone who is decently attractive and someone we can have fun with.

While this sounds like a reasonable criterion for finding someone to hang out with for a few years and maybe have a little bit of fun, there should probably be more in-depth, decision-making criteria in place when picking the person we'll spend the rest of our lives with.

Some of us are able to recognize this and try not to let our focus on physical appearance be the main thing that drives us. However, the one caveat that many people just don't consider as something that they should change is the fun category, and while I still agree that this needs to be at the forefront of any decision to spend time with someone, when we add the element of alcohol needed for fun, then we are somewhat rigging the system so that we'll be unable to truly know if this is the right person for us.

One of the reasons that alcohol is such an addictive drug is because it really works so well and can turn almost any situation into one in which you will convince yourself you had a good time. Alcohol has the ability to sugarcoat our senses in a way that will make us believe that almost any situation was fun and enjoyable.

What this means is that when you are on a date with someone and the element of alcohol is a strong variable in the course of the night, there is a good chance that the good time you had with that person was more a creation of the effect alcohol had on lowering your inhibitions and reservations, as opposed to this person really being a good compatible pick for you.

We may find ourselves enjoying this person's company because we are drunk as opposed to talking about the important topics in life and the opportunity for true connection.

Many times, individuals will get into relationships that are based mostly on looks and having fun and never really talk about the important topics of kids, finances, or life philosophies in general until somebody gets pregnant and then a big decision has to be made.

When we allow alcohol to be involved in our dating lives, we have the tendency to choose based on our physical desires and most base desire to have a good time, as opposed to truly discerning if this person is for us.

And the best way to prevent having to end a bad relationship is to never start one with someone you shouldn't have in the first place.

How to Avoid and Resolve Fights

Besides causing us to choose the wrong person, we then have to look at the way alcohol affects our relationships after that decision is made.

I'm sure we've all been in our fair number of arguments with a significant other, and it seems that very few things can match the intensity of these situations. Love's ability to stir up heated emotions is probably greater than anything else out there.

Whether it's from getting overly upset thinking our loved one is cheating on us or being mad about having to pick up after someone for the twentieth time, the closer two people are, often the greater their degree of anger can develop toward each other.

While this intensity is already strong enough and has led to many a situation that could potentially involve the police, when the dangerous variable of alcohol is added to the mix, it's like figuratively and somewhat literally adding fuel to the fire. Many times, an argument that would've been nothing more than two people being mad at each other for a certain amount of time turns into something completely different and potentially more dangerous when alcohol is involved.

For me, this didn't lead to any potentially dangerous situations, but it did create times in which disagreements that were nothing more than a simple difference of opinion turned into full-blown, I-don't-want-to-ever-speak-to-you-again type of fights.

When I was younger, I thought this was just the result of my believing in my point of view and not wanting to give up ground, but as I got older and began to look back on how ridiculous some of my arguments were, I recognized that alcohol played a tremendous part in my level of anger and how stubborn I was because of that anger.

Much of this had to do with how alcohol will often turn you back into a young adolescent as you navigate your emotions and feelings in a drunken state. Many times, you are going to focus on what is most important to you, and it is very hard to think of someone else's point of view during this time. Part of this has to do with the concept known as alcohol myopia,[133] a state in which our brains are typically focused mostly on the here and now and our ability to think about things in the distant future, i.e. consequences, is reduced due to our drunken state.

Relationships can be difficult anyway because you are working to coexist with someone, as you both are working to build your own individual lives but also fit each other into them since they are an intricate part. This, by itself, is going to potentially cause issues and conflict, as you can make decisions about your life much more easily when you don't have anyone else to consider in relation to them.

Therefore, when there is a time in which a more "tense" conversation has to take place for whatever reason, if alcohol is involved, it can make it much more difficult to have a productive conversation.

This can sometimes change benign situations into arguments in which things are said that cannot be unsaid. The reality is that whenever alcohol is involved, emotions seem to be heightened, and one of those things that can get out of proportion to the argument is anger.

While it is not the only trigger, it can be *a* trigger, as 55% of perpetrators[134] who engage in domestic abuse against their partners were drinking prior to the incident. While this is not an excuse for anyone, it is a good indicator that when one is drinking, there can be a tendency to ratchet up our response to something that makes us mad. I'm sure many of us have been a spectator or perhaps involved in a situation at a bar or a club in which a simple disagreement or spilling of someone's drink can lead to an all-out brawl that results in individuals going to the hospital and/or the police station.

When we allow alcohol to become too much of a part of our interactions with our significant other, it increases the chances that this same type of alcohol effect can take place, and we'll find ourselves doing or saying something from which we cannot come back easily.

At the end of the day, relationships can be challenging enough without alcohol involved, and by making it a large part of our lives with our significant other, we increase our chances of strife for really stupid reasons. Any long-term happy couple will tell you that one of the most important things you must avoid for any chance of success is fighting over things that don't matter. In other words, don't sweat the small stuff.

Relationships and Fidelity

Staying committed to one's partner and drinking excessively are often in direct conflict with each other. This is hard for many people to admit or even recognize as truth.

There are many stories of someone who "loves" their partner going out with friends one night and getting overly drunk, only to find themselves in a compromising situation that they would not want their significant other to find out about. Many times, the secret to not allowing such things to happen is to not put oneself in that type of situation in the first place. However, alcohol is not known as the drug of common sense and being prudent and cautious is not one of its side effects.

In fact, the chances that we will be overly confident in our ability to not do or say something we won't regret is highly likely, considering how our inhibitions are lowered dramatically and our confidence raised equally when we're in this state.

Sometimes, this may be something from which we can recover in a relationship and may not cause too much strife, depending on how far we go. Other times, once we cross a certain point and threshold, there is no putting the genie back into the bottle, and the relationship can never be the same.

For some, the harm caused might lead to tremendous guilt. It will always be over their head, until the point they finally confess. For others, it might be something more concrete, in which one of the people involved in the infidelity desires a full-blown relationship and won't let it go. Perhaps in what could be considered the worst-case scenario, someone becomes pregnant and there is an entirely new situation to deal with.

I will not in any way make excuses for individuals who are drinking, as this does not give one a free pass for decisions they make while drunk.

This is more so a warning that one should not put themselves in a situation in which they must try to fight off various temptations greatly heightened by the effects of alcohol.

Being transparent about the difficulties of relationships, fidelity is something that can be challenging to achieve even without any outside factors manipulating one's natural ability to resist it. With alcohol, we can then put ourselves in vulnerable situations with our ability to resist temptation reduced dramatically.

Recognizing this, it can only take one small slip-up to put ourselves in a situation that we will regret forever and could cause us to lose someone who could've been the love of our lives. It is hard to see how drinking and having a good night on the town could be worth losing love that would have lasted forever.

So now that we walked through all the ways that alcohol has been instilled in us from day one, as well as the way it creates the need for itself, along with all the tremendous benefits one will recognize if able to give it up, the question now becomes *how do you actually do it?*

No worries . . . you know I gotcha. I wouldn't give you all that knowledge without also giving you a way to remove yourself from this insidious trap that so many people are caught in so that you can completely change your life.

It's time to talk about The MEDS.

PART III

How Do You
Take Back Your Life?

CHAPTER TWELVE

I Need My MEDS

The Complete Holistic Mind/Body Approach to Quit Drinking

"Science is the process that takes us from confusion to understanding . . ."

—BRIAN GREENE

Your Problems
Lots

Your Prescription
The MEDS

When we have been indoctrinated with something since we were able to form memories and make associations between people's moods and external forces, it is going to take more than just a few words on a page to get us to completely reprogram our training and overcome the physical and mental connection that we have developed.

Understanding that, I was able to develop a very successful program that can help you overcome a lifelong connection to alcohol by following a step-by-step plan to guide you from living trapped and inhibited by alcohol to full freedom as the best version of yourself.

This program was developed over a four-year period in which I analyzed a number of different programs out there for individuals who were struggling with drinking. What I recognized was that many of these programs focused on people who were far down the road to alcoholism, as opposed to that person who just needed to understand alcohol was not the best decision for them long term.

Therefore, I analyzed what appeared to work for some of these programs and identified common themes that I could adapt to the more casual drinker who desired to quit BEFORE alcohol began to ruin their life. I also took feedback from a number of people about what worked and didn't work for them, as well as analyzed the various tips and tricks that greatly aided my own personal alcohol-consciousness journey.

The result was The MEDS, a program that has helped thousands of people overcome their casual relationship with alcohol to remove it from their lives forever and create the best version of themselves instead.

The plan allows everyone to customize it so that it makes the most sense for them and where they currently are on their journey. Some may be able to follow the same process of recovery that I did, while others may need to go back and forth between different steps until they find something that sticks and works for them.

Either way, the program is designed to give you the tools and strategies that will help you through this journey—but encourages everyone to figure out which of the tools gives them the best chance of quitting for the long term.

For this chapter, let's walk through each part of the process with a high overview and then we'll dive into each in more detail with examples and specific instructions in later chapters.

What Is The MEDS and Why Does It Work?

The MEDS is an acronym for the four parts of the holistic process.

Mental Re-engineering

M stands for Mental Re-engineering, and focuses on feeding your mind and doing the tough work of completely rewiring the way you think about alcohol and its effect on your life.

As shared earlier, much of what we think about alcohol was indoctrinated into us before we even had the chance to truly understand what we were learning. It has been drilled into our subconscious from a very young age and continues to become even more a part of our underlying psyche as we age and can truly grasp the nuance of what advertising and various mediums press upon us every day.

To think that you would be able to overcome years and probably decades of teachings by simply saying "that's enough" is not realistic. Therefore, in this first step of The MEDS, we focus on undoing these years of teaching and, instead, giving your mind the new view it needs to understand what alcohol is truly doing to it and where you may be headed if you don't make a change.

Exercise Commitment

The E stands for Exercise Commitment, and although many think this is unnecessary, I assure you, it is very important to one's success. The hold that alcohol can have on our lives is so strong that it likely encompasses all different parts of it.

When you quit drinking, one of the things you are going to find that you have more of than you could've probably imagined is time. It is one of the great finds of sobriety that many people find either pleasantly surprising or terrifyingly agonizing.

If you are used to spending so much time drinking and now you are living in a world where that isn't an option, trying to fill that void could be something of a struggle at first. Exercise is a great filler because it not only can be rather time-consuming, but it's also great for your recovery and the improvement of your general overall health.

We'll dive into this more as we get into the Exercise Commitment chapter, but different forms of exercise are great for reducing cravings and making it much easier to say no to that night out drinking because it will hurt your fitness regimen.

This is one of the reasons that The MEDS is a holistic mind AND body approach—because I strongly believe that your outer representation is often a reflection of how you are feeling on the inside. Of course, this is not true in all instances, as there are very fit and attractive people who are completely broken on the inside, but it doesn't seem the opposite of that is often true. You seldom find someone who is completely out of shape and overweight who is happy with everything about their lives.

For us, exercise commitment is not only a way to give you something else to do to occupy your time instead of drinking, but it will help you do the hard work of improving yourself in almost every aspect to ensure you are the very best version of you possible. This is so important to physically realize how much alcohol was holding you back from this endeavor and the second step, Exercise Commitment, will help you realize that.

Diet Improvement

The third letter is D and it stands for Diet Improvement. As most people can guess, exercising is only one-half of what one needs to do to create the body of their dreams and get in the best shape of their lives.

Honestly, for many, exercise is the easy part, as you will see people in the gym month after month, year after year, only to maintain a physique that is still very much not within the guidelines of healthy weight, cholesterol, or any other of the measurements doctors take to ensure one is physically fit. All the hard work they are putting in each week is somewhat wasted because they are only maintaining or worsening their physical status instead of improving it.

It's almost like running hard on a treadmill while trying to get to a destination. You are still putting in the same level of effort as someone who is running on the open road, but that person is going so much farther than you.

Staying committed to a diet ensures that the improvements you are making to your physical body mirror the same changes you are making within. When you decide to stop putting the poison of alcohol in your body every day, you have made a tremendous choice that will benefit your health tremendously.

To continue down that path, it only makes sense to begin to identify other healthy diet decisions that will give your body the fuel and energy it needs to create the best version of yourself possible. Being alcohol-conscious is an offshoot of being health-conscious in that you have decided that the negative things that you were doing to your body before no longer serve the long-term vision you have for yourself and your future.

By committing to changing your diet and coupling this with a new exercise regimen, you are restructuring who you were in the past to create a new lifestyle and version of yourself for this future. This change in diet and exercise will have a lot of positive benefits, with one of them being the extra energy and focus you need to pursue the last of the steps of The MEDS that I would consider the most important.

Success Seeking

S stands for Success Seeking, and the reason I often deem this the most important of the four steps is that this will require you to push yourself more than you ever have in the past. Of course, there are a number of negative aspects of drinking, but one of the things that truly hurts people without them realizing it is the mental stagnation that alcohol creates.

Many don't quite realize how their mental acuity has been softened due to alcohol's effects since they are so used to drinking all the time and the degradation happens slowly. Many never recognize the brain fog is even there until they have stopped drinking for at least a week or more. They often have no sense of how much alcohol hinders their mental clarity or ability to do deep, serious thinking.

The reason Success Seeking is so important is because it will require you to identify a goal that requires a higher level of mental clarity and agility than you could ever obtain or maintain with alcohol being a constant part of your life. There are a number of different goals that one can pursue, whether it be physical or purely mental, but it has to be something that requires a higher level of commitment and brain activity to achieve it.

All together, these four steps are part of a process that one should go through to decrease alcohol's stronghold on their mind and psyche and create a new way of thinking and lifestyle that will build a version of themselves beyond anything they could've previously imagined.

Now let's show you how.

CHAPTER THIRTEEN

Mental Re-engineering

Educate Yoself!

"If your mindset is defeated, the results will be the same
no matter how often you put up a physical fight."

—MAC DUKE, *THE STRATEGIST*

When we first make the decision to lead a different lifestyle from the norm, there are going to be a lot of forces fighting against us to try to keep us in the same place in life. Whether it's commercials on television, happy hours at work, or Friday texts from the crew, the pull to come out and drink to forget the sorrows of the day and just "enjoy life" are going to be strong and consistent from a number of different avenues.

However, if we are able to fight against these and put the work in to mentally reprogram the way our mind thinks and reacts to alcohol, we will be able to stave off these outside distractions and begin to move to the world of alcohol-consciousness.

DANIELLE

Danielle didn't think she had a problem with drinking at all, but felt she had gone a bit too hard over the holiday period and needed a life reset at the moment. From Thanksgiving week to the end of the year, she had a consistent itinerary of party after party and vacation after vacation.

She took the entire week of Thanksgiving off and visited her family back home in Tampa Bay. There, she saw a number of different friends and hit up all of her old spots in town. Between all the drinking and eating, she was in a daze by the time she got back to work.

Couple this with taking the last two weeks of the year off to travel to Australia with her boyfriend, and she figured she had probably put on 15 pounds during that month period. She wanted to go on a hard-core diet to get back into shape and figured coupling that with Dry January would probably be the best way to go to kill two birds with one stone. She thought a full detox was the best way to get the weight off.

Danielle didn't let everyone know that she made this choice, but she did share it with a few choice friends and co-workers whom she knew were going to be asking her to come out during the week and on the weekend to hang out. Of course, many people offered their support, letting her know they didn't think she had a drinking problem and that she doesn't "drink that much to them."

Danielle was surprised at this, as she never said she had a drinking problem. Why did everyone now begin to ask her questions like "How long has she felt this way?" or whether her family had a history of alcoholism?

She appreciated the support and those asking questions because it was obvious they cared about her, but she was taken aback. She didn't think she drank any more than any of her friends who now intimated she had a problem.

As the questions kept coming, she began to question whether she should take Dry January off, since so many people seemed to think she's an alcoholic now. She wanted to prove she can easily handle her alcohol without it being a problem.

As she bare-knuckled through not drinking for the first week, this was the main question in her mind as the upcoming Monday came around. Since she had decided to not go out Friday or Saturday night, she didn't really feel as if she'd had the chance to blow off any steam from the previous week, and this one was starting out to be a doozy.

One of her top customers had an order not show up as promised, and now they were threatening to pull their account. One of her top employers put in his two-week notice today because he found a job paying him almost twice what he was making now. Their back-office system was down, and she had to call all of their top customers to let them know that their orders would be delayed also.

As she worked through lunch to make as many calls as possible and troubleshoot the system with her back-office staff, she found herself dreaming of going home this afternoon and enjoying a nice Moscato to take her mind off work and make her feel good for a while. She remembered she was doing Dry January, but instantly thought that there was no way she was going to be able to make it through this week without some type of drinking to stay sane.

When she walked out of the office, she had no idea how she was not going to drink that night. She remembered reading on one of the blog posts from AINYF (Alcohol is NOT Your Friend) that podcasts were a great way to reprogram our mind to abstain from alcohol and the one by Annie Grace was highly recommended.

She decided to give it a listen on the way home to see if it would be the thing that could help bolster her resolve. If this didn't do it, she wasn't sure anything out there could, so she turned it on as she drove the 45 minutes in Atlanta traffic, hoping that it would help in some capacity.

As Annie talked about some of the traps that keep us drinking when we don't want to, she began recapping the exact scenario that Danielle was going through that day. We have all the will in the world until we have a bad day at work, and the only way we have been used to dealing with such bad days is to grab a drink and just zone out to easily get our minds off things. Instead, there are a number of other things that one can do to relieve such stress that don't involve drinking our sorrows away.

One of the suggestions was a workout to release some of the stress from the body and get our healthy endorphins going. Danielle thought she would give this a try and decided to go hit her gym for a quick 30-minute workout instead of just giving in to the idea of giving up Dry January.

After her HIIT (high intensity interval training) workout, she took a quick shower and realized that she did feel much better and was famished from hitting the gym so hard. She no longer felt like drinking *that night was a must-do, and she would continue with Dry January to see if she could make it the entire month. She also decided that she would start listening to Annie Grace's podcast every morning on the way to work and on the way home, as it had been a lifesaver today.*

All the tips and strategies shared were extremely helpful, but the biggest help was that it was almost as if Annie was reading her mind or was in her life in some respects. Any time Danielle had a thought that would try to convince her that she should no longer do Dry January, Annie had already told her that this was going to happen, so she was prepared for it. She recognized how her mind was working against itself to prevent her from staying committed to the decision she made and was, therefore, able to ignore it when it happened.

Just knowing that what she was thinking was normal, and that this was her body's way of just trying to convince her to give it what it wanted (the usual dopamine spike from drinking), she found it much easier to say no because she recognized it for what it was and knew that if she got through it, she would be able to withstand it much more easily in the future.

She didn't just end with listening to the podcast, however. Danielle picked up Annie Grace's book, This Naked Mind, *and began to devour it voraciously at night. She would read it each night before going to bed, and the more she read, the more she began to look at alcohol in a different light.*

Sure, she already understood that alcohol was probably not the best as it related to her future health and that she probably could not drink alcohol all the time if she was going to be healthier in her older age. What she didn't recognize, however, was how extremely bad it was for you regardless of what age you were.

In fact, the more she read about alcohol and its effects on your sleep, fitness, and overall emotional stability, the more she wondered why people did it in the first place. As the days turned into weeks and the weeks multiplied to bring her closer to the end of January, she began to seriously consider if she wanted to even start drinking again next month or ever again for that matter.

Mental Re-engineering

Dry January is probably one of the top reasons individuals decide to give up drinking for a short amount of time to start the beginning of the year. That time period from Thanksgiving through December can be prime time for indulging, as individuals tend to throw caution to the wind with all the back-to-back holidays and good food that come together during this period.

They think they can easily take a week or two break and then come back refreshed after cleansing themselves a bit. As a matter of fact, why not just try the whole Dry January thing out, as they have heard a lot of people say it's a great way to start the year with a clear mind to get ready for the year.

So they decide to commit to it at the beginning of the year and feel great going into January 1st. The first few days pass easily. No issues at all. They even tell a few people at the office that they are doing Dry January and are delighted when a few co-workers let them know that they are doing it, too.

Great. This is going to be easier than expected, since they now know there is going to be one less person inviting them out to drink after work or to "catch up" on anything. They get through the first week and as Friday comes around, they begin to think about what they are going to do this weekend since they are not drinking. The reality is that we have been drinking for so long at this point, trying to figure out something to do other than going out and partying can be extremely challenging.

For that reason, this first step in quitting drinking provides the foundation for an individual to successfully be able to fight off these tendencies and move toward a life of alcohol-consciousness. So many years of subconscious programming by so many different mediums is not something that one can shrug off lightly and forget about just because one no longer desires to drink.

In fact, this first step of mental re-engineering is something you should start exploring BEFORE you have even made the decision to stop drinking. I tell everyone that they should explore mental re-engineering to make sure they understand all the different aspects of what drinking can do to their body and truly understand the decision they are making each time they drink.

Many people have never been educated on all the negative effects that alcohol has on us, besides being a full-blown alcoholic and living on the street or drinking so much that we are at the hospital all the time with major liver problems. They have no concept of how alcohol actually ruins your sleep, decreases your mental capacity to learn and grow, and actually handicaps your ability to deal with anxiety as you age.

To begin to explore this step, the first thing one should do is read a few books or listen to a few audiobooks that give a great overview of all the ways that alcohol affects us physically, emotionally, and psychologically. There are a number of great books out there that do this in a way that is extremely informative and entertaining. My hope is that *Bamboozled* will become one of those books for many in the future.

The top books that one should explore are the following:

- *Drinking: A Love Story* by Carol Knapp
- *Alcohol Lied to Me* by Craig Beck
- *Drink? The New Science of Alcohol and Your Health* by Professor David McNutt
- *Sober For Good* by Anne M. Fletcher
- *This Naked Mind* by Annie Grace

There are a number of other books out there with great content that are very helpful as well, but these were the top five that I truly enjoyed, as they shined a light on all of the things that I had been programmed to believe about alcohol when I was very young and revealed that much of it was pure marketing designed to make us think that we need alcohol as a necessary part of our daily lives.

As I became more and more educated on the effects of alcohol and how, scientifically, it hurts us in so many ways, I slowly began to question if I would ever drink again. Up to that point, I thought I would just be giving up alcohol for about three months to see how it would affect me, and if I could see any positive results from it.

After reading *This Naked Mind*, I began to question why I would ever put in my body again something that has such negative effects on so many different areas of my life. Now that I was educated on all the different ways alcohol can affect you other than just being drunk or having a hangover the next day, I recognized that even though I didn't feel that I had developed a drinking problem up to that point, if I continued on the current path I was on, there was a good chance that a problem could develop.

My wife and I had stopped drinking on November 10th, 2018, and we left for Dublin, Ireland, on November 25th (roughly only two weeks into sobriety). Much of what we did on trips in the past was drink, so we were apprehensive about how this trip would go without it. However, as I sat on our plane to Dublin and continued to learn more and more about all the negative, short-term and long-term effects of drinking, I knew instinctively that I would never drink again.

When you read a bunch of different literature and listen to a number of different podcasts about the impact of drinking, you are educating yourself on a side of alcohol that is not advertised and that most people never really learn. The end result isn't about you not drinking again, but more so about you having the knowledge to decide if you want to risk all the negative results that could come from drinking long term.

It is why we use the term *alcohol-consciousness*. It's not about quitting drinking, as much as it is about making the conscientious decision to drink *after* having all the facts about what they are potentially giving up for it. The majority of us never truly have a grasp of how much we are giving up each time we decide to drink. In most of our minds, the only thing we have to worry about is money wasted at the bar buying drinks for other people and a little bit of lost productivity the next day while we nurse our hangovers.

What mental re-engineering does is open up our eyes to all the subtle effects of drinking alcohol excessively that can affect us short term and, more importantly, long term. By listening to all the different ways that alcohol can harm us both physically, mentally, and emotionally, we will finally start to see how much we are sacrificing by making this a consistent part of our lives.

There is a very good chance that this knowledge will not change anything for some, but for others, as they continue to hear about the different ways alcohol slowly changes us with time and affects our ability to do many things, we will find ourselves starting to question whether it is really worth all that it takes from us.

The change that needs to take place in most of us regarding our relationship with alcohol is not something that will happen overnight. It will take months and even years to dissemble all the social engineering that has taken place in our subconscious for us to be able to overcome it in our normal day-to-day activities.

The number of various habits that we have created over time and that have become entrenched in our psyche will be there under the skin, begging us to come back to our usual routines. We need something strong enough to stop our normal way of thinking and interrupt our patterns.

When we come home from work and 5:30 or 6:00 p.m. comes around, our body is going to begin to want that usual dopamine spike that comes from our favorite drink. The only way we are going to be able to fight against it is if we have planted something deep inside of our brains that will combat that feeling and make us think twice before moving forward with that natural habit.

Over time, the urge to drink will begin to dissipate a bit, but that will only be after consistent efforts to implant the new line of thinking in the way we look at alcohol as a whole. This is part of the reason that Danielle had to almost completely submerge herself in the information related to how bad alcohol could be for her.

When you first start going down this route, there will be a number of different times in which you will begin to question if this is the right decision for you. You will get calls and texts on Friday afternoon or

"Sunday Funday." You will be immensely tempted to go back on your word and just have a little "fun." This will not be easy at first, and the only way to give yourself the best chance of not allowing this to overtake you is to constantly ingest information educating yourself on all the ways alcohol hurts you in the long run.

By listening to different podcasts, as well as reading books, the knowledge will be consistently reinforced and you'll find it easier to say no when others try to get you to go back to your old self.

What this also will do is make you begin to think twice if you haven't made the decision to drink yet. For some, it takes a long time to truly allow the realization of what alcohol does to them to sink in, and they must see it for themselves.

For this reason, we usually suggest that you do NOT stop drinking when first implementing this step. We ask this so individuals can compare the negative scientific effects on your body and mind real time to know that what is shared in your readings/podcast is absolutely true.

Many times, when we are drinking, we are just enjoying the moment and are not very cognizant of our change in behavior as well as how we are affected the day after, other than the usual hangover. When we begin to scientifically analyze how alcohol affects us in the moment, as well as later, we can then see the subtle patterns of how we change as a person because of alcohol's effects on us.

By recognizing this, we are then able to consciously make the decision whether what we are giving up in terms of mental clarity, decision-making, and overall health is worth what we deem as the positives that we are getting from drinking alcohol.

This is what alcohol-consciousness is all about and the reason that the focus isn't on having everyone not drink, but rather ensuring that everyone is aware of what they are giving up or putting themselves at risk by making the decision to drink.

How to Reprogram Your Mind

This can be difficult for some, based on how busy all of our lives can be. For me, I was able to implement a pretty easy strategy that I think anyone can follow. As with anything in life, if you just say that you are going to do something, but don't have a specific plan as to HOW you are going to achieve it, then things will get left by the wayside.

This book is the first guide that will give you a step-by-step overview of how to begin your alcohol-conscious journey, with the what, the how, and the when to make implementing this foolproof in your life. As with anything that we start new, the most important time is going to be the first 30 days. Once you are able to get through that first initial wave of awkwardness and frustration, you'll begin to run on autopilot and do it without even thinking.

The most important part of starting a new habit is *consistency*. Regardless of how you are feeling that day and how little you may be able to get through a specific activity, the important part is to DO SOMETHING.

Doing a little bit of something at the same time each day is thousands of times better than skipping it altogether. Our brain is a very smart muscle, and just as it had gotten used to drinking alcohol every day at the same time and subtly began asking for it when you weren't even thinking about it, when you create a habit that takes place at the same time each day, your body will begin to feel a bit off when you skip it.

By staying committed to doing this as much as possible (ESPECIALLY on the days that you don't feel like it), your mind will begin to associate this as part of who you are and what you do to ensure you don't miss any days feeding your brain the constant positive knowledge it needs to be successful.

The What

Podcasts and books (or audiobooks) are a dynamic duo/trio for this endeavor.

I shared my top books earlier that I truly think are the best way to get started, but you can't go wrong if you read basically any type of quit-lit that will help you on your way. You can Google this term to find a large list of literature from which to choose.

Listening to podcasts in the car is another great strategy to consistently feed your mind with high-quality material as you drive in your car every day. Even though the world has changed from what it was pre-Covid, we all still drive from time to time, and a university on wheels is still a great way to obtain and retain a lot of information around alcohol-consciousness. Many of the books that you can find in a physical format will also have an audiobook version. And if that is not the case, there are many podcasts out there that one can listen to while driving.

The number of various sobriety podcasts are pretty extensive and growing every day, it seems, but here are some of the more prominent ones that have lots of listeners:

1. Soberful[135]
2. Tribe Sober[136]
3. Alcohol-Free Lifestyle[137]
4. That Sober Guy[138]
5. Recovery Rocks[139]

Make sure to do your research and get a feel for what each podcast offers to find the one that truly resonates with you and makes you ready to click play on the next episode each time.

The When

One of the most important aspects of starting a new habit is having a very specific time when you are going to do it every day. It is immensely important that this time remains consistent regardless of what is happening, if possible.

When you are reprogramming your mind with a new habit, the consistency of doing that same thing at the same time each day deeply ingrains it into the brain. When you do it at different times or only when you feel like it, the brain is not able to make the deeper connections to the surroundings or other specific characteristics of that time to make the mental connection stronger.

For example, if you always read first thing in the morning when you wake up or late at night before you go to bed, your mind is going to start associating the other specific task that you do around that time (waking up or going to sleep) with the habit of reading. Therefore, when you wake up and begin stretching for the day and meditating, your mind will automatically remind you that it's time to read. When you start your nighttime routine and begin brushing your teeth, your brain will begin to think about what you are going to read tonight, as well as probably remind you of something you read the previous night that was impactful and stood out. This will make the implementation of the habit much easier when other things try to come into your life to distract you from doing it.

I typically focused on podcasts and audiobooks to and from work. This gave me a sense of focus while I was feeding my mind with information that would work to improve my life in some way, similar to how we work to create a better future for ourselves.

If I wanted to listen to any type of general talk radio or music to relax a bit, I would leave that mostly to the weekends or late in the evening if I had to drive at night for some reason. It created a sense of obligation to continue to feed on the positive information I need to grow in my alcohol-consciousness when I may not feel as excited to do it every single day.

Making the Decision

Mental re-engineering is about recognizing what alcohol does to our lives and then deciding if we want to continue going down that path and allowing alcohol to have that effect on us, or if we might be better served long term by deciding not to partake in this harmful drug.

For some people, this is a decision that they can make easily after they begin to educate themselves on all the numerous ways that alcohol can negatively affect one's life. For others, this is a process that takes place over time. They need to experience situations that force them to realize a lot of the information that they are reading is actually beginning to come to fruition in their lives. Some people may not believe the physiological way their body can begin to change and desire alcohol at certain times of the day or in certain situations until they have experienced it enough times and have struggled to resist it. It is often only through experiencing this firsthand that we are able to understand how insidious the true nature of alcohol can be and make the decision if it is something that we should allow the rest of our lives to be dictated by.

Once the mental re-engineering has taken place and the decision to no longer allow alcohol to become a part of one's life has been made, the next step is very important to ensure that one is able to experience all the positive results of life that one can experience when alcohol is no longer a hindrance.

Let's move to the next chapter to discuss.

CHAPTER FOURTEEN

Exercise Commitment

*Move Your A**!*

"Good things come to those who sweat."

—ANONYMOUS

There are two different pictures of aging.

There is the aging that has us holding a cane everywhere we go and trying to remember the name of that nice boy at the grocery store who is always putting our groceries away, and then there's that Betty White aging, in which people are amazed at how spry and well put together we are, as well as how sharp our brains are.

As shared earlier, heavy binge drinking that results in blackouts at a young age (or almost any age) can result in major harm to our brain's ability to store and recall information in a timely manner. The ability to remember things quickly and correctly is what some would consider one of the first signs of "aging" and something that many people try to either prevent or reverse for fear of diseases such as dementia or Alzheimer's.

Exercise will give you a much better chance of experiencing this latter form of aging, and prevent the chance that you will be walking around Walmart trying to remember why you came into the store in the first place.

When you first stop drinking alcohol, the amount of free time that will be at your disposal will probably be scary. Who knew that you really wasted that much just drinking? However, when you think about all the time that usually goes into getting ready to enjoy a night out on the town, you see how it adds up. Case in point:

1. The happy hour to get the weekend started at 5 p.m.
2. Then pregaming at the house from 8–10 p.m.

3. Then meeting friends out from 10–12 a.m. before hitting the club.
4. Then partying at said club from 12–2 a.m.
5. Then finding food to eat so you don't wake up too hungover the next day from 2–4 a.m.
6. Then sleeping from 4-noon the next day because you need the extra sleep to recover from the hangover.

Put that all together and you have about a 19-hour window of time (or 11 hours, if you take out the sleep) in which you really need to find something to do that doesn't involve alcohol and partying.

Some people just have no idea how to fill this tremendous gap, as the thought of having so much time seems bizarre in a world in which everyone is trying to squeeze more hours in a day like New York drivers trying to get into a turning lane.

Exercise is a great filler of time because it provides even greater benefits beyond just filling this void.

KWABENE

Kwabene had lived a pretty hardcore life for the past ten years—he drank, smoke, and dipped tobacco like he was trying to kill himself.

Kwabene consistently only drank hard liquor and smoked about half a pack of cigarettes per day. He had been "dipping" tobacco ever since he was a high school baseball player and just found it challenging to give it up once he got older.

His lifestyle would be considered sedentary to say the least, as the last time he had seen a gym was when he was touring his apartment complex. It's not that he wouldn't be open to going to the gym, it's just that his body didn't care much for him going to the gym. He had gotten very used to his sedentary lifestyle and thought it was serving him pretty well up to this point.

Kwabene's doctor, however, disagreed. His doctor told him that his overall health was in bad shape and that drinking was not helping in any capacity—so Kwabene decided to try stopping.

Kwabene told his doctor that he only drank occasionally (once or twice per week), but when he did, he had a tendency to drink a fair amount and not quite remember everything that happened that night. He had woken up more than once on his couch with the final credits of an episode of Family Guy on the screen, having no idea of when and how he got in that position.

He agreed with the doctor that it was probably time to turn the corner in his life and live a bit healthier than he had before, and he figured cutting back on his alcohol was a good place to start.

As soon as he started, however, he had no idea how intense the desire to drink was going to be for him. He was just so used to drinking every Tuesday, Thursday, and Saturday that when those three nights rolled around, he found himself immensely pulled to the desire to pour a glass of whiskey. He joked to his co-workers that he knew what time of the day it was on those three days because his body started to say it was whiskey o'clock.

He needed to do something to occupy his mind so this wouldn't be such a problem. One of his friends offered to start working out with him every day at 5:30 p.m.

Kwabene figured if he worked out during this time, then he would probably be completely famished by the time he got home and would be more focused on eating than he would be on drinking. In the meantime, maybe he could lose a few pounds as well.

When Kwabene first started working out, he was amazed at two things:

First, he had no idea someone could possibly be that sore, as he had trouble getting out of bed two days after he started working out. Second, he was surprised that he did not think about alcohol by the time he got home after each of his workouts.

As he suspected, his body was more focused on getting food than it was on getting alcohol, and he needed something to replenish everything that he had lost during his workout. Often, his body craved *water more than anything else, and even the thought of drinking whiskey after working out made him a bit sick.*

The first few weeks, it was challenging for him to commit to going to the gym even just three days per week, as his mind would often try to use his soreness as an excuse to talk him out of it. However, he was able to persevere and work through the discomfort of those first 3–4 weeks to come out on the other side, and over time he found it was much easier to want to go to the gym on the appointed days.

He began losing some weight and started to notice a number of positive things happening. He was able to sleep so much better at night, as he found himself super tired by 9:00 p.m., whereas he used to stay up until at least 10:00 before. He started to have more energy during the day and found himself not having the same cravings that he had in the past after a few months or so.

The results were so encouraging that he decided to add Monday, Wednesday, and Friday to the mix to see if they would add any more benefits. He was now working out six days per week, and things were starting to change quickly.

He began to lose weight at an impressive clip, to the point that he found that his entire body was changing. Initially the decision was to stop drinking because it was so bad for him, but he found himself now giving up smoking and dipping as well, since it just didn't fit into his new healthy lifestyle.

As more and more time elapsed, his cravings completely dissipated, and he found himself a completely different person. He dropped 40 pounds and his doctor was amazed at his transformation.

As they sat and talked about all the changes he was making in his life and how he was able to give up alcohol, smoking, and dipping this time around when he had tried so many times in the past, he admitted that working out had been the missing link that he needed all of those years.

For him, committing himself to doing something that he didn't want to do consistently and then seeing the results of that commitment made him realize that this was what he needed to do in all areas of his life to be successful. Also, he realized that it got easier with time and now, he didn't see working out as something he HAD to do every day as opposed to something he GOT to do every day.

Giving up alcohol was extremely challenging at first, and he wasn't sure how he was going to get through it, but all of the positive effects of working out not only helped with filling his free time, so he wasn't overwhelmed with the desire to fill it with booze, but it even curbed the cravings tremendously over time.

As he sat back and thought about this decision, he kicked himself a bit, wishing he had done it sooner, but he was thankful that he finally realized it and was ready to now make the rest of his life the best of his life with this newfound truth.

The Positive Effects of Exercise Against Alcohol

When many people sit down and think about exercise, they often think about all of the pain that is associated with it and how so many people love it while others try to avoid it at all costs. When it comes to its effect on alcohol, however, and the numerous ways in which it can make a difference in one's journey of alcohol-consciousness, it is a wonder that all rehabilitation programs don't make physical fitness a required component.

Exercise helps with the mental, physical, and physiological changes that need to take place in one's body to truly put alcohol behind them and move on to that next chapter in their lives.

Let me walk you through how this is the case.

From a cravings perspective, alcohol is a great combatant against the physiological change that your mind and body takes once it becomes engrossed in alcohol's grip. The physiological pull of alcohol makes us feel like we need to drink, even though we may have told ourselves that this was no longer the choice we made for our lives.

Research shows that exercise can create a noticeable lessening of such desires. Without the usual stimulant, our bodies desire some type of replacement for the artificial high that we were used to getting while we were drinking.

By adding exercise to our daily regimen, our body will begin to experience the positive dopamine release[140] created from engaging in a tough workout that pushes us to our physical and mental limits. This natural release of dopamine will begin to help curb the artificial desire that our bodies may have been experiencing, as we look to lessen alcohol's control over us.

Another great benefit is the repair that exercise can actually do to our damaged brain cells from alcohol. When we drink excessively, our brain cells can be damaged tremendously by the excessive dopamine exposure. Exercise is known to improve the brain's health regardless of the need for it, but it is especially helpful in the case of repairing damaged brain cells from excessive alcohol use.

In a study conducted on rats, it was observed that subjects that exercised prior to being exposed to excessive ethanol toxicity experienced a smaller reduction in brain cells as opposed to those who did not exercise at all. From this observation, scientists have hypothesized that exercise could be a useful combatant to the decrease in brain cells from alcohol use as well as an avenue to potentially help regenerate them once one has given up drinking alcohol to that degree.

Another more obvious benefit of exercise is that it allows us to do something with all of that immense free time we get once we decide to stop allowing our lives to revolve around alcohol. There are so many things that turn into time-sucks that are a result of us either A. getting ready to go drink, i.e. pregaming, B. drinking (the act itself) or C. recovering from drinking, i.e., having a hangover (something that can take days to recover from).

When we have this much free time on our hands, we will begin to look for other things to do and our minds will ultimately begin to ask us if we are SURE we want to stop drinking. The mind has a tendency to not want to work if it can help it, and once we have a good routine in place, it is going to push us to stick to that if possible. The brain and body like familiarity, so as soon as you begin to do something that is outside of your normal habit, it will begin to sound alarm bells to ask what is going on.

This is part of what cravings are about. It's your brain's way of saying that you are going against your routine and there is something missing that it is so used to getting that it's now demanding it at the appointed time.

Therefore, you are going to need something to substitute that feeling and fill all of that now void time to make sure that you don't find yourself relapsing from boredom. Exercise is such a good filler of that void because not only does it combat the craving to allow you to not feel so overwhelmed when the moment arises, but there are so many other health benefits for your body and brain in general.

Better cognitive performance and better overall health in a number of different areas are just two of the small ways that exercise can benefit one's life. By implementing this activity, you could possibly find yourself having discovered a new love that could become something that consumes a lot of your time as well.

Many times, individuals who have experienced a strong affinity to drink excessively have what many would deem as addictive personalities. Once you like something, you REALLY like it and want to do it as much as you can. For this reason, many individuals who begin to use exercise as their coping mechanism or substitute of choice often find themselves as enamored with their new exercise lives as they were with their previous alcohol-filled ones.

This can be positive if one begins to fall in love with exercise, but one does need to be careful not to replace one addiction with another. The trick is to just make sure that one doesn't go overboard with working out to an unhealthy degree.

It's one thing to use exercise to work out every afternoon at 5:00 p.m. to prevent the desire to go to the bar. It's a completely different story if one is then working out every afternoon and morning for hours on end as an attempt to run from the craving of alcohol. There has to be a balance of exercise that makes sense with other activities and coping mechanisms, i.e., hobbies, new social activities, etc. that can make up the void.

You can't fill ALL of your time with exercise, but it is such a good start that we see it as a MUST-DO to truly allow you to become the very best version of yourself.

How to implement this

There are a number of different ways that one can go about implementing this step in their lives, but here are tips and strategies that will help you get started and create a system that will work for where you are and your lifestyle.

Frequency

The main thing here is consistency. They say to build a habit, it takes 21 days or more, but the reality is that you have to build a rhythm that makes building that habit almost bullet proof if you do it correctly.

Starting out, this could be rather challenging, as your body will be wondering why you made the decision to put it through so much pain after living a pretty sedentary life. It will try to find some way to get you to stop, mostly by causing a soreness unlike anything you may have ever experienced before.

The important thing here is to not stop working out or that soreness will linger and all be for nothing. However, if you are able to push through it and stay consistent on working out regardless of that soreness, you'll find that it will surely dissipate with time.

When you are first starting this fitness journey, you should try to build a habit of at least three days per week. That will be enough to generally get your mind and body in a consistent rotation to begin to feel that this is something that is going to happen more than just every now and then. Pick the three days that work best for you, and schedule those times in your calendar.

By picking those three days in advance, it will be easier for you to keep up with what days you work out, and prevent you from having to make a decision about when to work out based on how you feel.

VERY IMPORTANT: Do everything you can to NOT change these three days. Even though it will be tempting to say that something came up Tuesday, so you're going to work out on Wednesday, I highly advise against this.

You have to make your workouts non-negotiable in your life. Don't allow things to be able to trump them. I do understand that life will happen and sometimes there will be special occasions in which you will need to switch up a workout to attend a personal or work event, but these should be few and far between.

The reason for this is that your mind is very adept at trying to protect the body from feeling pain and if it can come up with a reason as to why you cannot work out today, it'll do so. You cannot fall into the trap of switching up what days you are going to work out because you don't really "feel" like it, as this will cause you to question if you should work out all the time.

Instead, you have to make up your mind ahead of time that these are the days that you are going to work out and there are very few things short of a zombie apocalypse (and maybe even not then, since you can get a good cardio workout in running from zombies!) that will stop you from doing so.

Three days per week is a good start to get your body used to working out, but as time progresses, the goal should be to work up to five days per week, as there are numerous positive attributes of exercising consistently.

Just as your body will adapt and begin to expect the effects of working out three days per week, it will also begin to adapt and expect the positive effects of the upped regimen. Working out five days per week will psychologically solidify the expectation of working out as something that you "do" and it will become more a part of who you are as a person.

I work out seven days per week because the benefits are so tremendous to start my day off right, but that isn't necessary as five days is enough for your body to really take to all the positive ways that exercise can change one's life.

Now, let's talk about how long you should work out.

Time

This can vary based on how many other obligations and responsibilities you may have that may make this challenging, but the ideal amount to get the best results is twice a day for 30 minutes each session.

Thirty minutes works well because it doesn't require one to commit to an extensive amount of time to get the body moving and see some results from one's actions relatively quickly (within a week or two) if one couples it with a steady, focused diet (more to come on that in the next chapter).

I typically suggest bookending your day with each session by doing one before work and the other immediately after. By bookending your days with exercising in the morning and the evening, you are ensuring that you are getting your day off to a strong start due to the numerous health benefits associated with working out in the morning.

By finishing the day with a workout as well, you give your mind and body something to do and somewhere else to be when you may be tempted to meet a group of co-workers at happy hour instead.

If you don't have anything to do, there's a chance you may think you are strong enough to join them and the temptation may overwhelm you when you're newly alcohol-conscious. However, if you already have a reason that you can't go and are looking forward to working off some stress after work or a long day of taking care of your family, this is a doubly helpful weapon to have in your tool bag to keep you on the straight and narrow as it relates to your sobriety.

The overall benefits of working out in the morning are so tremendous that if you have to pick one or the other to do based on your schedule, I would choose the morning every time. Some of the amazing benefits of working out in the morning are:

1. Fewer distractions with people in the gym or things that could pop up not allowing you to go ... most people are still sleeping, so you're good!
2. Beat the sun and heat ... if you're going to go for a run or do anything outdoors, doing it before the sun begins to blaze is always a smart idea.
3. Become more alert and ready to tackle the day ... working out in the morning is a great stimulant to your hormone known as cortisol[141] that keeps you alert and awake.
4. Appetite control ... exercising generally helps regulate appetite by reducing ghrelin,[142] the hunger hormone, and increases your satiety hormones[143] (the hormones that make you feel full), so it works on both sides of the equation.

The great part of all of this is that your body will adjust to waking up in the morning with a bit of time and consistency and soon, you'll be jonesing to wake up and work out once you experience all the positive effects that exercise has for your future.

Intensity

Intensity-wise, you need to do something that works up a decent sweat. You don't have to be sweating all over the place by the time it ends, but you should have pushed yourself to the point that you are wiping sweat off of your body.

I highly encourage individuals to work out outside whenever possible to experience the positive benefit of getting a healthy amount of sunlight consistently. When this happens and it's during the spring and summer, there is a good chance that you'll be drenched in sweat.

The purpose is to choose a set of exercises that require just enough level of focus from you that they are not easy but shouldn't be so challenging that you can't finish an entire set without stopping. The goal is that in the last 2–3 reps you WANT to stop, but you still have enough energy in the tank to finish strong.

When it gets to the point that those last 2–3 reps feel easy, then it's probably time to up the weight or the activity to another level of intensity.

Type of exercises

This really depends on your personal preference and what type of exercises excite you the most to do it consistently and not skip a day.

The one caveat to this is that you can't overly focus on one area of your body and skip other important aspects that will help you become well-rounded—in other words, don't be top heavy and have chicken legs.

When I used to go to the gym consistently, I would typically like workouts that included heavy lifting to start, with supersets toward the end because I felt like it allowed me to work on two aspects of a particular muscle at the same time, while also building the strength and endurance of that muscle. Coupling a heavy lift exercise with a superset of a different exercise hitting the same or ancillary spot of that muscle was typically excruciating from a "good" pain standpoint and would always work up a sweat relatively quickly. I would leave the gym with soreness from the initial heavy lifting, along with the increased muscular endurance of always supersetting as many times as I could in that workout window.

Due to Covid, I stopped going to the gym at all and began to do workouts at home to continue to stay in shape. This didn't allow me to continue to do the heavy lifting aspect of my workout, unfortunately (or maybe fortunately when you consider that I'm not getting any younger and those deadlifts were hard!), but they did add a very unique aspect to my life in the form of what is known as functional fitness.

Now, instead of lifting heavy and supersetting, I do a combination of calisthenics exercises with some calisthenics weightlifting exercises that allow me to keep various aspects of my body strong and in shape. These are in the form of what they call exercises for style and form (handstands) and exercises for strength and ability (planches).

There are a number of different programs that you can research that will give you a number of great workout options. I personally use the FIT app on my phone, in which you can purchase a number of different programs that fit where you are in your lifestyle journey.

Also, by searching for any type of calisthenics or home body workouts on YouTube, you should be able to find many good ones. I personally am a fan of Chris Heria's workouts,[144] as well as a lot of the content from Athlean-X.[145] They both have great content that you can adapt to meet where you are and give a combination of strength, endurance, and skill exercises that will keep your body guessing and growing over time.

As shared earlier, you have to make this your own, and, as someone who likes to lift heavy and is focused on strength, these recommendations may not resonate with everyone. However, there are a number of different ways you can go other than working out heavy or doing calisthenics. Yoga or simple aerobic full-body workouts are also a great way to begin, and there are many great fitness instructors like Krissy Cela,[146] Tone It Up,[147] or Yoga with Adrienne[148] who offer programs that will give you a full-body workout to keep you in shape.

How to bring it all together to adapt and grow

As also shared earlier, the most important thing about any exercise regimen is consistency, consistency, consistency. I can't stress enough how important it is not to allow your feelings to dictate whether you work out each day but rather focus on the commitment you made to yourself and your desire to build the best version of yourself possible. There are a lot of psychological tricks that your mind will play on you to convince you to procrastinate on working out or skip it altogether, and you have to fight them when you first go down this fitness journey.

However, as with anything, the more reps you have at doing something, the better and easier it will become, so the trick is to push through and persevere in those first 30 days to begin to make the daily activity of exercising a habit and as much a part of your day as brushing your teeth.

It might take more than 30 days, to be honest, but if you stay focused on the long-term goals and your desire for your future, you can get there.

While exercise is so important in regard to the mental and physical ways that it will allow you to improve yourself overall, there is a crucial next step that is equally important, as it relates to getting and staying in shape and allowing your outer change to represent the beauty of the inner change taking place.

Most people would say that this part is WAY harder than the exercise part, which usually makes it that much more important.

What is it? Let's turn the page to see.

CHAPTER FIFTEEN

Diet Improvement

*Don't Eat That Sh*t!*

"Exercise is king. Nutrition is queen.
Put them together and you've got a kingdom."

—JACK LALANNE

If you've ever been a regular at a gym, you've probably experienced the same thing that I have and were somewhat perplexed at times.

There is always that overweight person who seems to always be in the gym around the same time as you, and they always appear to be working out pretty hard and diligently. However, over the year or so that you may have witnessed this impressive consistent effort, they don't appear to have lost any weight.

Now, there is a good chance that they are not trying to lose any weight at all and simply prefer to improve their flexibility or heart health, but the likelihood of that being the case with the added weight hindering their health is not very good.

It is more likely, however, that they fall into the large category of individuals who are consistent gym goers because they enjoy all of the benefits that come along with working up a good sweat and relieving some stress, but they haven't made the commitment to control their daily eating habits to fully realize the fruits of their physical efforts.

Many of these people will want to eventually just give up on working out because they don't see any results, not fully grasping that you can work out all you want, but if you're not willing to switch that Big Mac and fries meals with a strawberry grilled chicken salad (one of my faves, BTW), you are putting in a lot of effort that you probably will never actually SEE any results from. No one wants to work out hard every day to look in the mirror to see absolutely no change.

As shared earlier, on the path to alcohol-consciousness and sobriety, your physical outside layer is very much a reflection of your inner change as well. This is why many people always show what they look like while drinking and afterward, so one can see the dramatic physical change that giving up alcohol can result in.

This typically happens without any other influence at all, due to how one's skin begins to become clearer and overall facial features aren't bogged down by the weight of Smirnoff vodka being infused in it every morning.

To take this up a notch, if one begins to implement the second step of The MEDS (Exercise Commitment), one will typically begin to see an even more dramatic change in one's overall appearance, as alcohol is one of the main reasons that many individuals have issues with getting into shape each year. Very few people actually want to wake up to do that 5:00 a.m. workout anyway, and this is very much less true when one is recovering from a barrage of fireball shots the night before (have I not been there once or twice or 90 times?).

Therefore, by removing alcohol from the equation, most people will find it immensely easier to keep their initial commitments to working out, whether it's early in the morning before work or in the evening when the workday is over.

Without the pain from last night's hangover lurking over our heads or the lure of the 5:00 p.m. happy hour telling us to skip that workout, it'll be much easier to stay focused on the fitness goals needed to ensure we can shed whatever amount of weight or gain whatever amount of muscle is desired.

However, the biggest obstacle that stands in so many people's way is the mental challenge of not eating food that will keep one in the same place physically as it relates to one's goals. While most people would assume that it is all about discipline and willpower to stop eating sh*t that goes against what you are trying to accomplish, that is only a part of the battle.

The reality is that discipline helps you build the character and resilience to turn down that cheeseburger and order the salad instead at a restaurant, but that discipline is only possible after you first implement two more important steps. These steps lay the foundation for progress and will allow you to build your discipline over time so that you will be successful at this endeavor long term.

Let's dive into those two.

CHRISTIE

Christie had been at her new company for two years now, and it showed.

It showed not only in her disheveled hair that she hadn't had the time to do in almost six months, but also in her waistline that was slowly starting to expand more than her bank account had over that same time period. Sure, she was making money and was doing well in her sales commission role, but the late-night dinners and afternoon happy hours were making it almost impossible to do anything other than crash when they were over.

She had never been much of a workout person because she felt she didn't need it. She felt she was blessed with a very high metabolism and could eat pretty much whatever she wanted without worrying about adding on any extra weight.

However, two years after her lifestyle changed dramatically with her new job, it didn't seem that her high metabolism alone was going to do the trick. She hadn't seen the inside of the gym since she was in high school and shuddered to think about how hard it would be to start going.

She remembered the last time she took a significant break from the gym and had the embarrassing moment of asking her then boyfriend to help her get off the toilet because her legs were literally so sore she could not do it herself.

She wasn't dating anyone now, so it seemed like the perfect time to get back to it and try to get her fitness life back on track.

She started back slowly per the advice of a few friends and only went three days per week to get her body used to the habit of it all.

Slowly her body began to get used to the soreness and stopped yelling at her daily about inflicting such pain on it. She was starting to feel more and more comfortable each day, and after about six months, was starting to actually enjoy the act of waking up three days per week to get her day started with a workout. It made her feel like she was more of a complete person, living a full-fledged adult life like you see in the movies.

However, as she was coming up on her fourth month of consistently going three days per week, she wasn't quite sure why she hadn't lost the weight that she thought she should during this time frame. She stayed consistent and felt like she was giving it her all when she was in there, so the fact that she hadn't lost any significant weight was beginning to depress her a bit.

She decided to increase her frequency to see if that would help. She increased her workout routine from three times to five times per week. She felt she was doing all the right things and found herself really working up a sweat in each workout, so she could not understand why she wasn't seeing the results that she thought she should be seeing at this stage. It was going on five months and she had only lost five pounds, not a significant amount to write home about by any means.

She was just about to give up working out altogether when one of her friends chided her at lunch for drowning her salad in ranch dressing and extra cheese.

"Well, I work out more than the average person," she shot back. "So, I definitely think I've earned it."

"Maybe," replied her friend, "but by earning it, do you also mean wasting it? You're not going to get anywhere in regard to your fitness goals if you eat like sh*t after you work out."

Christie scoffed at what she said in the moment, but later thought about it in more detail, as she had seemed to be running on a hamster wheel and getting nowhere fast. She started to do more research about the impact of diet and recognized that she had been putting herself at a tremendous disadvantage by not taking it as seriously as she should have.

There was no way she was going to hit any fitness goals unless she had a complete mind shift in regard to what and how much she was eating. From her research, she also recognized that certain foods would not only give her more energy but could improve her brain capacity as well, which she found rather exciting.

From that moment on, she started to research how she should go about constructing a diet that matched what she was doing in the gym to make sure that she was not wasting all of her hard work and sweat there. She started to eat much healthier overall and focused on understanding what worked for her body versus what hurt her ability to lose weight. She truly started to put more focus on what was serving her overall, and she was surprised at the number of things that she used to think were okay for her to eat that were clearly bad for her.

From what she was learning, she began to implement new foods into her daily diet and eliminate many of the things that she found out were terrible for her long term. Whereas in the past, she felt great about choosing a salad over a cheeseburger at lunch, she now realized that she needed to make sure she was light on the dressing and didn't overload it with cheese. She completely stopped drinking sodas and sugary fruit juices and reduced her sugar intake altogether.

As the days turned to weeks and weeks turned to months, she started to notice how much weight she was losing without feeling like she was killing herself at the gym. Sure, she wasn't perfect, but she was learning each week what foods helped her lose weight versus which ones kept her stagnant or held her back.

She saw the change take place slowly as her clothes began to fit much better and she realized her energy level was growing through the roof. As she looked at the scale and saw that she was down twenty pounds over the past six months, she realized that her life was forever changed and she would never go back.

How to do it

When it comes to implementing new diet guidelines in one's life, the trick is to not do too much at one time. The mistake many people make is trying to boil the ocean and change everything to completely become a different person overnight. It just doesn't work that way. It took you to whatever age you are right now in life (20 years, 30 years, 40 years or more) to build up all the eating habits you currently have, and, therefore, it's not very realistic to think that you are going to be able to break them in a week or two.

To make this change more easily, you should focus on taking baby steps to improve and learn what works and what doesn't work in relation to your body's ability to lose weight and your psychological fortitude to withstand said change.

To say to someone who is used to eating cookies and ice cream whenever they desire that now you cannot have ANY cookies or ice cream at all can be too much psychologically and could eventually lead some people to decide the diet is "too much" or just "not for them."

By breaking it up into baby steps, you will create bridges that allow you to make progress as you learn something new about yourself and how your body reacts to different foods. When you implement slowly, you will increase your chances of success.

Here are the following steps for diet change implementation:

Step 1: Track your calories for two weeks.

This step is important to allow you to understand what your current eating habits are. Fully understanding what you already do will help you successfully choose the right things to eat and stay away from the things that are hurting your diet.

Knowledge is the key. For two weeks, you should monitor everything that you typically eat by tracking it with a calorie tracking app that adds up the calories as you put in the food. My personal app of choice is MyFitnessPal[149] because it is extremely user-friendly and even includes the nutritional information of foods from a number of different well-known restaurants throughout the world.

This will make it much easier if you have a job like I did in sales in which you ate out the majority of the time.

This step is very important, as it sets the base for where you are now to be able to diagnose what you will need to do to change your diet to begin to move things in a positive direction. It will seem a bit tedious, but it is only for two weeks and your future self will thank you for staying diligent and committed.

Step 2: Identify the foods that are giving you the highest calorie/fat consumption.

There are two things that typically hurt your goal of weight loss when you start: calories in general and too much fat.

We all understand the concept of how calories in and calories burned works, but fat just typically seems to be more difficult to burn off than carbs due to the fact that your body requires more chemical reactions[150] to do so—meaning that you will have to work harder to burn off calories from fat than you would to burn off calories from carbs.

The other side of this is that fat consists of 9 calories per gram, while carbs only consist of 4 calories per gram, so something that contains a higher percentage of fat is likely to have twice the caloric density of something that is mostly made of carbohydrates. In other words, you can eat the same volume of two different things and get twice as many calories from the fat-laden item as you get from the carbohydrate-dense item.

Typically, fatty foods are going to be the foods that you like . . . a lot. Things like ice cream, potato chips, and creamy salad dressings. If there is something that gets you excited when you think about eating it, there's a VERY good chance it falls into the category of something you probably shouldn't be eating on a regular basis.

Don't worry, however, as we have a fix that will address that and NOT make you feel like the only thing you are eating is bland, terrible food.

Step 3: Substitute one to two items that are adding the most fat/calories to your diet with something that is better for you overall.

Rome wasn't built in a day, and you're not going to change everything about you overnight. Therefore, you need to only hold yourself accountable to changing a small portion of what you are currently doing with something that is a tad bit better to be able to make a significant impact on your diet.

I would suggest looking at what you like to eat consistently and identifying the one thing that you think will give you the most leverage as it relates to improving your lifestyle. What I mean by that is find the thing that is hurting you the most negatively and see if there is something that you can substitute for it. That will make a tremendous difference.

For me, it was fried foods.

That one change for me when I was 25 years old took me from a scrawny, skinny-fat 155-pound weakling to a relatively strong, muscular 155-pound man two years later. By eating less fried food and replacing it with grilled options instead, I was able to shed a lot of excess fat from my body and lean out tremendously.

Whereas before I didn't have a lot of muscular definition through my body, I began to see it very distinctly after changing this habit for about three months, and I could really see a major difference after six months.

For you, it might be ice cream, potato chips, or those amazingly good hot spicy Cheetos. Whatever it is, you should pinpoint that one thing and try to find a healthier alternative for it. There are so many different substitutions that you can make for it with all the different brands out there and the low-fat/no-fat phase that took place in the 1990s/2000s, there are going to be a lot of choices from which you can choose.

The one caveat to this is that you can't just eat foods that are labeled low fat and go crazy on them because many of them are loaded with sugar[151] that will ultimately do more harm than good, so you need to be cognizant of the long-term ramifications of this.

However, there are also a load of other healthier alternatives[152] you can choose from that will yield great results overall, as they are not only healthier for you from a fat/calorie perspective but also offer a ton of other nutritional benefits that will aid your overall health in a number of different ways.

Step 4: Give your body time to adapt and get used to the change.

Your body and mind are very powerful things. As shared in earlier chapters, when your body gets used to alcohol, it will do everything in its power to make you think you need it all the time.

However, as you begin to put more distance between yourself and your brain's memory of what alcohol did for you, you'll find yourself not thinking about it as frequently, if at all.

As it relates to your diet, give your mind and taste buds some time to get used to the new food you are going to be eating. At first, you will feel like the taste isn't as good as the fully fat-loaded foods. However, as time progresses and you become more accustomed to your new diet, you'll find yourself really liking the healthier foods and not missing the more fat-laden items much, if at all.

This was really the only change I made to my diet for the first year of my health journey. As I began to mature and think about what else I can do to improve my health across the board, a number of other changes began to reveal themselves as possibly having a big impact, and they did. The other three changes/substitutes that yielded equally impactful results were:

1. **Eating only low-fat or no-fat food.** This was extremely helpful in that it allowed me to actually eat more food while consuming way fewer calories than I had in the past, something that I just didn't realize before I started to count them consistently.

2. **Choosing 100% whole-grain wheat bread over white.**
I typically stay away from all bread if possible, but if I do happen to get a wrap or sandwich of any kind based on the circumstances, I do my best to always ensure that the bread is wheat (not white) and that it's whole-grain wheat if possible. The additional nutrients and reduced calories of whole grain will truly add up over time, especially if you are a heavy sandwich eater.

3. **Drinking sparkling water or water instead of juice/sodas/ milk.** Most people realize soda is just terrible for you and easily stay away from it. However, many people are still under the impression that milk and juice are good, when that is often not the case. First, you can just start with the extra calories of both that are unnecessarily adding more to your daily/weekly bottom line, which, in turn, becomes less food you can eat. Second, when you think of all the sugar[153] that is in most juices, as well as the plethora of problems[154] that many people experience from drinking milk long term, then it seems like a no-brainer to try one of the numerous low- to no-calories sparkling waters[155] that are on the market now that are so good they don't seem like a sacrifice at all.

Step 5: Consistently iterate and eat healthier with time.

As your body gets used to eating grilled food instead of fried and choosing low-fat/low-sugar items, you'll find that it'll become more of your baseline and what your body is used to. When this happens, you'll realize that you don't quite have the same craving for fried or highly fat-laden food that you used to and your body is beginning to accept that eating healthier is a part of who you are now and what you do.

As your body continues to get used to various changes to the diet and it doesn't seem like as much of a sacrifice anymore, you should then begin to look at any other diet changes you should be making as well to continue to improve your daily behavior related to health.

For example, when you first start on your journey, it may be acceptable to drink diet sodas all the time, but as you progress and realize that diet sodas tend to be as bad for you as non-diet sodas,[156] then you may want to begin weaning yourself off those.

The journey encompasses not being perfect from the very beginning at all, but consistently learning what works for you and what isn't working for you and making changes as you see fit. It will be difficult at first, but once you begin to see the results of your decisions and understand that you control exactly what you look like and how you feel based on what you decide to put in your mouth every day, the changes will become easier because of the results you're realizing from them.

The last step

What was shared in the past two chapters is just a very high-level overview of how health and fitness can be a tremendous aid to your recovery and why it is a significant part of the process. If interested in getting my complete fitness lifestyle change plan that goes into this in more detail, as well as getting access to my full workout plans and weekly diet, please check it out here on my website kenmmiddleton.com.

Now, let's move on to what I would consider the most important aspect of The MEDS process and the one that should not only challenge you day to day but will also keep you focused on staying alcohol-conscious for the rest of your life.

CHAPTER SIXTEEN

Success Seeking

Step Ya Game Up!

"The great danger for most of us lies not in setting
our aim too high and falling short; but in setting our aim
too low, and achieving our mark."

—MICHELANGELO

While all of The MEDS steps are important to give you a solid foundation for your alcohol-conscious journey, this last step is the glue that holds it all together and keeps us moving in the right direction when we may feel ourselves wanting to slip back for whatever reason.

The last step in The MEDS is the S, which stands for Success Seeking. This step is important because when you first begin your journey toward alcohol-consciousness, there are going to be many things that will get immediately better that will excite you about this change in your life and all of the amazing things it can bring. Your sleep will get better. Your mind and thinking will become so much clearer. And your overall feeling of stability and understanding of how much better of a person you are without alcohol will typically rise to the forefront. You will feel a little bit like you have superpowers now and as though there isn't anything you can't do.

However, with time, as with almost anything, this honeymoon period will wear off, and your feeling of being superhuman-like, while still there, will begin to feel a little less exciting, as it becomes your base-line and your body/mind gets used to the new (better) status quo.

This is the period of time in which a lot of people begin to realize the unexpected truth about giving up alcohol that they may not have quite realized before: it is NOT the answer to ALL of your problems and won't make EVERYTHING better.

For some people, this becomes too much for them to deal with as they then have to begin to deal with all the different things that can come with life that we all have to deal with from time to time; e.g. a bad relationship that needs work, a job that we don't particularly love, or not having all the money we would desire to do whatever we would like when desired.

It is during this time (it varies for all, but it is usually in the 3 to 6-month period) that people begin to question if giving up alcohol was the right thing to do and if it really is going to make any difference in their lives.

Sure, it helped with some of the immediate problems in life and resulted in positive outcomes such as better sleep, more money saved, and better clarity of thought, but all of the serious problems in life seem to still be there and are not going away. And now, not only are these issues still there, but now you can't just let loose and not think about all of these issues by turning to alcohol to drown out all of the noise for a while.

It is during this time that it is vitally important to recognize that the true benefits of our decision to give up alcohol will not take place in only the short 3 to 6-month stint immediately following this decision, (even though the benefits are still highly effective during that time), but that we need to have true LONG-TERM thinking to understand how this decision will truly impact and change our lives.

And one of the best ways to do that is to go on a quest that will require a greater version of yourself that would've been completely impossible with your pre-alcohol-conscious self. This is what success seeking is about.

MY STORY AGAIN

When I first stopped drinking, the overwhelming excitement that I experienced over getting better sleep and having more mental clarity was amazing.

To provide some context, we need to go back to the original reason I decided to stop drinking in the first place. The reason had everything to do with the lack of success I was experiencing in my venture to go out on my own and start my own staffing brand and model. I was about 18 months into the venture and was looking at the second straight year in which I was not on target to make much more than about 40k.

I was working long hours trying to build a brand called Your DevOps Recruiter, and was burning the candle at both ends trying to find business from my customers, and then recruit to find the candle as well. The number of hours that I was putting in on a weekly basis was extraordinary (70–80) without very much to show for it.

During this time, I was thinking about my overall lack of success and how I thought I would be doing much better by this time and began contemplating going back to corporate America and maybe even my former company. I thought about how devastating that would be for me. When I left, I believed the world was my oyster and I was excited about how I was going to create my future instead of building someone else's.

Now to go back and work again for a company I didn't own seemed like a tremendous failure. It felt defeating to admit that I wasn't as good or smart as I thought I was.

As I thought about what this would be like, I began to feel a bit better because I knew I had worked extremely hard to be successful and had put in a tremendous amount of time to uncover as many rocks as possible to see success. However, the more I began to think about all that I had sacrificed in the last 18 months, the more I realized there was one thing that was not helping my endeavor, and yet I had never before truly considered giving it up: alcohol.

My relationship with alcohol was love-love. I loved it and it loved me. For someone who worked 70–80 hours per week, having an outlet to blow off some steam and have a little fun was needed. I had always believed in the philosophy of YOLO and didn't want to miss out on too many things that could be a grand adventure.

The problem with this was that it just made it challenging to give the next day 1000% as I wanted to at times.

Sure, I still woke up at 5:00 a.m. after going to bed at 11:00 p.m. each night. However, the reality was that I was only a shell of myself when it came to getting the job done. I wasn't as sharp as I needed to be to drive business accordingly.

I'm sure there were numerous opportunities that I missed because mentally I was not as honed in as I should've been and verbally didn't have the skill needed to persuade a client to give me a shot or make a candidate feel that I had her/his best interest in mind.

I was still thinking about this on the night of November 10, 2018, while we were having dinner with one of our best couple friends. I wondered whether it was perhaps time to consider giving up drinking to see if it would really make a difference before I pulled the plug on my business.

I had given up drinking twice before for a three-month stint, so I knew I could do it, but I had never done it with the purpose of seeing how great I could be at my job. Therefore, I decided if I was going to throw in the towel and consider my entrepreneurship venture a bust, it was not going to be before I could unequivocally say I had truly given it EVERYTHING I could.

So the decision was made, and I was going to stop drinking for as long as I continued to see the positive results.

Fast forward three months, and man, what an amazing difference it made!

I woke up every day feeling refreshed and had very few episodes in which I didn't sleep soundly throughout the entire night. Over the first 3–6 months, I was amazed at how much I was growing each day and my mind was continuing to expand with my ability to think more holistically and clearly.

I began to see tremendous benefits in my physical health as well, as my focus on working out and eating right began to improve dramatically without the consistent slip-ups from alcohol that I had experienced in the past.

As time progressed, I began to see my business continue to improve dramatically as well. Due to my increased focus on maximizing my productivity every single day, I began to experience momentum based on being able to build upon the consistency of capturing the value from every conversation and not having any 70% or 80% days.

In the three months after I stopped drinking from November to January, I made three times as much money as I had made in the previous nine months. I was recognized by the company I was working with at the time as a top producer and continued to make strides in regard to my overall success.

Even though I was continuing to grow tremendously over time, a funny thing happened around the sixth month of my alcohol-consciousness. While I still felt as if I was much more clear-headed and able to do a number of things better and more efficiently, it was almost as if I plateaued in some way and was not experiencing the tremendous growth that I did over the first six months.

I couldn't quite understand why this was the case, as I was making such leaps and bounds before. As this occurred, I began to notice that there were still some areas that I needed to improve dramatically in my life and having stopped drinking did not solve them all automatically. I started to have second thoughts about whether giving up alcohol for the rest of my life was really something I wanted to do.

I was doing well in a lot of areas, but couldn't I just go back to drinking and keep it under control to still have fun and not allow the success I've been experiencing to go to the wayside? I thought about all the ways I was living life differently now and considered how many of those things I could continue to do if I went back to drinking.

I figured I could still do a few of them, but I would just have to be mindful of when and how much I drank.

I was consistently waking up at 4:30 a.m. every day and working out for an hour. I was reading and writing each morning and meditating three days per week. I figured there was no reason I couldn't continue to do that regularly, as long as I regulated my drinking only to the weekends and didn't go overboard.

There was one hobby I knew I would have a bit of trouble continuing to do if I started drinking again. This was something that I had decided to pick up because I felt I finally had the mental capacity to do it. It wasn't anything that I gave any special thought to or focused on as a big deal, but, ironically, it was in realizing the importance of keeping this hobby that I knew I could never go back to drinking again.

What was that thing?

Learning to speak Korean.

I chose Korean because my wife is Korean, and I thought it would be a great motivator to be able to communicate with her parents more effectively. Her parents immigrated to the US about 40 years ago, and while her mother speaks English fairly well, it was never something her father picked up. Therefore, this would be a great long-term goal for me, as I've wanted to learn a second language for about as long as I can remember.

I had waited tables at various restaurants for over seven years and many of our cooks spoke Spanish. I naturally picked it up over time and eventually began to understand it relatively decently.

However, I was never able to speak it fluently because I just didn't put in the time and energy that would be required to do so. I would dabble here and there, but I was too busy drinking and partying to sacrifice any time to really learn the different aspects of the language and immerse myself in it to speak it fluently.

Therefore, as the natural high of what life was like without drinking began to slowly wear off and my former feeling of superman-heightened mental clarity and sensitivity began to wear off, I found myself looking for something else to keep me motivated and focused.

What I recognized was that the newfound me was much smarter and focused than I ever was before, and while the day-to-day aspects of my current job (sales) were challenging enough to keep me somewhat interested, it wasn't mentally taxing enough to make me feel that I couldn't be successful at it still while drinking.

The fact that I had already done it for 10 years successfully, and that drinking had actually been a big part of that success with schmoozing my clients at happy hours and various entertainment events, was enough to even make me question if I would be less successful with some clients now that I didn't drink.

However, when I began to think about the mental focus and discipline I would need to begin to understand and comprehend the Korean language with its complex grouping of characters and pronunciation inflections, I knew that it would be the thing that I could commit to that would give me something long term to work toward that could keep me focused. There was no way I was going to learn Korean fully in a year or maybe even five years, but if I kept at it little by little and kept my mind alcohol-free to absorb as much of the language as possible, I felt confident that I would be able to in 10 years.

For me, this was the type of long-term, high-level challenge that I needed to help me understand that going back to drinking alcohol could not be an option if I wanted to see this to fruition.

Could I still be good at sales and operation management/leadership while drinking? Probably.

Could I be decent at fitness and writing while drinking (two of my other passions)? Probably as well.

Could I learn Korean fluently and be able to write and read it while drinking? No way in f*cking hell.

It was this realization that helped me understand this was the type of goal to which I had to commit to create a long-term *understanding of the type of person I could become if I were willing to put drinking behind me forever and keep moving forward to achieve other goals I would've never thought I was capable of.*

Why such a high-level goal?

The purpose of having such a high-level goal is that when you get through the honeymoon phase of abstinence and that sense of clarity and focus becomes what you are used to experiencing on a daily basis, you'll find yourself beginning to question how sober you actually need to be to commit to still leading the life you desire.

Something known as the "fading effect" bias will often begin to take place and you'll have to fight it to be able to remember why you decided to stop drinking in the first place.

The fading effect bias is a phenomenon that occurs whenever a significant amount of time passes between something negative affecting our lives at a moment in time and the present. This passage of this time has the tendency to make us then romanticize all the positive things about that particular person or experience in our lives and forget about all the negative things that made us not want to be in that situation in the first place.

This is one of the main reasons that many people end up in bad relationships after having some pretty damaging experiences. It's our mind's natural way of blocking out memories that are negative and wanting to remember and relive things that are positive.

In relation to alcohol, this is what happens typically when you are about at the six-month mark, and you are questioning if you should give up alcohol for good. Your mind will begin to tell you that you have proven you don't have a drinking problem and that your mind is so much clearer now that you've stopped drinking for a while.

Why can't you just take breaks every now and then instead of completely giving up on alcohol altogether?

This thought will run through your mind consistently and you'll find yourself deliberating whether occasional drinking is something you should consider.

You are working toward creating a high-level version of yourself, but the question becomes: does your current life require you to be this super person that no alcohol is allowing you to be every day? Do you really need immaculate mental clarity each day to do the things you need to do with school, work, or life?

The answer may be no for now if you are focused on doing everyday rudimentary things. Therefore, to ensure you don't allow this type of thinking to perpetuate and work to eventually convince you that your drinking self is "good enough" for the life you want to live, you have to focus on something that would require a much more enlightened and higher-level version of yourself that alcohol would in no way allow you to be.

How do you choose what your goal will be?

To accomplish this, you need to spend some time deciding, What does your ideal self look like? What type of person would you be if you could be the person that you've always dreamed of being? What characteristics does this person have and what are the attributes that you exhibit on a day-to-day basis? Think about who this person is. What is something about their life that you see as extremely challenging based on where you are right now in your life?

This attribute should be something that you almost could not see yourself doing today—something that feels out of reach right now—but if you stayed consistent and didn't allow all the negative impacts of alcohol to affect your life, then it could be a possibility.

This is the new goal and focus that you need for your life and what would be required of you to take your game to the next level.

You must know that whatever you are pursuing would not be something that you could ever accomplish if you were drinking for whatever reason. For some, this could be pursuing competitive bodybuilding, running a marathon, or pursuing your master's degree at Harvard.

Whatever the goal, it needs to be something big and aggressive enough that you know to achieve that goal, you are going to have to give 1000% of yourself every single day and you cannot allow the subtle mediocrity that alcohol creates in our lives to hold you back.

You can live a normal life by drinking alcohol, or you could become this amazing, idealized version of yourself by refusing to allow alcohol to keep you in mediocrity and pursuing this much higher version of yourself.

How do you begin working toward it?

The simplest way is to sit down and start writing out a plan for how you are going to get there.

As the saying goes, you can end up anywhere if you don't have a map of where you're going, so you need to make sure you have a solid understanding of the steps you need to take to achieve this goal and then begin to put this plan into action.

I have a simple 3-step goal-setting strategy that I always implement that helps ensure I am not just saying I want to achieve something but am realistically working toward it with a detailed plan each and every day.

1. Start with the end in mind. Think about what you want the end-goal version of yourself to look like and how you are going to get there.
    a. End goal: I want to speak fluent Korean to my in-laws, in restaurants, and in Korea when we visit.
2. Plan your steps to success backwards.
    a. Step 6 - Speak Korean fluently.
    b. Step 5 - Before I can speak Korean fluently, I need to know all the nuances and subtleties of the Korean language to be able to read and write it well and order from restaurants in my local area.

c. Step 4 - Before I know all the nuances, I need to get a tutor who will help me dive deeper into my understanding of all the various nuances of the language that I will not get from just being in a group class.

d. Step 3 - Before I get a tutor for the nuances, I need to be able to read and write well by immersing myself in a Korean class in which I am learning all the aspects of the culture and idiosyncrasies of the language.

e. Step 2 - Before I can join a class to immerse myself, I need to understand the basics of the Korean language and begin just working toward a general overall understanding of the different aspects of the language.

f. Step 1 - Find an app or online program that will allow me to begin learning the basics of the Korean language; I chose Pimsleur.

3. Begin implementing step 1 of your plan and take it day by day.

Remember, this needs to be a BIG goal, so this is not something that you are going to accomplish in three months or so. This has to be something that you can see yourself doing in 3–5 years, if not longer.

I am a little over two years into my journey to learn Korean, and I am still very far from being fluent. I have a number of different strategies I have to implement to get better, but I'm thinking this is going to be a 5 to 10-year road for me to truly get to a place where I feel that I can speak at the level that I desire. It is this mindset that keeps me grounded and lets me know that drinking is not something that will be in my future in any shape, form, or fashion.

The great thing about having a goal such as language adoption is that the farther I am along the journey, the more I have to lose if I were to ever go back to drinking. As I have learned over time and grown my mental abilities to be able to read, write, and speak the language, the thought of drinking again and losing all of that hard work makes it something I cannot even consider.

When you focus on a goal that requires a different level of achievement and success in yourself, you are creating a version of yourself that is so different from who you used to be that the thought of going back to that old version may even be a bit frightening.

When you level up with focus on your future and refuse to be anything less than your absolute best, your old standards will not be reasonable to the new you and you'll find yourself continuing to ensure that you are maximizing your abilities as much as possible.

By keeping a high-level goal in the forefront and pushing yourself to shoot for the stars, you are creating a future in which alcohol cannot be an option. Once that goal is finally achieved, however, and you feel that you are at a stable point in your commitment to forgo alcohol, then the question becomes, What is next?

The answer to that is simple . . . the next goal and a life that you would have only dreamed of before.

The way to really bring this all together and build a life that is beyond anything you could've ever thought possible before you stopped drinking is related to a new philosophy that I created that, if you truly embrace it, can change your life forever.

This philosophy is called Decagism.

CHAPTER SEVENTEEN

The Practice of Decagism

It's All About Perspective and It's NEVER Too Late

"Your 40s are good. Your 50s are great. Your 60s are fab.
And 70 is fucking awesome."

—HELEN MIRREN

"F*ck it, I'm too old!"

That was my sister's response to my request that she stop eating a large bag of Doritos and clean her orange powder-covered hands.

This last chapter to wrap up *Bamboozled* is not so much about being tricked by alcohol through society, nor is it strategies or tips to help you overcome the mental and physical urges that could come from drinking alcohol for a long period of our lives. Instead, it is focused on a principle philosophy and perspective on life that can be an absolute game changer.

It is something that I discovered while comparing my current level of success at the time to my current age. I have always been a little obsessed with achieving things at a clip that I feel is in line with where I am chronologically. I think about the age milestones of 30 and 40 and have always compared where I was to where I thought I would be at that time.

How much money I have saved toward retirement, as well as where I am in regard to my professional career are two consistent barometers that I assess myself against related to my age.

This idea started because, when I was growing up, I always had the feeling I was a bit of a late bloomer in life. I was constantly playing catch up to get myself back on track and make up for the time that I had lost not being focused on my goals like I should've been. I felt I was a little behind in knowing how to talk to someone to whom I was attracted and was always trying to make up how to do this correctly, probably until the age of about 30.

My original undergrad degree was in English Education and then I waited tables for two years of my life, so I didn't get started in my professional career of sales and business until the age of 26.

I got my first Director job at 35 and then resigned at 36 to try to become an entrepreneur on my own. This in turn led me to spend a lot of money over a 2.5-year period that put my 401k and retirement savings back from where I thought they should be. Therefore, at 38, when I decided to give up alcohol forever and come back to corporate America, I once again felt like I was behind and had to make up for lost time to get myself back on track career-wise and financially.

I thought about the newfound focus and clarity I had and I began to wish that I had made the decision 10 years earlier at 28. I started to think of all the mistakes I made with my time and money over those past 10 years and imagined where I could be in life and in my career if I had the focus then that I had now.

There was no doubt in my mind that in that 10-year period, I would have achieved some of the most amazing things ever because I would not have had the distraction of alcohol to take me off my path or make me lose focus.

Just thinking through the entire scenario, I felt that I could easily have amassed a $2–5 million dollar net worth if I had the focus I had now and understood what I needed to do and how alcohol was not helping in any manner.

That's when it hit me.

The average lifespan in the U.S. is 78–79 years old. So let's just say 80 to make it a round number.

Have you looked at pictures of individuals who are 80 versus individuals who are 70? There are some who are as spry as a spring chicken at 80, while there are others who can barely walk or do anything at 70.

The reason I use those two numbers is because if that number is the end game (game over … no more lives … no restart), if I'm able to live a healthy life that puts me in the category of one of those "young" 80-year-olds, then I am really giving myself at least 10 more years to make up for a "late" start in life.

What that means is regardless of where I am now, if I just treat my mentality like I am really 10 years younger (because I live a healthy lifestyle to ensure I am able to get there), then it doesn't really make a difference that I didn't do all of these things earlier in my life. The main point is that I know better NOW, and 10 more years are going to pass whether I'm creating the life I desire or not, so why don't I just ACT like I'm 10 years younger and begin to incorporate everything that I wish I told my 10-year-younger self?

I'm not going to let the relative concept of age hold me back from thinking young, acting young, and having the excitement my younger self would have had with this knowledge.

The equation was simple when I thought about it to myself.

I was 38 at the time, and if I got to 48 in 10 years, and had a net worth of $5 million with 25–30% of that liquid, wouldn't that still be a pretty good place to be at 48 years old? How many people have amassed that kind of wealth at 48?

And if I were completely honest, $5 million was on the low end of my dreams. If I really applied myself over the next 10 years—if I were focused and really pushed myself hard to think strategically and put into place all the different investment opportunities from real estate to writing to crypto/NFT investments—there was a good chance that I could blow that number out of the water.

This is when the concept of Decagism was created.

Decagism (pronounced Dé/ cā/ gism) is the practice of looking at your life now and focusing on two distinct ways of thinking:

1. What would you tell yourself if you could go back 10 years about what is important in life and what things you should be doing with your time, energy, and focus?

2. What would your life look like 10 years in the future if you actually listened to yourself and did those things? What goals will you have accomplished? How different would your life be?

You're only as old as you *think* you are.

Don't allow the relative concept of age to hold you back. Age is a construct that we created as a society to help us understand how much time has passed in life, but it is not something you should allow to determine where you should be in life or what you *must* do at a certain time in your life.

Ten years is not a long time in the grand scheme of things and just because you may not have done everything that you wish you could've when you were younger, it doesn't mean you can't figure it out now and start doing the things you know you should do TODAY to build that life 10 years from now.

I began to think about how I would feel about life if I were 48 and had accomplished a net worth of at least $5 million. I thought about the average retirement age being 65 and thought about how I could easily see myself retiring at 55 years old—ten years early!—over the next seven-year period if I continued to apply all the lessons I had learned and grow as I know I should.

That would then make me retire at a Decage of 45 years old, and that sounded like a pretty f*cking good deal over the grand scheme of things. If I lived to be 70 in decage years (80 years in normal time), that would give me 25 years to do whatever I wanted to do with my life.

If you then took my societally accepted age of 55 and had me living until 80, then I still had the same 25 years to do what I wanted to do with the rest of my life.

So the time frame of living the life I desire is the same, so who cares that it came a bit later than others. It was still much earlier than most.

How to begin practicing Decagism

To begin your journey exploring Decagism, you can follow the same steps I shared in my experience:

Step 1 - Think about all the lessons you've learned over the past 10 years and all the mistakes that you may have made at work, with fitness, or just in life in general.

Sit down and take some time to think through these things. You don't have to worry about every single lesson that you ever learned, but I would focus on the major ones that could've made a big difference in my life and career.

Outside of not drinking alcohol, I wished I had not spent so much time having fun on the weekends, and instead had spent more time building my future. I also wished I had way more confidence in my own abilities and didn't always feel like I had to "prove" myself to others to be a leader and do the type of things that leaders do.

You should come up with at least three big lessons of things that you wish you did differently that would've made a dramatic impact on the outcome of where you are currently in life.

Step 2 - Now think 10 years in the future and imagine what your life would look like if you actually did all the things that you know you should do in the future for the next 10 years without wavering.

What would the future hold for you if you made an unwavering commitment to focus on these things completely and be the person that you have always dreamed about becoming? By focusing on this, you should be able to visualize what is possible if you just commit to these things from now going forward.

Great things are still very much possible in your future.

Step 3 - Start doing these things ASAP. That's it.

Begin implementing all the things that you know you should be doing and working toward the future that you know is yours. You'll be surprised at how exciting this will be if you truly embrace it.

Let go of society's time constraints and labels and really think about all that you can accomplish and become in a 10-year period if you just truly commit to doing the things you know you should on a day-to-day basis. It's almost like you have a time machine so you can go back in time and have a do-over.

You control if you use it or not, so the question becomes, What are you going to do with it?

What Decagism Looks Like

Decagism looks like you NOT allowing anything to hold you back from achieving your dreams.

It is you deciding what you would have done if you could've done things differently from the beginning, and then going out and doing those things. It's you not allowing the thought or concept of you being too "old" or it being too "late" to cross your mind in any capacity.

As you begin living with this mindset, you may find yourself in rooms of people who might be a bit younger than you, but you have what they don't have that you can use to your ultimate advantage: your time machine of experience.

Whereas they are still in the process of learning all of their lessons about life and making many of the same mistakes that you made in life, you have already been there and done that.

You don't have to worry about not saying the right thing or letting an opportunity slip through the cracks. You've already done that before, and you know how that story plays out.

Now, you can focus on doing all the different things that you know you should've always done.

Never finished that college degree? Time to go finish it.

Always wanted to get in the best shape of your life but just never committed? Now is the time.

Wanted to start that entrepreneurial business or start-up to build the company that you've always dreamed of running. Why not now?

Decagism looks like you saying that you can do anything you are willing to put your mind and energy into.

It's about thinking about what an ideal life for you would look like and then taking the day-to-day steps to build it. It's not about bemoaning the past or wishing that you had done things differently.

It's about *doing* things differently.

At the end of the day, Decagism is about you refusing to give up on your dreams and opportunities and realizing that if you work today as if you're 10 years younger, you have a great chance of becoming the person of your dreams 10 years from now.

Ten years are going to pass one way or the other, so why not allow it to pass while building a future you will be proud of?

A real-life example

I wanted to end this chapter and, subsequently, this book, with one last story that sums up both of them quite nicely as the perfect embodiment of what giving up alcohol can look like, how it's never too late, and what it can mean for your future.

This story is perfect because it's not something that I created to make a point, but it's the true story of an amazing woman who made the decision to quit drinking "later" in life but yet has gone on to do amazing things, not only for herself but for the world.

But instead of me retelling it for her, I'll rather let you hear it directly from her, so you can understand the impact this decision truly had on her life.

JANET'S STORY (IN HER OWN WORDS)

While I was climbing the greasy pole of corporate life, my mantra was "work hard, play hard" and I certainly did. I would occasionally indulge in a little daydream about retirement. I had a very clear picture in my head which involved sitting in a sun-drenched garden with a large glass of wine in my hand.

So fast forward to my early fifties and there I was living in Cape Town — so that took care of the sun-drenched garden. Trouble was, I got rather bored doing nothing and even I couldn't drink wine and read books 24/7. So I started an HR consultancy which I ran for 10 years, reverting to my default position of "work hard, play hard."

In my early 60s I tried again to retire. I sat in that sun-drenched garden with glass(es) of icy white wine and everything was perfect — or was it?

Well, it would have been if it weren't for that nagging voice in my head. The voice that kept saying:

"You're drinking too much. I think we might have a problem here . . ."

I had managed to integrate Sauvignon Blanc into my life to such an extent that the first drink would often be just before midday and would morph seamlessly into a couple more large glasses with lunch. By the time 5:00 p.m. came around, another cork would pop to see me through the (early) evening.

Just another quiet day at home.

If I successfully engineered an evening out, the drinking would step up a notch. Anyone unable to keep up with my enthusiastic pace would be left behind.

Always the last one to leave any social event, I felt like I was "living the life." I had, of course, completely lost the plot but back then it didn't feel like it.

It felt pretty damn good, actually.

Then there were the blackouts, the injuries, the dramas, and the horrible depressions. Surely everyone got those when they overdid it—didn't they?

For me, rock bottom came in the form of a walking, talking blackout while on a weekend away with friends. I had absolutely no recollection of an entire afternoon even though apparently I'd been functioning in a relatively normal way.

That was the moment when I finally accepted that I had to end my relationship with alcohol.

I'd always known that I was harming my body—after all, I'd had breast cancer to prove it. The realization that my brain had been so soaked in alcohol that it couldn't even create memories drove it home.

I was done with alcohol — finally, it was over...

All I had to do then was to work out how to stop drinking.

I tried Alcoholics Anonymous, but found it hard to relate to the people there — although I was putting away a bottle of wine a night, I wasn't pouring vodka on my morning cornflakes (yet).

I kept looking for help and eventually found a workshop in London that was perfect for me. I found other women with good jobs and nice families, also sinking a bottle of wine every evening. I'd found my people and we were able to keep each other on track.

We opened our hearts to each other about just how unhappy alcohol was making us. We realized we couldn't do this alone, so we supported each other and connected on a deep level.

I now understand that **"connection is the opposite of addiction."**

My ongoing connection with the people I met enabled me to stay on track. I used the workshop tools and continued to educate myself. Reading books like This Naked Mind by Annie Grace helped me to understand that the key to sustaining my sobriety was mindset rather than willpower. Only when I felt that I was no longer "missing out" by not drinking was I able to begin to thrive in my alcohol-free life.

The benefits of sobriety for me have been numerous. My health has improved dramatically and my fitness has improved. I sleep so much better and wake up full of energy and eager to start the day.

I strongly believe that giving up drinking is one of the best things we can do for our health and happiness as we get older. Of course, sobriety is no guarantee that I will stay cancer-free, but the odds of a recurrence of my breast cancer are greatly reduced. The evidence of the link between alcohol and breast cancer is now well known.

Although I have lost some friends (drinking buddies), I have made many new ones and connect with them on a deeper level. My long-suffering husband is thrilled that I have (finally) given up drinking and I am closer to my son.

However, by far the most significant benefit for me has been to find more purpose and meaning in my life. One of my favorite quotes is by Viktor Frankl, who says:

"Life is not primarily a quest for pleasure, as Freud believed, or a quest for power as Adler taught, but a quest for meaning. The greatest task for any person is to find meaning in their life."

That shift from seeking pleasure to seeking meaning has been real.

Although I had dreamed of a leisurely retirement, I now realize that would not have made me happy. What HAS made me happy is setting up and running an international sobriety group.

I quit drinking in May 2015 and in early 2016, I founded tribesober.com.

I used my 25 years of experience in training and development to design a workshop to help others to quit drinking. These workshops were well attended and the participants wanted ongoing support and connection. That's why we created a membership program which now includes people who have been sober for years and are busy inspiring and advising the newer members.

As a qualified executive coach, I was able to retrain as a recovery coach so we could include coaching as part of our support. The Tribe Sober team grew organically as some people who had gotten sober with us wanted to stick around to help others to change their lives.

Just as AA had not been right for me, I felt sure that there would be more people who were looking for a different and more modern approach.

People who would understand that quitting alcohol could mean an opportunity to thrive rather than a life of deprivation.

People who would realize that they were not "broken" with a life-time struggle on their hands.

People who felt that an individually tailored program would suit them better than the generic "12 steps."

One of the reasons people stay trapped in their drinking is that they feel that sobriety is going to be a dull and miserable place — and that it's going to be a "lifetime struggle" to stay alcohol-free.

Nothing could be further from the truth.

After working with hundreds of people at Tribe Sober, we have discovered that the usual pattern is that a few months of hard work and commitment has enabled them to make the change.

Apart from leading Tribe Sober I have become a podcaster and have released more than 100 episodes of the Tribe Sober podcast.

Guests include experts, authors, and people with inspiring recovery stories. The podcasts are reaching people from all over the world, which means that we are becoming more and more international. Covid pushed us to run our workshops online which means we can reach many more people who need our help.

Creating and managing a sobriety group has kept me busy and fulfilled. There is nothing that makes me quite so happy as seeing someone ditch the drink and change their life!

—Janet Gourand, tribesober.com, janet@tribesober.com

Janet's story is proof that it's NEVER too late to stop drinking and create an amazing future for yourself. She stopped drinking at 63, founded Tribe Sober at 64, and has been an amazing force in the alcohol-conscious movement ever since.

At 70-plus years young, the future is still very bright for Janet and can be for you if you make the decision to give alcohol-consciousness a try.

So that only leaves us with one final question…

PART IV

Who Are You
Going to Become?

CHAPTER EIGHTEEN

Red or Blue Pill?

"This is your last chance. After this, there is no turning back.
You take the blue pill - the story ends, you wake up
in your bed and believe whatever you want to believe.
You take the red pill - you stay in Wonderland
and I show you how deep the rabbit-hole goes."

—MORPHEUS FROM *THE MATRIX*

WHICH PILL WOULD YOU CHOOSE?

RED PILL   BLUE PILL

There are very few scenes as iconic as the one in which Lawrence Fishburne's character in the Matrix offers Neo, played by Keanu Reeves, the chance to decide what he wants to do with his future.

Up until that time, Lawrence has just revealed to Neo that he is living in a simulated world known as the Matrix, in which everything has been fabricated. An alien host is living on the bodies of human beings while they remain in this dreamlike, comatose state, thinking all is well with the world.

Neo now has to decide if he wants to move forward and help them fight these creatures and reclaim the freedom of the world, or go back to living his happy-go-lucky dream life in which all appears to be perfect.

If we are lucky, sometimes we get these types of choices in life when we learn something of which we were not previously aware and we have to decide if we are going to take this knowledge and do anything with it, or if we are going to go back to our world of ignorance and act like we still don't know.

Hopefully, *Bamboozled* has been that eye-opening experience for you.

The information here is available anywhere to anyone who decides to look for it. However, hopefully, it's been presented in such a manner that now you truly understand the decision you are making every day by allowing alcohol to trick you into believing that all is "right" with your world.

Society's focus on making alcohol an everyday, *needed* aspect of life is a lie, and it is only by recognizing that this is not a truth we need to subscribe to can you break the chains of societal pressure that tries to get everyone to stay within this box of acceptance.

Now that you know this to be the case and can understand the tremendous trick that alcohol plays in making you think it's helping you when it is really inhibiting your ability to grow and become the best version of yourself possible, the question now remains, what . . . will . . . you . . . do?

Take the blue pill and put this book down, and you can go back to living the life that you were living before, with the happy hours, weekend hangovers, and booze-filled vacations.

Or take the red pill, and begin a journey that will be much more difficult at first, but will give you the opportunity to experience a life that you could've never thought possible had you continued on the current path of alcohol-unconsciousness.

Today is your day. The decision is yours. What decision will you make for your future?

FAQs

In this section, I'll address some of the most frequently asked questions and situations related to alcohol-consciousness that I may not have covered in the book. I'll refer to specific parts of the book that will help give added context and information. If there are other questions this book doesn't answer that you think are important and need to be addressed, feel free to email me directly at ken@kenmmiddleton.com.

Science

How do you become addicted to alcohol? - Chapter 4

Alcohol creates the need for itself over time. Alcohol is a depressant because it dampens the nervous system upon injection into our bloodstream, thus slowing our speech and motor skills.

However, it also creates a tremendous spike in endorphins in our body that makes us feel good. This artificial spike in endorphins is more than what our body is used to, and to combat this, our body releases a counter-balancing chemical known as dynorphins. The dynorphins' job is to take us back to baseline, or homeostasis, as our body does not like staying in an endorphin-spiked state for too long, as this heightened sense of excitement puts too much stress on our body over time.

When we build a pattern of alcohol consumption, our body becomes used to alcohol and two things happen that could lead to addiction.

1. We build a tolerance and we have to drink more alcohol to build the same effect. This, in turn, causes more dynorphins to be released into our body to counterbalance it, which creates a continuous cycle of the need to drink more to achieve the same results.

2. Once our body becomes so used to experiencing the endorphin spike at the same time of the day or week, it will begin to preempt the release of your dynorphins in anticipation of the endorphin spike coming. When this happens, you will begin to experience a low depressed state from the dynorphin and will then need to drink to even get back to baseline.

The combination of the two debilitating cycles above is what eventually leads to alcohol creating the need for itself over time, and, ultimately, addiction.

Does alcohol make it harder to remember and learn new things? - Chapter 10

One of the main areas of the brain that alcohol affects consistently is your hippocampus. The hippocampus is the small brain-like looking part of your brain that sits in the back of the head. It is the structure that stores our short-term memories and then eventually transfers them to our long-term memory function.

When we drink, the functioning of this piece of our brain is impaired greatly, and we sometimes lose the ability to transfer those short-term memories to our long-term bank. This is one of the reasons we experience blackouts and can remember part of what happened, but not all of it.

The disconnect relates to your hippocampus either not fully creating and storing the memories in the first place or in its inability to fully transfer them from your short-term to long-term memory bank. This, in turn, will make it more challenging to remember what happens when you drink and has been shown to affect your ability to remember and learn new things over time, even when you're not drinking.

Is there an age at which I should absolutely stop drinking alcohol? - Chapter 10

Yes. The absolute age that no one should drink anymore is after 40. Many of these reasons are related to the physiological and psychological way your body and brain changes after 40 that makes it more dangerous to continue to drink. This is also the age range (35–50) in which most people begin to develop alcohol use disorder (AUD) because of the length of time most have been drinking by this point in their lives.

How much alcohol is too much to drink? What does a moderate, "normal" amount look like? - Chapter 10

Any amount of alcohol can be too much, as more and more studies are coming out that show there are no true health benefits (only risks) from drinking alcohol in almost any amount. However, the recommended amount from the CDC is 2 drinks or less for men and 1 drink or less for women. This amount per day would equal 7–14 drinks per individual per week, which would automatically put this person in the top 30% (meaning 70% of the population would consume less alcohol than you) of all the people in the world.

Social Aspects of Quitting

How do you handle the peer pressure of having to drink at social events?

There are numerous ways that one can handle this, but the most straightforward way is to remove yourself from the situation if it becomes too much. Peer pressure is one of the biggest reasons that most people begin drinking in the first place, and when one makes the decision to quit, this is one of the biggest reasons that individuals will keep drinking or relapse.

To give yourself the best chance to maintain your commitment to alcohol-consciousness, the best advice is to not put yourself in situations where you think you will be tempted until enough time has elapsed that the desire to drink has subsided substantially enough that you feel you are safe. This can vary for different people. For some, it could be six months, while for others it may be never. It all depends on how far along you may have been on the scale of alcohol dependence.

If you do decide to go to a social event, here are a few practical tips that can help:

1. Bring a friend or meet someone there who knows you are no longer drinking. Having someone that you can connect with and just talk about things other than why you're not drinking will help tremendously. Preferably, this person also should not be drinking, so as to prevent them from becoming inebriated and forgetting they are there to help support you.

2. Keep a non-alcoholic beverage in your hand as much as possible. This may sound weird, but your body is so used to drinking that it won't miss the alcohol as much as it'll miss you having a glass in your hand and drinking "something" during a social event. Our minds are so hard-wired to crave patterns that if you don't have something in your hand during a party, it will begin to freak out, and you might find yourself feeling extremely anxious. Funny enough, putting a club soda or Coke Zero in your hand is more than enough for your brain to begin to calm down because it'll begin to recognize something that it's used to. Over time, this will subside, but initially, it will be very important for you to feel comfortable in these scenarios.

3. Be honest. Some people may disagree with this, but I'm not of the mindset of lying about the fact that I'm not drinking.

Some people use the argument that you should lie because it's no one's business other than your own, but that logic seems flawed because you typically only lie to someone when you *do* care about what that person is thinking about you. That's the reason you tell the lie—to put yourself in a better light. By being honest in these situations, you help yourself in two ways: 1) You don't have to keep remembering what lie you told to whom to ensure you're not caught before the end of the night and 2) It allows you to relax because no one (but a jerk) is going to try to get you to drink when you've already been clear that it is not something you're choosing to do anymore. This now allows you to let your guard down and just enjoy the night for what it is.

How do you stop drinking and still have a career in which you're supposed to entertain your clients, e.g. sales? - Chapters 3 and 4

When it comes to sales, there is definitely an aspect of the job that involves meeting clients out for drinks and schmoozing them a bit on the company tab. While it can be more challenging for one to figure out how to do this without drinking, the silver lining is that it can actually make your interactions with your clients much stronger if you do this in the right manner.

Most of your competitors are going to have the same idea of how to go about getting to know their clients. It's typically the easy way out. Even if you don't have a whole lot in common with someone, if you can manage to share a few beers with them, you feel like you can cross relationship-building bridges quickly.

While this is true, since you don't drink and won't have that as easily to fall back on (even though you can still take them to a bar and drink club soda like I did if you want), a much better solution is to try to figure out what your client likes to do that is more unique than just going to a bar and drinking the evening away.

If your client likes rock climbing, see if you can go with them to your local climbing gym. If they like yoga, join them for a class. There are so many things that you could do other than just trying to get someone to join you at a local bar like all the other salespeople do. By taking a genuine interest in them and what they care about, you will stand out from the crowd and still be able to land those million-dollar deals without having to break your promise to yourself.

What do you say when your friends ask why you're not drinking?

As shared earlier, honesty is always the best policy. Don't make up some story about being on medication or having to get up early the next morning. It will be too hard to try to keep track of all the time, and what if you decide that you're having a good time and actually want to stay longer? You put yourself in a box by not being able to do so.

People typically lie about things of which they're ashamed, and there's nothing to be ashamed of for deciding that you no longer want to drink. Being alcohol-conscious is just realizing that your health and your future are much better served by not putting ethanol down your throat anymore. It's no different from making the decision to no longer eat fried food or sugar.

Do you feel the need to lie to someone about why you don't want to eat either of these things? No. Then why should you be afraid of someone else judging your decision to no longer ingest poison?

How do you still go out when you first quit drinking?

This one can be tricky because it depends on where you are on the quitting spectrum.

If you are still very new (less than a month in), I would not recommend going into any atmosphere that can make you feel like you want to drink.

Remember, your body is a machine that works on memory and patterns. If you put yourself in an environment where you used to drink consistently, your body is going to automatically begin to release signals that are going to make you want alcohol very badly.

If you are newly alcohol-conscious, this could easily be too much for you to handle. Therefore, ensuring that you don't put yourself in these situations is the best way to prevent having to try to overcome them.

Depending on where you were on the spectrum before you quit drinking, it could take 30 days or 30 months. It's hard to say. It took me about three months before I was relatively comfortable in most environments and six months until I was completely comfortable.

Once you do get to a good spot to go out, having a club soda or your favorite diet soda in your hand is a great strategy to allow you to trick your brain into thinking that you are still drinking and to subdue any nerves that may be awakening from old memories. You can use this trick in a number of different scenarios.

How important is it to have a friend when you're quitting?

Finding someone who can do things when you first quit drinking is extremely important. The reason for this relates to two things: 1. How much more free time you will probably have that you never had before, and you'll have to find something to do to fill, and 2. The realization that many of your previous "fun" activities all involved alcohol.

Going to a birthday party? People are probably drinking there.

Night on the town? Definitely drinking.

Going to watch a sporting event? Alcohol will be consumed in droves.

Without having someone with whom you can do things other than alcohol-related activities, you might find yourself very much alone and bored. This is dangerous, as boredom can slowly begin to trick you into believing you didn't really need to quit drinking and that drinking a little bit will be fine.

Having someone willing to do things with you that do not involve alcohol will be important to get a sense of what your life can be like without it and to be able to see yourself building a future in which alcohol has no part.

A spouse or significant other would probably be the most ideal in this scenario, but any good friend that you know you can trust and who will be supportive and open to doing things with you that don't involve alcohol will work just fine.

Who should you tell about your decision to stop drinking?

This is another tricky one because it goes back to the lying question. I stand by my advice not to lie to anyone about your decision to no longer drink. However, with that being said, this doesn't mean you have to go around telling everyone you know that you've made this decision.

Some people will be happy for you; some will be curious; others will be downright scared (if YOU thought you needed to stop drinking, what does this mean for them?). All of these reactions could result in some interesting ways they could respond to your decision. Some could be supportive, while others may not be as supportive due to how your decision may make them negatively reflect on themselves.

Therefore, you should be judicious as to whom you share this information with for support. If it comes up in natural conversation and it's the choice to share or lie, I would choose to share every time.

However, when you are thinking about sharing this with people whom you are going to need for support to do things with that don't involve alcohol, or whom you want to understand why you're turning down the chance to go out with them for a third time in a row, you need to make sure this is a friend or a group of friends that you trust explicitly, and who have your best interests in mind.

This group should be easy for you to recognize. The rule of thumb: if you question whether someone fits in this group or not, then they probably don't.

Will you lose friends when you quit?

The short answer is yes, but the long answer is a bit more complicated.

You probably won't lose any friends that you think would fall in the category above. Those friends will stick beside you and support you because they care about you more than just the good times that you may have had together. These people will stick by you and will typically be there despite your decision to become alcohol-conscious.

The friends you will probably lose, however, are those casual acquaintances that you shared with a number of people whom you wouldn't put in your category as your best friends (and you probably didn't think to tell them you decided to quit drinking), but you would find yourself out with them from time to time just because you both liked to drink and do some of the same things.

This group of people will eventually fall by the wayside, as you'll find yourself not really having a reason to interact with them as much anymore. Since much of your relationship was based on alcohol-related activities, there just won't be as many opportunities for you to interact with these people as there were in the past, and eventually, these relationships will dissipate.

The one other caveat that I have to be honest about is that there is a chance you will lose some of your previous true-blood friends as well. The sad reality of quitting drinking is that it will level you up in a number of ways that you might not have even expected yourself.

One change that I just didn't anticipate but happened naturally is that my emotional maturity increased dramatically in regard to what was important to me on a number of different planes. This, in turn, made a number of my friendships harder to maintain with individuals who continued to live in a world of emotional superficiality. I was just growing in a different direction from them, and the more I began to use my alcohol-consciousness as a springboard to holistic wellness, the more I realized that we just didn't share as many things in common anymore.

The reality is that you'll lose some friends because they no longer want to hang out with you when you're not drinking, and you'll lose others because you'll make the same decision about them.

Fitness

How does alcohol make getting in shape difficult? - Chapter 9

There are two specific ways this is true. One is scientific, while the other is more behavior-based.

We'll start with science first. Scientifically, the body's physical reaction to alcohol is pretty straightforward. We all recognize it when we wake up the next day and don't feel the best, as our body attempts to remove alcohol from our bloodstream.

The feeling of "bleh" and extreme dehydration is our body doing everything it can to get the poisonous effects of the ethanol out of our bodies as quickly and efficiently as possible. As you can imagine, this must affect other aspects of how our body operates to focus such a massive amount of our energy to do this, and you would be correct.

One of the main by-products of this redirection of energy resources is the significant decrease of our body's natural metabolic processes related to the food that we eat. Since the body is working tremendously hard to metabolize the alcohol out of our system, it does not have the capacity to do that AND metabolize that cheeseburger or pizza that you ate when you got home at 3:00 a.m.

Therefore, instead of breaking those fats and carbs and quickly converting them into energy that our body can use, it ignores it and allows it to remain in the body, eventually turning into fat that is stored in the body.

From a behavior-based perspective, the fact that you decided to eat a cheeseburger or pizza at 3:00 a.m. is not going to help any fitness desires long term. Had you not been drinking, there is a very good chance you would be asleep at 3:00 a.m. and would not have the desire or thought of consuming the additional 700–1000-plus calories from that meal, which will destroy any diet.

Also, when we are drinking, we have a tendency to make terrible choices in what we eat at night or even in the morning. Our body seems to typically crave greasy or carb-heavy foods to "soak up the alcohol" in an attempt to help us feel better by sobering us faster. These types of foods are definitely not going to help us hit those fitness goals any faster.

How does exercise help one with quitting alcohol? - Chapter 14

The concept of exercising to help with quitting is a combination of pragmatism, physiology, and psychology all working in conjunction to aid you in your alcohol-conscious journey.

From a pragmatic perspective, when you quit drinking, you are going to have a lot of free time on your hands and need to take on some type of hobby or new habit that will allow you to shore up that free time with something positive.

There are very few habits that are as positive as exercising consistently, and adding this to your daily regimen will be a great way to take your mind off of drinking and place it on the new person that you are building through these efforts.

Physiologically, when you stop ingesting alcohol to create that artificial dopamine spike, your body is going to be looking for something to potentially replace it. While exercise will not allow you to achieve quite the same high as ethanol would, you can still create a feeling of excitement and exhilaration from exercising that could offset this desire a bit. From the recognized dopamine spike of a runner's high or that positive feeling you get from a good sweat after a grueling workout, exercising has been known to give those trying to quit drinking an outlet that not only gives them an alternative to replace what alcohol used to give them, but it also reduces the cravings for said alcohol.

Lastly, psychologically, creating a new version of yourself is a lot about feeling good inside, but it is also about seeing a physical change in the person you see in the mirror every day. While feeling better internally is the ultimate indicator of success, being able to look in the mirror or having someone comment on the positive change they can witness in you is a great external motivator that will keep one excited about the decision to stop drinking.

By exercising consistently and creating this new physical version of yourself, you are stoking the fire so your flames of motivation always stay ablaze.

What does diet have to do with giving up alcohol? - Chapter 15

Just like exercising is so important to the creation of the physical new you, eating the right type of foods is imperative to be able to see and experience this actual change. If you work out consistently but still eat terrible food, there is a good chance that you won't see any change despite all the hard work you might be putting in at the gym.

This, in turn, can be depressing and could eventually lead to the loss of motivation to work out and may even get you to go back to drinking. By coupling exercise and diet, you give yourself the best chance to experience the psychological motivating boost that comes with being able to physically see the results of your efforts and to know that the same type of change and improvement is also taking place inside of you.

Ways to Quit

What is the best way to quit? - Chapter 12

There is really no ONE way to quit. There are so many ways that one could be successful in quitting that it really comes down to what feels the best for you.

If you google "ways to quit alcohol," you will be inundated with a number of different programs that you could possibly join to help in this endeavor. The biggest thing you need to look for is the right type of fit with any of these groups, as many are slanted to a specific demographic or group of people.

I was able to quit "cold-turkey" without any help from any one program, but I did implement all the different aspects of The MEDS daily to help me in this endeavor.

It was by following these steps of Mental Re-engineering, Exercise Commitment, Diet Improvement, and Success Seeking that kept me focused on what I wanted to achieve in life and why giving up alcohol was the right thing for me.

Whatever program you choose to go with (if any), the biggest thing you are going to have to figure out and become very clear on is your WHY. You are going to need a clear and focused reason that you no longer want to allow alcohol to hold you back from all the things you can achieve in life. If you are clear on this, I believe you can be successful with just about any program out there.

What are some of the best books to read?

While podcasts provided the daily mental food and motivation I needed to stay on my alcohol-conscious journey, it was reading books and truly digesting the lessons they were teaching me about what alcohol was doing to my body that was the initial jolt I needed to wake up and realize there was a better way to live.

While there are a number of books that will do a good job of helping you see the way alcohol negatively affects your life, there are a few that have always stood out to me because of their heavy focus on the science behind what alcohol does and the fact-based strategies to help the reader quit. Here are my top ones:

- *This Naked Mind* by Annie Grace
- *Alcohol Lied to Me* by Craig Beck
- *Alcohol Explained* by William Porter
- *The Unexpected Joy of Being Sober* by Catherine Gray
- *Drinking: A Love Story* by Caroline Knapp
- *Allen Carr's Easy Way to Control Alcohol* by Allen Carr
- *Unwasted: My Lush Sobriety* by Sacha Z. Scoblic

Should I worry about sugar cravings? - Chapter 15

The answer is yes and no.

Let's start with the NO first.

The reason I am not jammed up on anyone having intense sugar cravings when you first stop drinking is that this is perfectly natural. Depending on how long you have been drinking and where exactly you fall on the spectrum, your body is going to be so used to getting that artificial dopamine spike, that it is not going to be screaming for something to replace it initially.

This will be one of your biggest saviors when you first stop drinking. If you're anything like me and are used to a work hard/play hard culture, you are going to be used to intense bouts of focus and hard work with the promise of some type of reward at the end of the day or the week.

Of course, the reward for me was alcohol that I allowed myself to partake in every other day or hard on the weekends. This having something to look forward to gave me the focus and commitment I needed to push through 50 to 60-hour weeks with no problem.

If you have a similar pattern, you are going to need something that you can then replace alcohol with that will allow you to feel like you are still rewarding yourself in some capacity and not giving up everything at once. One of my biggest pieces of advice for someone who is trying to quit is to NOT try to be perfect in everything. You just made a big decision to stop doing something that you may have been doing for a long time and your body is almost chemically attached to it.

Therefore, it's okay to give yourself a break and choose the "lesser of two evils" as a substitute for as much time as needed to allow the craving for alcohol to pass.

Now, on to the YES.

The caveat here is that you have to be cognizant of the phrase "as much time as NEEDED" and not too much more. Fair warning, truly recognizing when you no longer need sugar and need to remove it as a substitute can be very challenging, as it has been recognized as a highly addictive substance as well.

In all transparency, it took me almost two years before I was able to finally recognize the effects of sugar were becoming as bad of a pattern as alcohol was and I needed to reduce my consumption dramatically, if not completely. Too much sugar on a consistent basis is tied to a number of chronic diseases (e.g., diabetes, obesity, cardiovascular disease, etc.), so long-term excessive consumption is not an option.

In the short term, however, if it allows you to take your mind off of alcohol long enough for it to lose its physiological effects on your psyche and body, then you can tackle the sugar problem later with the same approach you took to quitting alcohol, starting with Mental Reengineering. When you are ready to make that transition, a great book to read is *Breaking Up With Sugar* by Molly Carmel.

How long until I should not think about drinking anymore?

There's no one answer to this, of course, as everyone is different.

Also, I don't think anyone will ever get to the point that they never *think* about drinking. It's around us too much and too often for that to ever happen.

However, if the question is how long did it take me to realize that alcohol no longer has the same effect on me or I didn't actively get a tingling when thinking about the idea of drinking again, it was six months.

I remember that my wife and I were both in a funny space at about the six-month spot. It was the longest we had ever been without drinking (I had two previous three-month stints) and the positive results of the decision were continually compounding.

However, the other side of doing something for longer than you ever have before is the subtle belief that now you have it figured out and are more in control than you ever have been in the past. Therefore, I started to think that perhaps it would be okay for me to drink again, as long as I didn't overdo it.

I decided this type of thinking was wrong and dangerous, however, and pushed through that six-month period, and never even considered the thought of drinking again after that.

Should I count days?

Once again, this is a personal choice, but I found that NOT counting days helped me the most.

As shared in an answer to a different question, at around the six-month point, I found myself considering if I would give drinking another shot since I had made it further than I ever had before and was clearly in control now.

I decided the answer to that question was no at the time and instead decided to sign up for another six-month stint to see where it led me.

This is a strategy that I created called "commitment batching." What this means is that I would decide how long I was going to commit to something and then once I reached the end of that time frame, I would then consider if I would continue on the same path or not.

This name is derived from the productivity strategy in which you "batch" the same type of activity for a certain time frame to increase your efficiency and hopefully create a state of flow at some point. For me, I liked to do this in periods that would increase by factors of either two or three.

For example, when I first stopped drinking, I said I was only going to do it for 30 days and then re-evaluate at that time. After 30 days, I then decided I would push it out to 90 days because the positive effects were so apparent. After 90 days, I then said I would give it another 90 days to push it to 6 months to see how that played out. After six months, I then said I would sign for another six months to make it a full year. After a year, I then knew that this was going to be a forever lifestyle for me.

What commitment batching allowed me to do was to take away the anxiety of having to make the decision every single day whether I was going to drink or not. I only had to begin considering close to the time frame when my commitment batch was coming to an end.

This would help me ensure that I would give myself enough time to truly allow the positive effects of the decision to take place, while also removing the pressure that could come with having to grapple with making this decision each day.

Three months easily turned into six months, which turned into a year, which turned into a lifetime.

I don't think counting the days would've worked as well for me, but this is only my strategy. You have to do what motivates and keeps you committed long term.

Does journaling help?

I would say this is an emphatic yes.

I started *AINYF (Alcohol is NOT Your Friend)* as a way to help others learn the lessons I did from my alcohol-conscious journey and to help them realize the same positive effects that I did.

This decision helped me grow in my knowledge of all things related to giving up alcohol and helped me see how far I had come from a growth standpoint to become the person I am at this very moment.

You don't have to publish your thoughts publicly like I did, but putting your thoughts on paper and having something to refer to in your weak moments or just as a moment of pride in your growth is a great motivator to keep you focused and committed to the long-term journey of who you are becoming.

What if I relapse?

It's okay.

Relapsing doesn't mean the world is over or that you can't decide to give up alcohol again.

I had two three-month stints of giving up alcohol before I decided it was going to be a forever decision, and I learned a lot about myself and living an alcohol-conscious lifestyle during both of those times that helped me when I finally decided to do it long term.

The key here is that whenever you have a slip-up, you have to spend the time to cerebrally walk through exactly what happened and what caused the mistake. You have to understand where you think you went wrong that caused you to drink again when it wasn't a decision you said you wanted to make.

Was it the environment you put yourself in? Subscribe to not go to that place again until you know you're able to handle it.

Was it a friend who encouraged you to drink, and you just couldn't say no? I would say that you should stop hanging out with that friend until you are strong enough to resist.

Was it an experience or event that made you so sad or depressed, you felt you HAD to drink? You should ask yourself, is there another legal substitute that you could've used that would've helped alleviate this sadness without making you break your commitment?

Everyone's journey is different, and as long as you are learning what works for you versus what doesn't work for you each time you slip up, you are getting closer to creating the rubric that will unlock your alcohol-consciousness forever.

The key is not being perfect . . . the key is not ever EVER giving up.

Notes

1. "Alcohol Facts and Statistics." *National Institute on Alcohol Abuse and Alcoholism (NIAAA)*. https://www.niaaa.nih.gov/publications/brochures-and-fact-sheets/alcohol-facts-and-statistics. 2022, March 3.

2. https://www.who.int/news-room/fact-sheets/detail/alcohol.

3. "Harmful use of alcohol kills more than 3 million people each year, most of them men." *World Health Organization.* (2018, September 21) https://www.who.int/news/item/21-09-2018-harmful-use-of-alcohol-kills-more-than-3-million-people-each-year--most-of-them-men.

4. *Roots (TV Mini Series 1977).* IMDb. https://www.imdb.com/title/tt0075572/.

5. "History of alcoholic drinks." *Wikipedia, The Free Encyclopedia,* Wikimedia Foundation. https://en.wikipedia.org/wiki/History_of_alcoholic_drinks. 2022, June 25.

6. "An ancient thirst for beer may have inspired agriculture, Stanford archaeologists say." *Archeologists.* https://news.stanford.edu/press-releases/2018/09/12/crafting-beer-lereal-cultivation/. 2018, September 12.

7. "Alcohol among the Greeks and Romans: They Enjoyed Drinking." *Alcohol Problems and Solutions.* https://www.alcoholproblemsandsolutions.org/alcohol-among-the-greeks-and-romans/. 2022.

8. "Ancient Greece - Alcohol Consumption." *Global Healthcare.* https://www.globehealth.net/alcohol-consumption/ancient-greece.html. 2022, June 15.

9. "Aristotle Drunkenness: Drunkenness and Punishment Essay Example." *GraduateWay.* https://graduateway.com/aristotle-drunkenness-drunkenness-and-punishment/. 2022.

10. "General Data Protection Regulation (GDPR) Guidelines BYJU'S." *BYJUS.* https://byjus.com/chemistry/fractional-distillation/ 2022.

11. Ritchie, H. and M. Roser, "Alcohol Consumption." *Our World in Data.* https://ourworldindata.org/alcohol-consumption. 2018, April.

12. "War of the Grand Alliance | European history." *Encyclopedia Britannica.* https://www.britannica.com/event/War-of-the-Grand-Alliance.

13. Abel, E. L. (2001). "THE GIN EPIDEMIC: MUCH ADO ABOUT WHAT?" *Alcohol and Alcoholism, 36*(5), 401–405. https://doi.org/10.1093/alcalc/36.5.401.

14. Vorel, J. (2020, January 22). "The Gin Craze: When 18th Century London Tried to Drink Itself to Death." *Pastemagazine.com.* https://www.pastemagazine.com/drink/alcohol-history/the-gin-craze-britain-1700s/#life-in-the-gin-craze.

15. *The History Press* | "The land of the 'free': Criminal transportation to America." (2020, March 4). English. https://www.thehistorypress.co.uk/articles/the-land-of-the-free-criminal-transportation-to-america/.

16. *Statista.* (2022, June 14). "Per capita alcohol consumption of all beverages in the U.S. 1850–2020." https://www.statista.com/statistics/442818/per-capita-alcohol-consumption-of-all-beverages-in-the-us/#:%7E:text=Per%20capita%20alcohol%20consumption%20in,ethanol%20per%20capita%20in%202019.

17. "The History of Alcohol Throughout The World." (2022, July 18). *Recovery.org.* https://recovery.org/alcohol-addiction/history/.

18. "Disulfiram." *Wikipedia, The Free Encyclopedia,* Wikimedia Foundation. (2022, July 12). https://en.wikipedia.org/wiki/Disulfiram.

19. Pollard, M. S., PhD. (2020, September 29). "Changes in Adult Alcohol Use and Consequences During the COVID-19 Pandemic in the US." *Addiction Medicine* | JAMA Network Open | JAMA Network. https://jamanetwork.com/journals/jamanetworkopen/fullarticle/2770975.

20. *College Gazette.* (2021, November 16). "Check Out the 10 Best Party Schools in the US." *Collegegazette.com.* https://collegegazette.com/best-party-schools-in-the-us/.

21. "Understanding Binge Drinking." *National Institute on Alcohol Abuse and Alcoholism (NIAAA).* (2021, April 4). https://www.niaaa.nih.gov/publications/brochures-and-fact-sheets/binge-drinking.

22. The University of Nevada, Reno. (2020, July 23). "Is Binge Drinking in College Worth a Lifetime of Damage and Health Issues?" https://onlinedegrees.unr.edu/blog/binge-drinking-in-college/#:%7E:text=The%20Health%20Effects%20of%20Binge,crashes%2C%20falls%2C%20or%20burns.

23. "Fall Semester—A Time for Parents To Discuss the Risks of College Drinking." *National Institute on Alcohol Abuse and Alcoholism (NIAAA).* (2021, July 2). https://www.niaaa.nih.gov/publications/brochures-and-fact-sheets/time-for-parents-discuss-risks-college-drinking.

24. "Consequences of College Drinking." (2020, September 3). *NIAAA.* https://www.collegedrinkingprevention.gov/statistics/consequences.aspx.

25. "The ages your brain peaks at everything." (2017, July 31). *Business Insider Nederland.* https://www.businessinsider.nl/smartest-age-for-everything-math-vocabulary-memory-2017-7?international=true&r=US.

26. Markel, H. (2016, December 5). "A symphony of second opinions on Mozart's final illness." *PBS NewsHour.* https://www.pbs.org/newshour/health/symphony-second-opinions-mozarts-final-illness.

27. "10 Facts about Michelangelo's Statue of David in Florence, Italy." (2021, December 6). *Context.* https://www.contexttravel.com/blog/articles/ten-facts-about-the-statue-of-david.

28. "Early Drinking Linked to Higher Lifetime Alcoholism Risk." (2006, July 3). *NIAAA.* https://www.niaaa.nih.gov/news-events/news-releases/early-drinking-linked-higher-lifetime-alcoholism-risk.

29. Silveri M. M. "Adolescent brain development and underage drinking in the United States: identifying risks of alcohol use in college populations." *Harvard Review of Psychiatry.* 2012 Jul-Aug;20(4):189–200. doi: 10.3109/10673229.2012.714642. PMID: 22894728; PMCID: PMC4669962.

30. Sripada, C. S., Angstadt, M., McNamara, P., King, A. C., & Phan, K. L. (2011). "Effects of alcohol on brain responses to social signals of threat in humans." *NeuroImage, 55*(1), 371–380. https://doi.org/10.1016/j.neuroimage.2010.11.062.

31. Squeglia, L. M., Jacobus, J., & Tapert, S. F. (2014). "The effect of alcohol use on human adolescent brain structures and systems." *Handbook of Clinical Neurology*, 501–510. https://doi.org/10.1016/b978-0-444-62619-6.00028-8.

32. Paturel, Amy (December 2011). "The effects of drinking on the teenage brain." *Brain and Life.* https://www.brainandlife.org/articles/how-does-alcohol-affect-the-teenage-brain/.

33. Hernandez, Anna. "Hippocampus." *Osmosis*, https://www.osmosis.org/answers/hippocampus. Accessed 22 October, 2022.

34. "Brain Map: Temporal Lobes." *Queensland Health*, 12 July 2022. https://www.health.qld.gov.au/abios/asp/btemporal_lobes. Accessed 22 October 2022.

35. "Amygdala." *Wikipedia, The Free Encyclopedia*, Wikimedia Foundation, 19 October 2022. https://en.wikipedia.org/wiki/Amygdala.

36. Baxter, Mark and Paula Croxson. "Facing the role of the amygdala in emotional information processing." *Proceedings of the National Academy of Sciences.* Vol. 109, No. 52, 26 December 2012, pp 21180 - 21181, https://doi.org/10.1073/pnas.121916711 epub: 14 December 2012.

37. McGaugh, James, Larry Cahill, and Benno Roozendaal. "Involvement of the amygdala in memory storage: Interaction with other brain systems." *Proceedings of the National Academy of Sciences.* Vol. 93, No. 24, 26 November 1996, pp 13508 - 13514. https://doi.org/10.1073/pnas.93.24.13508 epub: 26 November 1996.

38. "Thalamus." *Wikipedia, The Free Encyclopedia*, Wikimedia Foundation, 1 September 2022. https://en.wikipedia.org/wiki/Thalamus.

39. "Thalamus." *Cleveland Clinic*, https://my.clevelandclinic.org/health/body/22652-thalamus 30 March 2022. Accessed 22 October 2022.

40. "Hypothalamus." *Wikipedia, The Free Encyclopedia*, Wikimedia Foundation, 11 October 2022. https://en.wikipedia.org/wiki/Hypothalamus.

41. Burdakov, Denis, and Daria Peleg-Raibstein. "The hypothalamus as a primary coordinator of memory updating." *Physiology & Behavior*, Vol. 223, 2020, https://doi.org/10.1016/j.physbeh.2020.112988. 1 September 2020.

42. Guy-Evans, Olivia. "Limbic System: Definition, Parts, Functions, and Location." *Simply Psychology*, 22 April 2021. https://www.simplypsychology.org/limbic-system.html. Accessed 22 October 2022.

43. Dutta, Sanchari. "The Limbic System and Long-Term Memory." *News Medical Life Sciences*, 24, August 2021. https://www.news-medical.net/health/The-Limbic-System-and-Long-Term-Memory.aspx. Accessed 22 October 2022.

44. Mewton, L., Lees, B., & Rao, R. T. (2020). "Lifetime perspective on alcohol and brain health." *BMJ*, m4691. https://doi.org/10.1136/bmj.m4691.

45. López-Caneda, E., Cadaveira, F., Correas, A., Crego, A., Maestú, F., & Rodríguez Holguín, S. "The Brain of Binge Drinkers at Rest: Alterations in Theta and Beta Oscillations in First-Year College Students with a Binge Drinking Pattern." *Frontiers in Behavioral Neuroscience, 11.* https://doi.org/10.3389/fnbeh.2017.00168. 2017.

46. Meda, S. A., Dager, A. D., Hawkins, K. A., Tennen, H., Raskin, S., Wood, R. M., Austad, C. S., Fallahi, C. R., & Pearlson, G. D. "Heavy Drinking in College Students Is Associated with Accelerated Gray Matter Volumetric Decline over a 2 Year Period." *Frontiers in Behavioral Neuroscience, 11.* https://doi.org/10.3389/fnbeh.2017.00176. 2017.

47. Lees, B., Meredith, L. R., Kirkland, A. E., Bryant, B. E., & Squeglia, L. M. "Effect of alcohol use on the adolescent brain and behavior." *Pharmacology Biochemistry and Behavior, 192,* 172906. https://doi.org/10.1016/j.pbb.2020.172906. 2017.

48. Sterling, J. "The Illicit, Underground History of the Happy Hour." *Thrillist.* https://www.thrillist.com/drink/history-of-happy-hour. 2017.

49. Sitterley, A. "As Restaurants Struggle, Some States Ask: Why is Happy Hour Still Banned?" *InsideSources.* https://insidesources.com/as-restaurants-struggle-some-states-ask-why-is-happy-hour-still-banned/#:%7E:text=A%20well%2Dknown%20feature%20of,and%20Vermont%20are%20the%20others. 2021.

50. Contributor, W. E. K. "Drinking on the job is now a part of the office culture at some startups." *WCPO.* https://www.wcpo.com/news/insider/drinking-on-the-job-is-now-a-part-of-the-office-culture-at-some-startups. 2017.

51. Helmore, E. "WeWork calls time on free beer and wine at North American sites." *The Guardian.* https://www.theguardian.com/business/2020/jan/30/wework-ends-free-beer-wine-north-american-sites. 2020.

52. Murphy, D. A., Hart, A., & Moore, D. (2016). "Shouting and providing: Forms of exchange in the drinking accounts of young Australians." *Drug and Alcohol Review, 36*(4), 442–448. https://doi.org/10.1111/dar.12444.

53. Chen, Siyi. "The complete guide to business drinking in China." *Power Moves.* https://qz.com/701395/the-complete-guide-to-drinking-in-china/ 2016.

54. "How alcohol affects driving ability." *NHTSA.* https://www.nhtsa.gov/risky-driving/drunk-driving. 2022.

55. "Drunk Driving Fatality Statistics." *Responsibility.org.* https://www.responsibility.org/alcohol-statistics/drunk-driving-statistics/drunk-driving-fatality-statistics/. 2022.

56. *Traffic Safety Facts.* "Alcohol-Impaired Driving." https://crashstats.nhtsa.dot.gov/Api/Public/ViewPublication/812864. 2018.

57. Baldwin, J. M., Stogner, J. M., & Miller, B. L. "It's five o'clock somewhere: An examination of the association between happy hour drinking and negative consequences." *Substance Abuse Treatment, Prevention, and Policy, 9*(1). https://doi.org/10.1186/1747-597x-9-17 2014.

58. Drug. *The Merriam-Webster.Com Dictionary.* https://www.merriam-webster.com/dictionary/drug 2020.

59. "Drug Scheduling." *DEA.* https://www.dea.gov/drug-information/drug-scheduling 2020.

60. "What Is Dopamine?" *WebMD.* https://www.webmd.com/mental-health/what-is-dopamine 2019.

61. Ma, H., Zhu, G. "The dopamine system and alcohol dependence." *Shanghai Arch Psychiatry*. 2014 Apr;26(2):61-8. https://www.ncbi.nlm.nih.gov/pmc/articles/PMC4120286/.

62. *Harvard Health*. "Endorphins: The brain's natural pain reliever." https://www.health.harvard.edu/mind-and-mood/endorphins-the-brains-natural-pain-reliever 2021.

63. Dynorphin. *Wikipedia, The Free Encyclopedia*, Wikimedia Foundation. https://en.wikipedia.org/wiki/Dynorphin#:%7E:text=Dynorphins%20(Dyn)%20are%20a%20class,%2F%CE%B2-neo-endorphin. 2020.

64. Schrader, Jessica. "Alcohol and sleep. What you need to know." *Psychology Today*. https://www.psychologytoday.com/us/blog/sleep-newzzz/201801/alcohol-and-sleep-what-you-need-know 2022.

65. Mcleod, S. "Pavlov's Dogs." *Simplypsychology.org*. https://www.simplypsychology.org/pavlov.html#:%7E:text=Pavlov%20showed%20that%20dogs%20could,an%20unconditioned%20(innate)%20response. 2018.

66. "Homeostasis." *Britannica*. https://www.britannica.com/science/homeostasis. 2022

67. "Early Drinking Linked to Higher Lifetime Alcoholism Risk." *National Institute on Alcohol Abuse and Alcoholism (NIAAA)*. https://www.niaaa.nih.gov/news-events/news-releases/early-drinking-linked-higher-lifetime-alcoholism-risk 2006.

68. *BD Wong*. [Video]. IMDb. https://www.imdb.com/name/nm0000703/.

69. "Television on Television Violence: Perspectives from the 70s and 90s." *GBH Openvault*. (2009, March 3). https://openvault.wgbh.org/exhibits/television_violence/article 1960.

70. *Statista*. "Advertising spending in North America 2000–2024." https://www.statista.com/statistics/429036/advertising-expenditure-in-north-america/#:%7E:text=It%20was%20calculated%20that%20the,about%20296.4%20billion%20U.S.%20dollars. 2022.

71. Vansteelant, A. "What is reference marketing and when do you need it?" *Livingstone.eu*. https://blog.livingstone.eu/what-is-reference-marketing-and-when-do-you-need-it. 2019.

72. "Research: Drunk People Are Better at Creative Problem Solving." *Harvard Business Review*. https://hbr.org/2018/05/drunk-people-are-better-at-creative-problem-solving. 2020.

73. *Jessica Jones* (TV series). *Wikipedia, The Free Encyclopedia*, Wikimedia Foundation. https://en.wikipedia.org/wiki/Jessica_Jones_(TV_series) 2022.

74. *Strike* (TV series). *Wikipedia, The Free Encyclopedia*, Wikimedia Foundation. https://en.wikipedia.org/wiki/Strike_(TV_series) 2022.

75. "Alcohol advertising: What are the effects?" *10th Special Report to the U.S. Congress on Alcohol and Health*. https://pubs.niaaa.nih.gov/publications/10report/chap07c.pdf. 2022.

76. "Alcohol Use in Films and Adolescent Alcohol Use." *PEDIATRICS, 135*(5), X7.https://www.researchgate.net/publication/274965892_Alcohol_Use_in_Films_and_Adolescent_Alcohol_Use. 2015.

77. Hanewinkel, R., Sargent, J. D., Hunt, K., Sweeting, H., Engels, R. C., Scholte, R. H., Mathis, F., Florek, E., & Morgenstern, M. "Portrayal of Alcohol Consumption in Movies and Drinking Initiation in Low-Risk Adolescents." *Pediatrics, 133*(6), 973–982. https://doi.org/10.1542/peds.2013-3880. 2014.

78. Muldoon, Michael. "Alcohol in Movies." *Alcohol Rehab Guide*. https://www.alcoholrehabguide.org/alcohol/alcohol-in-popular-culture/movies. 2022.

79. Behm-Morawitz, E., & Mastro, D. E. "Mean Girls? The Influence of Gender Portrayals in Teen Movies on Emerging Adults' Gender-Based Attitudes and Beliefs." *Journalism & Mass Communication Quarterly*, *85*(1), 131–146. https://doi.org/10.1177/107769900808500109. 2008.

80. Mastro, D. E., Behm-Morawitz, E., & Kopacz, M. A. "Exposure to Television Portrayals of Latinos: The Implications of Aversive Racism and Social Identity Theory." *Human Communication Research*, *34*(1), 1–27. https://doi.org/10.1111/j.1468-2958.2007.00311.x. 2008.

81. Kimmerle, J., & Cress, U.. "THE EFFECTS OF TV AND FILM EXPOSURE ON KNOWLEDGE ABOUT AND ATTITUDES TOWARD MENTAL DISORDERS." *Journal of Community Psychology*, *41*(8), 931–943. https://doi.org/10.1002/jcop.21581 2013.

82. Brozovic, A. Opinion letter regarding the article Arch Toxicol https://doi.org/10.1007/s00204-018-2240-x. *Archives of Toxicology*, *92*(10), 3241. https://doi.org/10.1007/s00204-018-2272-2. 2018.

83. Gillig, T. K., Rosenthal, E. L., Murphy, S. T., & Folb, K. L. "More than a Media Moment: The Influence of Televised Storylines on Viewers' Attitudes toward Transgender People and Policies." *Sex Roles*, *78*(7–8), 515–527. https://doi.org/10.1007/s11199-017-0816-1. 2017.

84. "Classification System in Nazi Concentration Camps." *Holocaust Encyclopedia*. https://encyclopedia.ushmm.org/content/en/article/classification-system-in-nazi-concentration-camps. 2018.

85. "Canada DUI Entry: 2019 Changes." *Canada Border Crossing Services*. http://bordercrossing.ca/canada-dui-entry-2019-changes/. 2021.

86. Emberson, J. R., & Bennett, D. A. "Effect of alcohol on risk of coronary heart disease and stroke: causality, bias, or a bit of both?" *Vascular Health and Risk Management*, *2*(3), 239–249. https://www.ncbi.nlm.nih.gov/pmc/articles/PMC1993990/. 2006.

87. Ferraro, P. M., Taylor, E. N., Gambaro, G., & Curhan, G. C. "Soda and Other Beverages and the Risk of Kidney Stones." *Clinical Journal of the American Society of Nephrology*, *8*(8), 1389–1395. https://doi.org/10.2215/cjn.11661112. 2013.

88. Beckman, L. J., & Ackerman, K. T. "Women, Alcohol, and Sexuality." *Recent Developments in Alcoholism*, 267–285. https://doi.org/10.1007/0-306-47138-8_18. 2002.

89. "Heavy Drinking Heightens Immediate Risk for Heart Attack and Stroke." *CardioSmart*. https://www.cardiosmart.org/news/2016/3/heavy-drinking-heightens-immediate-risk-for-heart-attack-and-stroke. 2016.

90. "Can Alcohol Cause Kidney Stones?" *American Addiction Centers*. https://americanaddictioncenters.org/alcoholism-treatment/kidney-stones 2022.

91. Chiolero, A., Faeh, D., Paccaud, F., & Cornuz, J. "Consequences of smoking for body weight, body fat distribution, and insulin resistance." *The American Journal of Clinical Nutrition*, *87*(4), 801–809. https://doi.org/10.1093/ajcn/87.4.801. 2008.

92. Ramirez, E. Study: "No Amount Of Drinking Alcohol Is Safe For Brain Health." *Forbes*. https://www.forbes.com/sites/elvaramirez/2021/06/01/study-no-amount-of-drinking-alcohol-is-safe-for-brain-health/?sh=123570667eaa 2021.

93. "Alcohol use and burden for 195 countries and territories, 1990-2016: a systematic analysis for the Global Burden of Disease Study 2016." *The Lancet*, 392 (10152) 1015-1035. https://doi.org/10.1016/S0140-6736(18)31310-2. 2018.

94. "Study says no amount of alcohol is safe, but expert not convinced." *Harvard Chan School News.* https://www.hsph.harvard.edu/news/hsph-in-the-news/alcohol-risks-benefits-health/ 2019.

95. Galea, S., & Maani, N. "The cost of preventable disease in the USA." *The Lancet Public Health*, 5(10), e513–e514. https://doi.org/10.1016/s2468-2667(20)30204-8 2020.

96. Androus, B. R. A. N. "Healthcare Costs & Spend: Rising by Age, Gender, and Race." *RegisteredNursing.org.* https://www.registerednursing.org/articles/healthcare-costs-by-age/ 2021.

97. "Human alcohol dehydrogenase: Design of a secondary alcohol dehydrogenase using Crystallography and Mutagenesis." *Protein Engineering, Design and Selection.* https://doi.org/10.1093/protein/6.supplement.44-a 1993.

98. "Alcohol & Aging: Impacts of Alcohol Abuse on the Elderly." *American Addiction Centers.* https://americanaddictioncenters.org/alcoholism-treatment/elderly 2022.

99. *Fallen.* IMDb. https://www.imdb.com/title/tt0119099/ 2022.

100. *NHS website.* "Alcohol-related liver disease." Nhs.Uk. https://www.nhs.uk/conditions/alcohol-related-liver-disease-arld/#:%7E:text=Drinking%20a%20large%20amount%20of,drinking%20at%20a%20harmful%20level. 2022.

101. Underferth, D. "Does alcohol cause cancer?" *MD Anderson Cancer Center.* https://www.mdanderson.org/cancerwise/does-alcohol-cause-cancer.h00-159383523.html#:%7E:text=We%20know%20that%20alcohol%20increases,less%20you%20drink%2C%20the%20better. 2020.

102. "Does Alcohol Affect Your Lungs?" *The Recovery Village Drug and Alcohol Rehab.* https://www.therecoveryvillage.com/alcohol-abuse/does-alcohol-affect-your-lungs/#:%7E:text=Alcohol's%20damage%20to%20lung%20cells,lower%20parts%20of%20the%20airway. 2022.

103. *British Heart Foundation.* "Effects of alcohol on your heart." BHF. https://www.bhf.org.uk/informationsupport/heart-matters-magazine/medical/effects-of-alcohol-on-your-heart 2018.

104. "How Alcohol Affects Metabolism / Fitness / Weight Loss." *Fitness.* https://www.fitday.com/fitness-articles/fitness/weight-loss/how-alcohol-affects-metabolism.html 2018.

105. Aho, Christy. "What exactly is the Tom Brady diet?" *Inquirer.Net.* https://usa.inquirer.net/82489/the-tom-brady-diet. Accessed September 14, 2021.

106. LaMotte, Sandee. "Global study finds surprising results for alcohol consumption." *CNN Health*, 14 July 2022, https://www.cnn.com/2022/07/14/health/alcohol-by-age-study-wellness/. Accessed 20 October 2022.

107. "Dietary Guidelines for Alcohol." *Centers for Disease Control and Prevention*, 19 April, 2022. https://www.cdc.gov/alcohol/fact-sheets/moderate-drinking.htm. Accessed 20, October 2022.

108. Ingraham, Christopher. "Think you drink a lot? This chart will tell you." *The Washington Post.* 25 September 2014. https://www.washingtonpost.com/news/wonk/wp/2014/09/25/think-you-drink-a-lot-this-chart-will-tell-you/. Accessed 20 October 2022.

109. "Red wine and resveratrol: Good for your heart?" *Mayo Clinic*, 14 Jan 2022. https://www.mayoclinic.org/diseases-conditions/heart-disease/in-depth/red-wine/art-20048281. Accessed 20 October 2022.

110. GBD 2016 alcohol Collaborators. "Alcohol use and burden for 195 countries and territories, 1990-2016: a systematic analysis for the Global Burden of Disease Study 2016." *The Lancet*, vol 392, issue 10151, pp 1015-1035. 22 September 2018. https://doi.org/10.1016/S0140-6736(18)31310-2. Accessed 20 October 2022.

111. Meade, Robert, et al. "Aging Attenuates the Effect of Extracellular Hyperosmolality on Whole-body Heat Exchange During Exercise-heat Stress." *The Journal of Physiology*, Nov 12, 2020, https://doi.org/10.1113/JP280132. Accessed 15 October 2022.

112. Gilbertson, Rebecca, et al. "Effects of Acute Alcohol Consumption in Older and Younger Adults: Perceived Impairment Versus Psychomotor Performance." *Journal of Studies on Alcohol and Drugs*, Volume 70, Issue 2, 2009. https://doi.org/10.15288/jsad.2009.70.242. 2022.

113. "David Hasselhoff eating an hamburger." *YouTube*, uploaded by Mario Tapia Ramirez, 10 August 2017, https://www.youtube.com/watch?v=pqPoREAM9ZM.

114. "Acetaldehyde." *Wikipedia, The Free Encyclopedia*, Wikipedia Foundation, 11 October 2022, https://en.wikipedia.org/wiki/Acetaldehyde.

115. "Aldehyde." *Wikipedia, The Free Encyclopedia*, Wikipedia Foundation, 11 October 2022, https://en.wikipedia.org/wiki/Aldehyde.

116. Setshedi M, Wands JR, Monte SM. "Acetaldehyde adducts in alcoholic liver disease." *Oxid Med Cell Longev*. 2010 May-Jun;3(3):178-85. doi: 10.4161/oxim.3.3.3. PMID: 20716942; PMCID: PMC2952076.

117. "Alcohol Metabolism: An Update." *National Institute on Alcohol Abuse and Alcoholism*. July 2007, https://pubs.niaaa.nih.gov/publications/aa72/aa72.htm. Accessed 20 October 2022.

118. "Alcohol poisoning." *Mayo Clinic*. 19 January 2018. https://www.mayoclinic.org/diseases-conditions/alcohol-poisoning/symptoms-causes/syc-20354386. Accessed 20 October 2022.

119. "Alcohol's effect on the body." *HSI*. 11 August 2019. https://www2.hse.ie/wellbeing/alcohol/physical-health/alcohols-effect-on-the-body/the-liver.html. Accessed 20 October 2022.

120. Wetherill R. R., Fromme K. "Acute alcohol effects on narrative recall and contextual memory: an examination of fragmentary blackouts." *Addictive Behaviors*. 2011 Aug;36(8):886-9. doi: 10.1016/j.addbeh.2011.03.012. Epub 2011 Mar 25. PMID: 21497445; PMCID: PMC3101897.

121. "Interrupted Memories: Alcohol-Induced Blackouts," *National Institute on Alcohol Abuse and Alcoholism*. 2021 March. https://www.niaaa.nih.gov/publications/brochures-and-fact-sheets/interrupted-memories-alcohol-induced-blackouts. Accessed 20 October 2022.

122. McLeod, Saul. "Multi-Store Model of Memory." *Simply Psychology*, 2021. https://www.simplypsychology.org/multi-store.html. Accessed 20 October, 2022.

123. Rundell, O. H, and H. L. Williams. "Effect of alcohol on recall and recognition as functions of processing levels." *Journal of Studies on Alcohol*, 45(1), 10-15 (1984). https://doi.org/10.15288/jsa.1984.45.10. Epub 2015 Jan 4.

124. Ray, Suchismita and Bates, Marsha. "Acute effects of alcohol on intrusion errors in free recall tasks." *International Journal on Disability and Human Development*, vol. 6, no. 2, 2007, pp. 201-206. https://doi.org/10.1515/IJDHD.2007.6.2.201.

125. White, Aaron. "What Happened? Alcohol, Memory Blackouts, and the Brain." *Alcohol Research and Health*. 2003; 27(2) 186-96. https://pubs.niaaa.nih.gov/publications/arh27-2/186-196.htm. Accessed 20 October 2022.

126. Ling, J. et al. "Effects of Alcohol on Subjective Rating of Prospective and Every Memory Deficits." *Alcoholism: Clinical and Experimental Research*. Vol 27. Issue 6, June 2003, pp 970-974. https://doi.org/10.1111/j.1530-0277.2003.tb04422.x Epub 2006 May 30.

127. Bradimonte, Einstein, & McDaniel, 1996; Kerns, 2000. "Prospective memory is defined as the ability to remember to carry out intended actions in the future." *Advances in Child Development and Behavior*, https://www.sciencedirect.com/topics/neuroscience/prospective-memory. Accessed 20 October 2022.

128. "Explicit memory." *Wikipedia, The Free Encyclopedia*, Wikimedia Foundation, 13 June 2022, https://en.wikipedia.org/wiki/Explicit_memory.

129. Bettio LEB, Rajendran L, Gil-Mohapel J. "The effects of aging in the hippocampus and cognitive decline." *Neuroscience & Biobehavioral Reviews*. 2017 Aug;79:66-86. doi: 10.1016/j.neubiorev.2017.04.030. Epub 2017 May 2. PMID: 28476525.

130. Topiwala, Anya and et al. "Associations between moderate alcohol consumption, brain iron, and cognition in UK Biobank participants: Observational and mendelian randomization analyses." *PLOS Medicine*, 14 July 2022. https://doi.org/10.1371/journal.pmed.1004039. Accessed 4 November 2022.

131. "Cognitive decline can begin as early as age 45, warn experts." *the bmj*, 5 January 2012. https://www.bmj.com/press-releases/2012/01/05/cognitive-decline-can-begin-early-age-45-warn-experts. Accessed 20 October 2022.

132. Kubala, Jillian. "14 Natural Ways to Improve Your Memory." *Healthline*, 17 May 2022. https://www.healthline.com/nutrition/ways-to-improve-memory. Accessed 20 October 2022.

133. "Alcohol myopia." *Greenfacts.org*. https://www.greenfacts.org/glossary/abc/alcohol-myopia.htm#:%7E:text=%22Alcohol%20myopia%22%20refers%20to%20the,to%20myopia%20which%20is%20nearsightedness). 2022.

134. "Alcoholism and Domestic Abuse: Finding Help." *Alcohol Rehab Guide*. https://www.alcoholrehabguide.org/alcohol/crimes/domestic-abuse/#:%7E:text=Alcohol%20And%20Domestic%20Abuse%20Statistics,more%20likely%20to%20abuse%20alcohol. 2022.

135. Valli, Veronica and Chip Somers. *Soberful*. https://soberful.com/episodes/ 2022.

136. Gourand, Janet. *Tribe Sober*. https://www.tribesober.com/podcasts/ 2022.

137. English, Victoria and James Swanick. *Alcohol-Free Lifestyle*. https://alcoholfreelifestyle.com/ 2022.

138. Ramer, Shane. *That Sober Guy*. https://www.thatsoberguy.com/ 2022.

139. *Recovery Rocks Podcast - SobrieTea Party - Tawny and Lisa*. SobrieTea Party. http://www.sobrieteaparty.com/podcast/ 2020.

140. "Benefits of Exercise in Addiction Recovery." *The Recovery Village Drug and Alcohol Rehab*. https://www.therecoveryvillage.com/recovery/wellness/6-proven-benefits-exercise-addiction-recovery/#:%7E:text=Research%20shows%20that%20exercise%20releases,endorphins%20back%20into%20their%20body. 2022.

141. "What Is Cortisol?" *WebMD*. https://www.webmd.com/a-to-z-guides/what-is-cortisol 2017.

142. "Ghrelin." *You and Your Hormones from the Society for Endocrinology*. https://www.yourhormones.info/hormones/ghrelin/ 2018.

143. Gunnars, K. B. "Leptin and Leptin Resistance: Everything You Need to Know." *Healthline*. https://www.healthline.com/nutrition/leptin-101 2012.

144. *CHRIS HERIA*. [Video]. YouTube. https://www.youtube.com/c/CHRISHERIA.

145. *ATHLEAN-Xâ„¢*. [Video]. YouTube. https://www.youtube.com/c/athleanx.

146. *Krissy Cela*. [Video]. YouTube. https://www.youtube.com/c/KrissyCelaa.

147. *Tone It Up*. [Video]. YouTube. https://www.youtube.com/c/toneitup/videos.

148. *Yoga With Adriene*. [Video]. YouTube. https://www.youtube.com/user/yogawithadriene.

149. *MyFitnessPal | MyFitnessPal.com*. https://www.myfitnesspal.com/ 2018.

150. Tremblay, Sylvie. "Fat Burning vs. Carbohydrate Burning." *Livestrong.com*. May 2019. https://www.livestrong.com/article/32587-fat-burning-vs.-carbohydrate-burning/.

151. Schneider, Sarah. "The history of the low-fat diet." *Nourish Your Life*. October 2016. https://nourishyourlife.org/the-history-of-the-low-fat-diet/.

152. Meixner Ms, M. R. "13 Low-Fat Foods That Are Good For Your Health." *Healthline*. https://www.healthline.com/nutrition/healthy-low-fat-foods 2018.

153. Petre, M. A. S. "Is Fruit Juice as Unhealthy as Sugary Soda?" *Healthline*. https://www.healthline.com/nutrition/fruit-juice-vs-soda#sugar-content 2019.

154. Dr. Verma. "Why You Should Stop Drinking Milk Right Now." *The Daily Meal*. (2014, January 30th). https://www.thedailymeal.com/why-you-should-stop-drinking-milk-right-now/013014.

155. Yu, C., & Felbin, S. "The 15 Best Sparkling Water Brands, According To Registered Dietitians." *Women's Health*. https://www.womenshealthmag.com/food/g29829930/best-sparkling-water-brands/ 2022.

156. "Why Diet Soda is Bad for You." *Penn Medicine, Health and Wellness*. (2017, March 1st). https://www.pennmedicine.org/updates/blogs/health-and-wellness/2017/march/diet-soda.

ABOUT THE AUTHOR
Ken Middleton

Ken Makimsy Middleton is obsessed with helping people build the best versions of themselves. Ever since he experienced a tremendous turn-around from an entrepreneurial endeavor when he gave up alcohol on November 10th, 2018, his mission has been to help others realize alcohol is probably the one thing that is holding them back from realizing all of their dreams. He started the Medium publication *AINYF (Alcohol is NOT Your Friend)* in May of 2020 for this reason and then decided to write *Bamboozled – How Alcohol Makes Fools of Us All*, which exposes the subtle tactics and traps of alcohol and the alcohol industry, while also giving the reader the tools to overcome them. He lives in Atlanta, GA, with his wife, Lena, and their Siamese cat, Tony.